knitting motifs, blocks, projects & ideas

201 knitting motifs, blocks, projects & ideas

Nicki Trench

CICO BOOKS
LONDON NEW YORK

This edition published 2018 by CICO Books
An imprint of Ryland Peters & Small Ltd
20–21 Jockey's Fields, London WC1R 4BW
341 E 116th St., New York, NY 10029
www.rylandpeters.com

10 9 8 7 6 5 4 3 2 1

First published in 2010 by CICO Books

A CIP catalog record for this book is available from the Library of Congress and the British Library.

978 1 78249 571 0

Printed in China

Copy editor: Marie Clayton
Design: Jerry Goldie
Illustration: Kate Simunek, Stephen Dew
Photography: Martin Norris
Style photography: Emma Mitchell
Styling: Rose Hammick

contents

introduction

I teach knitting and home crafts, and over several years of meeting knitters of all standards, I've found that with just a little encouragement and confidence even the most basic knitter can turn a little ball of yarn into something clever, cute, or magnificent. Knitting is more than just a hobby; it can easily become a real passion. I hope you will use this book to kindle or rekindle interest in a craft brought up-to-date by the contemporary designs in the Blocks and Projects sections. I've not only included an abundance of different stitches and techniques in the Blocks section, but also created 50 charming projects and ideas in the final section that I hope you'll find tempting and inspiring.

working with blocks

The Blocks section is divided into different techniques based around a 6in. (15cm) square. The sections offer practice in different stitches and techniques, from Basics to Fair Isle, giving you a great opportunity to experiment and create your own patchwork—or simply to extend your knitting knowledge. Blocks are just perfect for our modern lifestyle; they can be as quick or slow to knit as you like. Some basic blocks will take minutes, others are more challenging, but all are perfect for doing while sitting in front of the television, listening to music, or while on vacation. Some of the squares—particularly the Fair Isle and Intarsia—are like miniature stand-alone projects. If you don't want to make anything in particular with them, try framing them; after all, they are pieces of art. If the blocks inspire you to create your own patchwork, try using the same square in different color combinations or make a variety of different stitches and techniques and join them together.

the projects

Many of the projects use the designs and stitches in the Blocks section. I have used a variety of yarns to give an interesting mix of texture and color and there are even simple felted projects, such as the Felted Bag (page 159), which you wash in a machine after knitting to get amazing effects. If you like to combine your knitting and sewing skills, there are lined bags (pages 128, 156, and 159), a Beaded Purse (page 125), and an adorable Knitting Needle Roll (page 136). If you're knitting for a baby, see the Child's Pompom Hat (page 152) or Baby Cot Blanket (page 96), as well as the cutest bibs in 100% cotton (page 122), so you can throw them in the washing machine after mealtime mayhem. There are also many projects for the home, some small, quick, and fun; the two mug cozies (page 114) or the fantastic Springtime Teapot Cover Flowers (page 105) will cheer anyone's kitchen. You don't even have to stick with traditional yarn: there's a Bath Mat knitted using giant needles and strips of fabric (page 145). It's always fun to experiment and this just proves how basic knitting is. After all, it's really just a combination of knots and has been practiced since the beginning of time.

I hope you will use this book to inspire you to transform a traditional craft into a contemporary pastime and to extend and develop your knitting skills for a lifetime's satisfaction.

part one

blocks

Traditionally blocks were made to use up spare yarn, and each of the designs in this section uses only around 1oz (28g) of yarn. The size of each block is based on a 6in. (15cm) square, but will vary according to your gauge (tension) so you can adjust this until you achieve the size square that you need.

basic squares

This section demonstrates just how many textures you can get from simply working in knit and purl stitches. These blocks are perfect for increasing your stitching confidence and discovering the interesting dimensions and shapes you can create with basic knitting.

seed stitch

Seed (moss) stitch can come in various forms. It's a strong and flat stitch that is good for borders and edgings.

materials

Rooster Almerino DK, shade 204 Grape
Needle size: US 6 (4mm)

instructions

Cast on 35 sts.
*K1, p1, rep to last st, k1.
Rep this row until work measures 6in. (15cm).
Bind (cast) off.

blanket check

A lovely textured check that is knitted in just one color makes a very subtle and interesting design.

materials

Rooster Almerino DK, shade 210 Custard
Needle size: US 6 (4mm)

instructions

Cast on 30 sts.
Row 1 *[K1, p1] twice, k6; rep from * to end.
Row 2 *K5, [p1, k1] twice, p1; rep from * to end.
Rows 3, 5 As Row 1.
Rows 4, 6 As Row 2.
Row 7 *K6, [p1, k1] twice; rep from * to end.
Row 8 *[P1, k1] twice, p1, k5; rep from * to end.
Rows 9, 11 As Row 7.
Rows 10, 12 As Row 8.
Rep these twelve rows until work measures 6in. (15cm).
Bind (cast) off.

little knots

There's something about lots of little bobbles—this is a very cute, happy stitch.

materials
Rooster Almerino DK, shade 201 Cornish
Needle size: US 6 (4mm)

special abbreviation
MB (make bobble)—knit into front, back and front of next stitch, turn and K3, turn and P3, turn and K3, turn and sl 1, K2tog, psso (bobble completed).

instructions
Cast on 35 sts.
Rows 1–4 Work in stockinette (stocking) stitch, starting with a knit row.
Row 5 K7, *MB, k9; rep from * to last 8 sts, MB, k7.
Rows 6–10 Work in stockinette (stocking) stitch.
Row 11 K2, *MB, k9; rep from * to last 3 sts, MB, k2.
Row 12 Purl.
Rep these twelve rows until work measures 6in. (15cm).
Bind (cast) off.

loubie lou

A bobble stitch that creates very rounded little bobbles on a plain background of simple garter stitch.

materials
Rooster Almerino DK, shade 211 Brighton Rock
Needle size: US 6 (4mm)

instructions
Cast on 35 sts.
Rows 1–4 Knit.
Row 5 K5, *[k1, p1, k1, p1] loosely into next st, k5; rep from * to end.
Row 6 K5, *sl 3, k1, pass 3rd, 2nd and first of slipped sts separately over last knitted st, k5; rep from * to end.
Rows 7–10 Knit.
Row 11 K8, *[k1, p1, p1, p1] loosely into next st, k5; rep from * to last 3 sts, k3.
Row 12 K8, *sl 3, k1, pass 3rd, 2nd and first of slipped sts separately over the last knitted st, k5; rep from * to last 3 sts, k3.
Rep these twelve rows until work measures 6in. (15cm).
Bind (cast) off.

rippled chevrons

This square can be used with either side facing—the pattern will be reversed.

materials

Rooster Almerino DK, shade 204 Grape
Needle size: US 6 (4mm)

instructions

Cast on 33 sts.
Row 1 K1, *p7, k1; rep from * to end.
Row 2 P1, *k7, p1; rep from * to end.
Row 3 K2, *p5, k3; rep from * to last 7 sts, p5, k2.
Row 4 P2, *k5, p3; rep from * to last 7 sts, k5, p2.
Row 5 K3, *p3, k5; rep from * to last 6 sts, p3, k3.
Row 6 P3, *k3, p5; rep from * to last 6 sts, k3, p3.
Row 7 K4, *p1, k7; rep from * to last 5 sts, p1, k4.
Row 8 P4, *k1, p7; rep from * to last 5 sts, k1, p4.
Row 9 As Row 2.
Row 10 As Row 1.
Row 11 As Row 4.
Row 12 As Row 3.
Row 13 As Row 6.
Row 14 As Row 5.
Row 15 As Row 8.
Row 16 As Row 7.
Rep these 16 rows until work measures 6in. (15cm).
Bind (cast) off.

ridged stitch

This stitch looks rather like a rib, but with lines of small chevrons.

materials

Rooster Almerino DK, shade 201 Cornish
Needle size: US 6 (4mm)

special abbreviations

Tw2R (twist 2 to the right)—pass needle in front of first st, knit second st, knit first st and slip both sts off needle
Tw2L (twist 2 to the left)—pass needle behind first st, knit second st, knit first st and slip both sts off needle

instructions

Cast on 36 sts.
Row 1 *K4, Tw2R, Tw2L; rep from * to last 4 sts, k4.
Row 2 Purl.
Rep these two rows until work measures 6in. (15cm).
Bind (cast) off.

busy bees

A very busy, wiggly, and textured pattern that is great for adding interest in a single color yarn.

materials

Rooster Almerino DK, shade 207 Gooseberry
Needle size: US 6 (4mm)

instructions

Cast on 33 sts.
Row 1 (wrong side) Knit.
Row 2 K1, *K1B, k1; rep from * to end.
Row 3 Knit.
Row 4 K2, K1B, *k1, K1B; rep from * to last 2 sts, k2.
Rep these four rows until work measures 6in. (15cm).
Bind (cast) off.

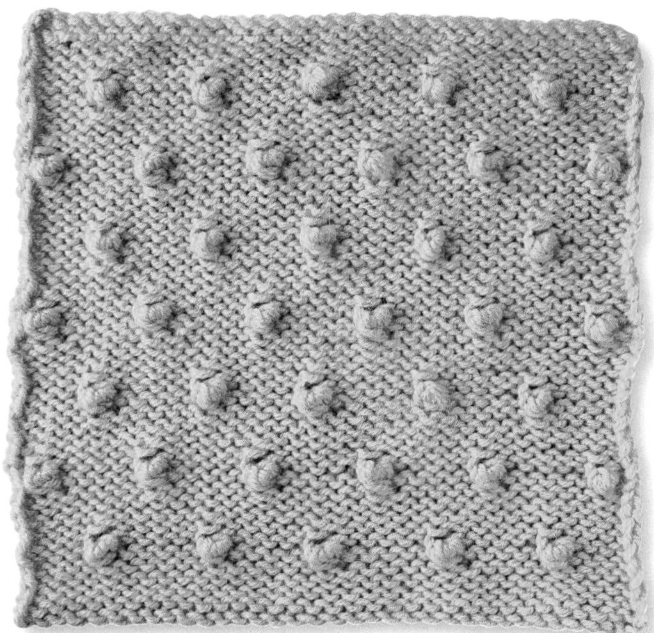

nipples

This stitch creates very subtle little bumps that give an interesting and sensual feeling to the block.

materials

Rooster Almerino DK, shade 210 Custard
Needle size: US 6 (4mm)

instructions

Cast on 35 sts.
Rows 1–4 Work in stockinette (stocking) stitch.
Row 5 K5, *[k1, p1] twice into next st, k5; rep from * to end.
Row 6 P5, *sl 3, k1, pass 3 slipped sts separately over last st (knot completed), p5; rep from * to end.
Work 4 rows in stockinette (stocking) stitch.
Row 11 K2, *[k1, p1] twice more into next st, k5; rep from * to last 3 sts, [k1, p1] twice into next st, k2.
Row 12 P2, *sl 3, k1, pass 3 slipped sts separately over last st (knot completed), p5; rep from * to last 6 sts, sl 3, k1, pass 3 slipped sts over as before (knot completed), p2.
Rep these twelve rows until work measures 6in. (15cm).
Bind (cast) off.

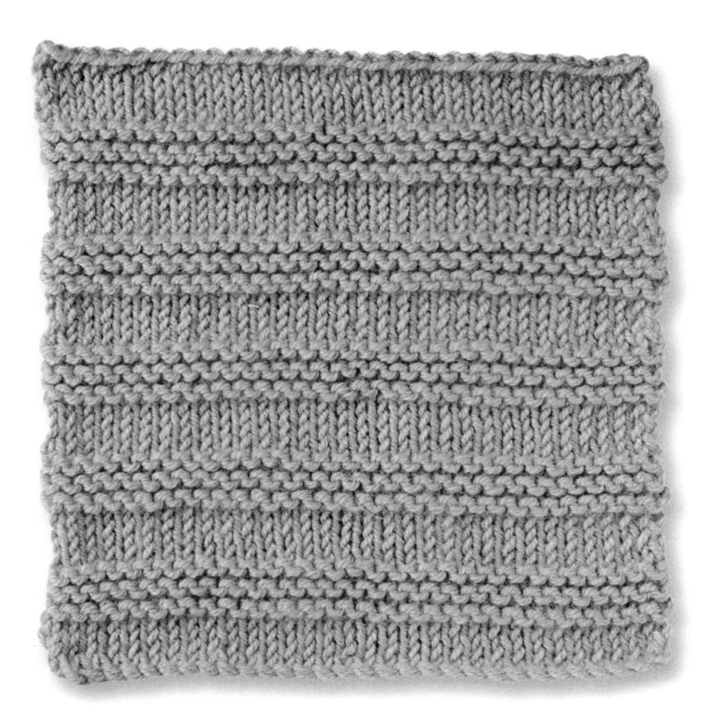

horizontally ridged

This is a square that forms very neat, small, horizontal stripes.

materials

Rooster Almerino DK, shade 203 Strawberry Cream
Needle size: US 6 (4mm)

instructions

Cast on 32 sts.
Row 1 (right side) Knit.
Row 2 Purl.
Rep these two rows once more.
Rows 5–10 Purl.
Rep these ten rows until work measures 5½in. (14cm). Rep Rows 1–4 once more.
Bind (cast) off.

looped honeycomb

An attractive heavily textured design with repeating shapes just like a honeycomb.

materials

Rooster Almerino DK, shade 210 Custard
Needle size: US 6 (4mm)

instructions

Cast on 42 sts.
Row 1 *Sl 1 purlwise, k2, psso, k3; rep from * to end.
Row 2 *P4, yrn to inc by 1 st, p1; rep from * to end of row.
Row 3 *K3, sl 1 purlwise, k2, psso; rep from * to end.
Row 4 *P1, yrn to inc by 1 st, p4; rep from * to end.
Rep these four rows until work measures 6in. (15cm).
Bind (cast) off.

brighton pebbles

There is no wrong side to this attractive square—the pattern will work well either way round.

materials

Rooster Almerino DK, shade 201 Cornish
Needle size: US 6 (4mm)

instructions

Cast on 31 sts.
Row 1 (right side) Purl.
Row 2 K4, *p3, k7; rep from * to last 4 sts, k4.
Row 3 P4, *k3, p7; rep from * to last 4 sts, p4.
Row 4 As Row 2.
Row 5 Purl.
Row 6 Knit.
Row 7 K2, *p7, k3; rep from * to last 2 sts, k2.
Row 8 P2, *k7, p3; rep from * to last 2 sts, p2.
Row 9 As Row 7.
Row 10 Knit.
Rep these ten rows until work measures 6in. (15cm).
Bind (cast) off.

fencing

These vertical ridges, which look like a row of fence posts, are very easy to create.

materials

Rooster Almerino DK, shade 202 Hazelnut
Needle size: US 6 (4mm)

instructions

Cast on 39 sts.
Rows 1, 3 (right side) Knit.
Rows 2, 4 Purl.
Rows 5, 7 K1, *p1, k2; rep from * to last 2 sts, p1, k1.
Rows 6, 8 P1, *k1, p2; rep from * to last 2 sts, k1, p1.
Rows 9, 11 *P2, k1; rep from * to end.
Rows 10, 12 *P1, k2; rep from * to end.
Rep these twelve rows until work measures 6in. (15cm).
Bind (cast) off.

sea groines

This stitch creates a series of little vertical dashes in offset stripes.

materials

Rowan Pure Wool DK, shade 037 Port
Needle size: US 6 (4mm)

instructions

Cast on 37 sts.
Row 1 (right side) P3, k1, *p5, k1; rep from * to last 3 sts, p3.
Row 2 K3, p1, *k5, p1; rep from * to last 3 sts, k3.
Rep Rows 1–2 once more.
Row 5 K1, *p5, k1; rep from * to end.
Row 6 P1, * k5, p1; rep from * to end.
Rep Rows 5–6 once more.
Rep these eight rows until work measures 6in. (15cm).
Bind (cast) off.

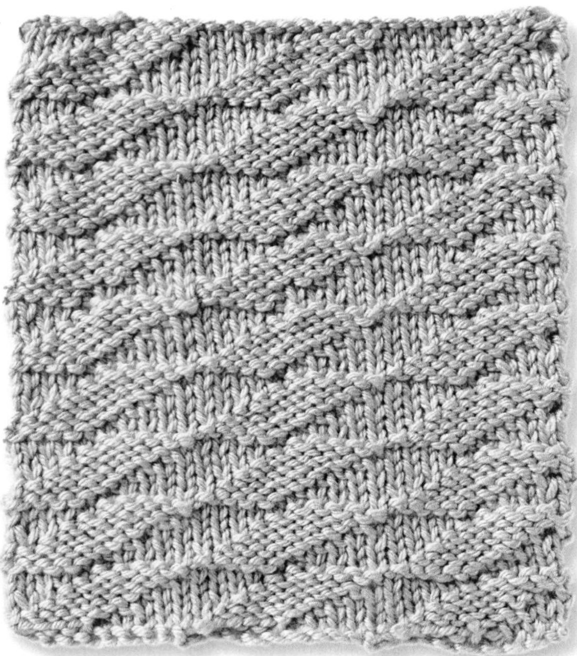

slip sliding away

A soft and wavy stitch, created here in a beautifully soft, pastel-colored yarn.

materials

Rooster Almerino DK, shade 203 Strawberry Cream
Needle size: US 6 (4mm)

instructions

Cast on 30 sts.
Row 1 *K5, p5; rep from * to end.
Row 2 K4, *p5, k5; rep from * to last 6 sts, p5, k1.
Row 3 P2, *k5, p5; rep from * to last 8 sts, k5, p3.
Row 4 K2, *p5, k5; rep from * to last 8 sts, p5, k3.
Row 5 P4, *k5, p5; rep from * to last 6 sts, k5, p1.
Row 6 *P5, k5; rep from * to end.
Rep these six rows until work measures 6in. (15cm).
Bind (cast) off.

waffles

A textured shape that looks rather like the waffles often served at breakfast.

materials

Rooster Almerino DK, shade 207 Gooseberry
Needle size: US 6 (4mm)

instructions

Cast on 34 sts.
Rows 1–2 Knit.
Rows 3–4 *K1, p1; rep from * to end.
Rep these four rows until work until work measures 6in. (15cm).
Bind (cast) off.

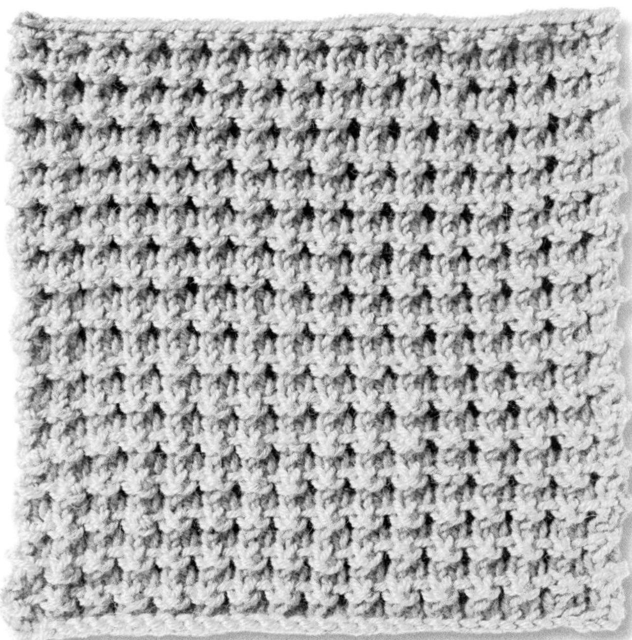

planting seeds

The little holes in this square resemble the regular series of openings in trays for planting seeds.

materials

Rooster Almerino DK, shade 210 Custard
Needle size: US 6 (4mm)

instructions

Cast on 32 sts.
Row 1 Knit.
Row 2 Purl.
Row 3 K2tog across row.
Row 4 *K1, pick up loop before next st and knit; rep from * to end.
Rep these four rows until work measures 6in. (15cm).
Bind (cast) off.

reversed out

This is a very simple little pattern that is just five stitches of knit and then five stitches of purl repeated.

materials

Rowan Pure Wool DK, shade 029 Pomegranate
Needle size: US 6 (4mm)

instructions

Cast on 35 sts.
Row 1 K5, *p5, k5; rep from * to end.
Row 2 P5, *k5, p5; rep from * to end.
Rows 3, 5, 6, 8 As Row 1.
Rows 4, 7, 9 As Row 2.
Row 10 K5, *p5, k5; rep from * to end.
Rep these ten rows until work measures 6in. (15cm).
Bind (cast) off.

seeded diamonds

A very delicate, feminine stitch with subtle diamond shapes.

materials

Rooster Almerino DK, shade 201 Cornish
Needle size: US 6 (4mm)

instructions

Cast on 31 sts.
Row 1 (right side) K3, *p1, k5; rep from * to last 4 sts, p1, k3.
Row 2 P2, *k1, p1, k1, p3; rep from * to last 5 sts, k1, p1, k1, p2.
Row 3 K1, *p1, k3, p1, k1; rep from * to end.
Row 4 K1, *p5, k1; rep from * to end.
Row 5 As Row 3.
Row 6 As Row 2.
Rep these six rows until work measures 6in. (15cm).
Bind (cast) off.

snakes and ladders

A really unusual pattern with a horizontal ridge and a hidden vertical stripe—perfect for snakes!

materials

Rooster Almerino DK, shade 202 Hazelnut
Needle size: US 6 (4mm)

instructions

Cast on 32 sts.
Row 1 *Yrn to inc by 1 st, p2tog, p6, rep from * to end.
Rows 2, 4, 6 *K7, p1; rep from * to end.
Rows 3, 5, 7 *K1, p7; rep from * to end.
Row 8 Purl.
Row 9 P4, yrn to inc by 1 st, p2tog, p2; rep from * to end.
Rows 10, 12, 14 *K3, p1, k4; rep from * to end.
Rows 11, 13, 15 *P4, k1, p3; rep from * to end.
Row 16 Purl.
Rep these 16 rows until work measures 6in. (15cm).
Bind (cast) off.

staircase

This very geometric square resembles a bricked staircase.

materials

Rooster Almerino DK, shade 201 Cornish
Needle size: US 6 (4mm)

instructions

Cast on 32 sts.
Row 1 and every alt row (right side) Knit.
Rows 2, 4 *K4, p4; rep from * to end.
Rows 6, 8 K2, *p4, k4; rep from * to last 6 sts, p4, k2.
Rows 10, 12 *P4, k4; rep from * to end.
Rows 14, 16 P2, *k4, p4; rep from * to last 6 sts, k4, p2.
Rep these 16 rows until work measures 6in. (15cm).
Bind (cast) off.

embossed diamonds

One of my favorite stitches, which you can see on the needle case on page 154. A really pretty and delicate stitch that is easy to work but looks so clever!

materials

Rooster Almerino DK, shade 202 Hazelnut
Needle size: US 6 (4mm)

instructions

Cast on 33 sts.
Row 1 (right side) P1, k1, p1, *[k3, p1] twice, k1, p1; rep from * to end.
Row 2 P1, k1, *p3, k1, p1, k1, p3, k1; rep from * to last st, p1.
Row 3 K4, *[p1, k1] twice, p1, k5; rep from * to last 9 sts, [p1, k1] twice, p1, k4.
Row 4 P3, *[k1, p1] 3 times, k1, p3; rep from * to end.
Row 5 As Row 3.
Row 6 As Row 2.
Row 7 As Row 1.
Row 8 P1, k1, p1, *k1, p5, [k1, p1] twice; rep from * to end.
Row 9 [P1, k1] twice, *p1, k3, [p1, k1] 3 times; rep from * to last 9 sts, p1, k3, [p1, k1] twice, p1.
Row 10 As Row 8.
Rep these ten rows until work measures 6in. (15cm).
Bind (cast) off.

blue flag

A lovely stitch to work, and either side of this design can be used as the right side.

materials

Rooster Almerino DK, shade 205 Glace
Needle size: US 6 (4mm)

instructions

Cast on 33 sts.
Row 1 (right side) *P1, k10; rep from * to end.
Row 2 *P9, k2; rep from * to end.
Row 3 *P3, k8; rep from * to end.
Row 4 *P7, k4; rep from * to end.
Row 5 *P5, k6; rep from * to end.
Row 6 As Row 5.
Row 7 As Row 5.
Row 8 As Row 4.
Row 9 As Row 3.
Row 10 As Row 2.
Row 11 As Row 1.
Row 12 *K1, p10; rep from * to end.
Row 13 *K9, p2; rep from * to end.
Row 14 *K3, p8; rep from * to end.
Row 15 *K7, p4; rep from * to end.
Row 16 *K5, P6; rep from * to end.
Row 17 As Row 16.
Row 18 As Row 16.
Row 19 As Row 15.
Row 20 As Row 14.
Row 21 As Row 13.
Row 22 As Row 12.
Rep these 22 rows until work measures 6in. (15cm).
Bind (cast) off.

garter stitch

Basic and very easy to work, yet this stitch gives a lovely texture.

materials

Rooster Almerino DK, shade 210 Custard
Needle size: US 6 (4mm)

instructions

Cast on 32 sts.
Work in garter stitch (knit every row) for 57 rows, or until work measures 6in. (15cm).
Bind (cast) off.

stockinette stitch

The most popular stitch of all—also known as stocking stitch. A lovely flat stitch and so easy to work that you can watch the television at the same time.

materials

Rooster Almerino DK, shade 204 Grape
Needle size: US 6 (4mm)

instructions

Cast on 32 sts.
Row 1 Knit.
Row 2 Purl.
Rep these two rows until work measures 6in. (15cm).
Bind (cast) off.

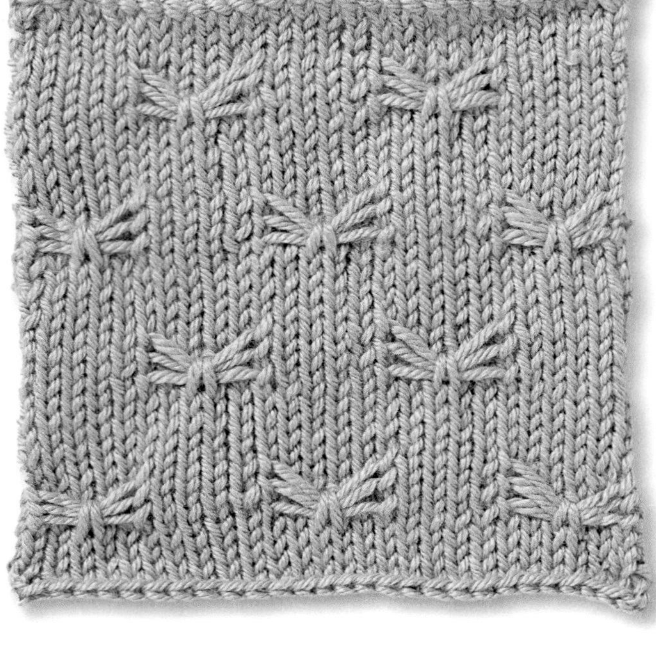

holiday

Well, you don't have to work this one while you are on vacation, but it will make you feel as if you are relaxing away from home.

materials

Rooster Almerino DK, shade 201 Cornish
Needle size: US 6 (4mm)

instructions

Cast on 39 sts.
Row 1 *P5, k1, p1; rep from * to last 4 sts, p4.
Row 2 and every alt row Knit the K sts and purl the P sts.
Row 3 *P5, k1, p1; rep from * to last 4 sts, p4.
Rows 5, 7 *P4, k1, p1, k1; rep from * to last 4 sts, p4.
Row 8 As Row 2.
Rep these eight rows until work measures 6in. (15cm).
Bind (cast) off.

kiss

This simple little pattern resembles little kisses or bows. It's a very simple pattern; use it to brighten up a child's cardigan or blanket.

materials

Rowan Pure Wool DK, shade 006 Pier
Needle size: US 6 (4mm)

special abbreviation

Make Kiss—slip right needle under 3 strands knitwise, knit next st pulling the loop through downward and under strands

instructions

Cast on 27 sts.
Row 1 Purl.
Row 2 Knit.
Row 3 Purl.
Row 4 Knit.
Row 5 P6, *wyib, sl 5 sts, wyif, p5; rep from * to last st, p1.
Row 6 Knit.
Row 7 As Row 5.
Row 8 Knit.
Row 9 As Row 5.
Row 10 K8, Make Kiss, k9, Make Kiss, k8.
Row 11 Purl.
Row 12 Knit.
Row 13 Purl.
Row 14 Knit.
Row 15 P1, *wyib, sl 5 sts, wyif, p5; rep from * to last 6 sts, wyib, sl 5 sts, p1.
Row 16 Knit.
Row 17 As Row 15.
Row 18 Knit.
Row 19 As Row 15.
Row 20 K3, *Make Kiss, k9; rep from * to last 4 sts, Make Kiss, k3.
Rep Rows 1–20 once.
Row 41 Purl.
Row 42 Knit.
Bind (cast) off.

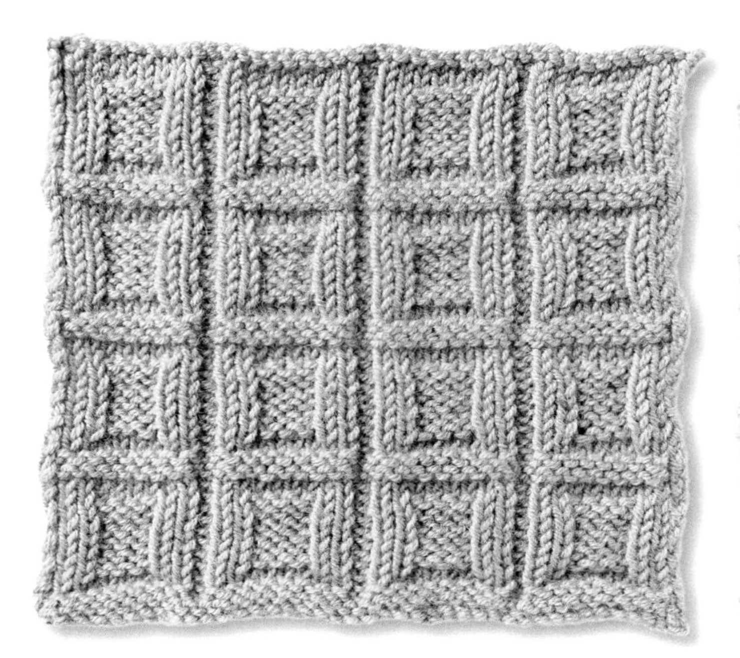

window view

This stitch has a raised border and gives a series of little window shapes.

materials
Rooster Almerino DK, shade 202 Hazelnut
Needle size: US 6 (4mm)

instructions
Cast on 42 sts.
Row 1 (right side) Knit.
Row 2 Purl.
Row 3 K2, *p8, k2; rep from * to end.
Row 4 P2, *k8, p2; rep from * to end.
Rows 5, 7, 9 K2, *p2, k4, p2, k2; rep from * to end.
Rows 6, 8, 10 P2, *k2, p4, k2, p2; rep from * to end.
Row 11 As Row 3.
Row 12 As Row 4.
Rep these twelve rows until work measures 6in. (15cm).
Bind (cast) off.

ridged bricks

This textured stitch is the perfect project to give beginners a taste of the interesting ways they can use knit and purl stitch.

materials
Rooster Almerino DK, shade 205 Glace
Needle size: US 6 (4mm)

instructions
Cast on 33 sts.
Row 1 and every alt row Knit.
Row 2 Knit.
Rows 4, 6 P3, *k3, p3; rep from * to end.
Rows 8, 10 Knit.
Rows 12, 14 K3, *p3, k3; rep from * to end.
Row 16 Knit.
Rep Rows 1–16 twice more.
Rep Rows 1–9 once more.
Bind (cast) off.

textured motifs

This is a subtle way of creating a motif pattern, but using just one color of yarn. The motif usually stands above the main fabric, making a lovely textured feel, particularly for a baby item because the child can feel and trace the shape of the motif.

textured diamond

Just by changing a knit to a purl or a purl to a knit, you can make interesting designs or motifs. This diamond square is a subtle and classic design.

materials

Rooster Almerino DK, shade 201 Cornish
Needle size: US 6 (4mm)

instructions

Cast on 32 sts.
Work 42 rows following the chart.
Bind (cast) off.

◆ = knit on RS, purl on WS
☐ = knit on WS, purl on RS

textured star

This square has a hidden star with a delicate texture.

materials

Rooster Almerino DK, shade 201 Cornish
Needle size: US 6 (4mm)

instructions

Cast on 32 sts.
Work 42 rows following the chart.
Bind (cast) off.

◆ = knit on WS, purl on RS
☐ = knit on RS, purl on WS

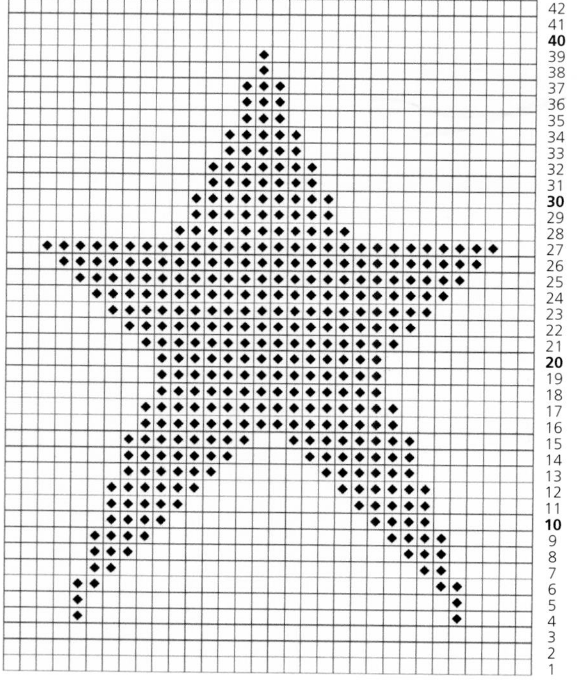

textured leaf

A lovely textured design, which can be viewed either as a leaf or a tree.

materials

Sublime Cashmere Merino Silk DK, shade 106 Egg Nog
Needle size: US 6 (4mm)

instructions

Cast on 32 sts.
Work 42 rows following the chart.
Bind (cast) off.

◆ = knit on WS, purl on RS
□ = knit on RS, purl on WS

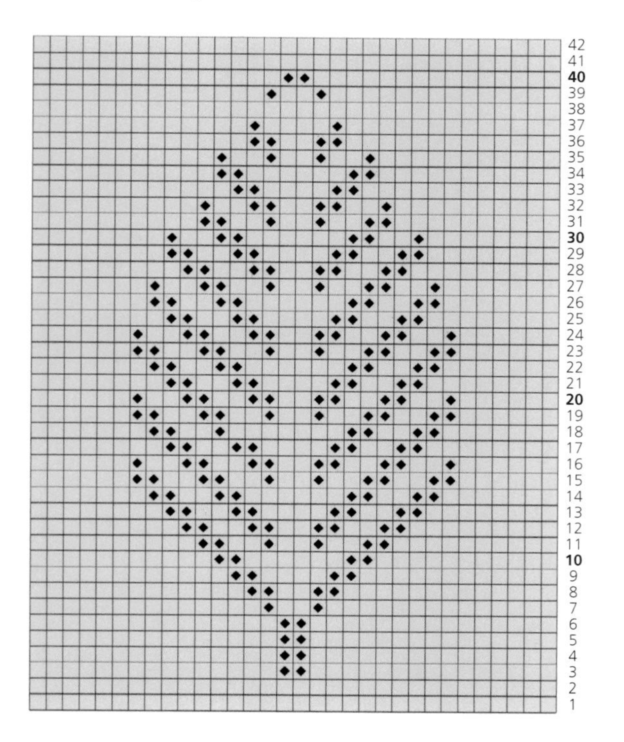

textured heart

This textured square has a narrow seed (moss) stitch edging and a romantic heart motif.

materials

Rooster Almerino DK, shade 207 Gooseberry
Needle size: US 6 (4mm)

instructions

Cast on 32 sts.
Work 42 rows following the chart.
Bind (cast) off.

◇ = knit on RS, purl on WS
□ = knit on WS, purl on RS

cables

Cabling creates a warm fabric, and is made by twisting lines of several stitches using a cable needle. You can make many different size cable patterns and they form a popular part of the traditional "Aran" patterns historically knitted and worn by fishermen. Use a cable needle around the same size as your knitting needles.

cable and rib

A little twisted cable alongside ribbing stitches gives a very professional look.

materials

Debbie Bliss, Rialto DK, shade 02 Off White
Needle size: US 6 (4mm)
Cable needle

special abbreviations

C4B (cable 4 back)—slip next 2 sts onto a cable needle and hold at back of work, knit next 2 sts from left hand needle, then knit sts from cable needle
K1B—knit into back of st on right side rows
P1B—purl into back of st on wrong side rows

instructions

Cast on 32 sts.
Row 1 (right side) P2, K1B, p2, *k4, p2, K1B, p2; rep from * to end.
Row 2 K2, P1B, k2, *p4, k2, P1B, k2; rep from * to end.
Row 3 P2, K1B, p2, *C4B, p2, K1B, p2; rep from * to end.
Row 4 As Row 2.
Rep these four rows until work measures 6in. (15cm).
Bind (cast) off.

cable fabric

A series of wide open cables with a wavy look.

materials

Rowan Pure Wool DK, shade 005 Glacier
Needle size: US 6 (4mm)
Cable needle

special abbreviations

C4B (cable 4 back)—slip next 2 sts onto a cable needle and hold at back of work, knit next 2 sts from left hand needle, then knit sts from cable needle
C4F (cable 4 front)—as C4B, but hold sts on cable needle at front of work

instructions

Cast on 32 sts.
Row 1 Knit.
Row 2 and every alt row Purl.
Row 3 *K2, C4B; rep from * to end.
Row 5 Knit.
Row 7 *C4F, k2; rep from * to end.
Row 8 Purl.
Rep these eight rows until work measures 6in. (15cm).
Bind (cast) off.

woven lattice cable

A crisscross, checked cable that gives a thick, cozy knitted fabric.

materials

Debbie Bliss Rialto DK, shade 02 Off White
Needle size: US 6 (4mm)
Cable needle

special abbreviations

C4B (cable 4 back) – slip next 2 sts onto a cable needle and hold at back of work, knit next 2 sts from left hand needle, then knit sts from cable needle
C4F (cable 4 front) – as C4B, but hold sts on cable needle at front of work
T4F (twist 4 front) – slip next 2 sts onto a cable needle and hold at front of work, purl next 2 sts from left hand needle, then knit sts from cable needle

instructions

Cast on 38 sts.
Row 1 (wrong side) K3, p4, *k2, p4; rep from * to last st, k1.
Row 2 P1, C4F, *p2, C4F; rep from * to last 3 sts, p3.
Row 3 As Row 1.
Row 4 P3, *k2, T4B; rep from * to last 5 sts, k4, p1.
Row 5 K1, p4, *k2, p4; rep from * to last 3 sts, k3.
Row 6 P3, C4B, *p2, C4B; rep from * to last st, p1.
Row 7 As Row 5.
Row 8 P1, k4, *T4F, k2; rep from * to last 3 sts, p3.
Rep these eight rows until work measures 6in. (15cm).
Bind (cast) off.

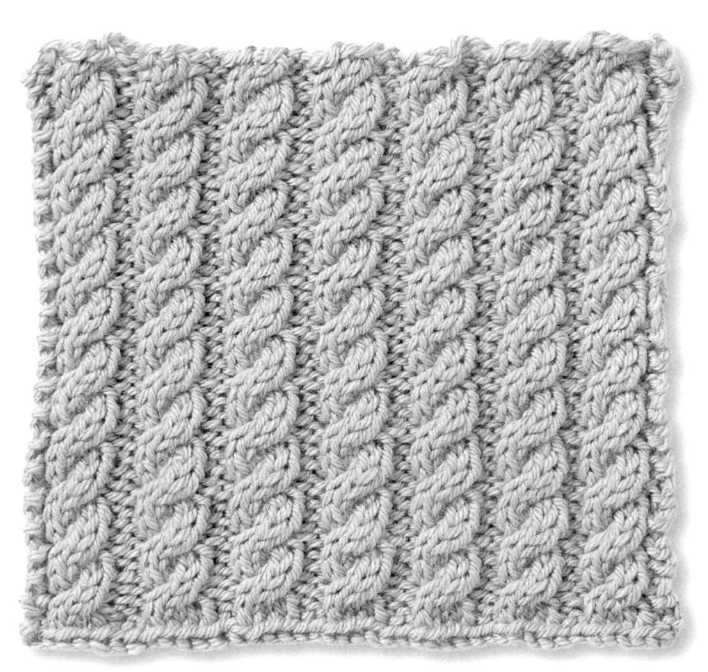

baby cables

These are very sweet little cables that work well on smaller garments. Try them on beanie hats, scarves, or incorporated into a baby blanket.

materials

Rowan Classic Cashcotton DK, shade 601 Cool
Needle size: US 6 (4mm)
Cable needle

special abbreviation

C4B (cable 4 back)—slip next 2 sts onto cable needle, hold in place at the back of the work and knit next 2 sts from left-hand needle, then knit sts from cable needle

instructions

Cast on 44 sts.
Row 1 K1, p1 *k4, p2; rep from * to last 6 sts, k4, p1, k1.
Row 2 K2, *p4, k2; rep from * to end.
Row 3 K1, p1, *C4B, p2; rep from * to last 6 sts, C4B, p1, k1.
Row 4 K2, *p4, k2; rep from * to end.
Rep Rows 1–4 ten times more, ending with a Row 4.
Bind (cast) off.

ribbing

When working ribbing, the stitches make a vertically ridged pattern, but these patterns still use the basic stitches of knit and purl. Ribbing is used often for socks and other garments as it can make a stretchy and sturdy fabric, fitting well into the shape of the body.

2 x 2 ribbing

This is the most common ribbing that is often used on cuffs and the bottom hem because it is a very stretchy stitch.

materials

Rowan Wool Cotton, shade 974 Freesia
Needle size: US 6 (4mm)

instructions

Cast on 58 sts.
Row 1 *K2, p2; rep from * to end.
Row 2 *P2, k2; rep from * to end.
Rep these two rows until work measures 6in. (15cm).
Bind (cast) off.

ripples

The stitch in this square resembles little ripples drifting toward the shore.

materials

Rooster Almerino DK, shade 203 Strawberry Cream
Needle size: US 6 (4mm)

instructions

Cast on 34 sts.
Row 1 K3, *yo, skpo, k2; rep from * to last 3 sts, yo, skpo, k1.
Row 2 P3, *yrn, p2tog, p2; rep from * to last 3 sts, yrn, p2tog, p1.
Rep these two rows until work measures 6in. (15cm).
Bind (cast) off.

fisherman's delight

It's not only fish that are the fishermen's delight; this stitch makes a super thick fabric to keep them warm at night.

materials

Rooster Almerino DK, shade 201 Cornish
Needle size: US 6 (4mm)

instructions

Cast on 36 sts.
Row 1 Purl.
Row 2 *P1, k next st in row below; rep from * to last 2 sts, p2.
Rep Row 2 only until work until measures 6in. (15cm).
Bind (cast) off.

seafarer

This stitch makes little rows of scallop shells, great for a project with a seashore theme.

materials

Rowan Baby Alpaca DK, shade 208 Southdown
Needle size: US 6 (4mm)

instructions

Cast on 47 sts.
Row 1 P2, *k3, p2; rep from * to end.
Row 2 K2, *p3, k2; rep from * to end.
Row 3 P2, *sl 1, k2tog, psso, p2; rep from * to end.
Row 4 K2, *[p1, k1, p1] in front and back of next st, k2; rep from * to end.
Rep these four rows until work measures 6in. (15cm).
Bind (cast) off.

seed ribbing

A lovely simple stitch for beginners to try out; it is more textured than a traditional ribbing. Seed stitch is also known as moss stitch.

materials

Rooster Almerino DK, shade 203 Strawberry Cream
Needle size: US 6 (4mm)

instructions

Cast on 36 sts.
Row 1 *K3, p1; rep from * to end.
Row 2 *K2, p1, k1; rep from * to end.
Rep these two rows until work measures 6in. (15cm).
Bind (cast) off.

perforated ribbing

This is a slightly more sophisticated and complex ribbing design, but still very easy to work.

materials

Rowan Pure Wool DK, shade 029 Pomegranate
Needle size: US 6 (4mm)

instructions

Cast on 39 sts.
Row 1 (right side) P1, k1, p1, *yrn, p3tog, yrn, p1, k1, p1; rep from * to end.
Row 2 K1, p1, k1, *p3, k1, p1, k1; rep from * to end.
Row 3 P1, k1, p1, *k3, p1, k1, p1; rep from * to end.
Row 4 As Row 2
Rep these four rows until work measures 6in. (15cm).
Bind (cast) off.

pique ribbing

An interesting ribbing stitch, with a mix of different textures and stitch stripes.

materials

Rooster Almerino DK, shade 205 Glace
Needle size: US 6 (4mm)

instructions

Cast on 33 sts.
Row 1 (right side) K3, *p3, k1, p3, k3; rep from * to end.
Row 2 P3, *k3, p1, k3, p3; rep from * to end.
Row 3 As Row 1.
Row 4 Knit.
Rep these four rows until work measures 6in. (15cm).
Bind (cast) off.

little bobble ribbing

Lines, bobbles, and ridges combined together make a very neat, lined square.

materials

Rooster Almerino DK, shade 202 Hazelnut
Needle size: US 6 (4mm)

instructions

Cast on 43 sts.
Row 1 (right side) K3, *p2, [p1, k1] twice into next st, turn, k2tog twice, turn, p2tog (bobble completed), p2, k3; rep from* to end.
Row 2 P3, *k5, p3; rep from * to end.
Row 3 K3, *p5, k3; rep from * to end.
Row 4 As Row 2.
Rep these four rows until work measures 6in. (15cm).
Bind (cast) off.

double eyelet ribbing

This is a ribbing stitch, but it resembles a lace stitch. A very pretty stitch that is easy to work.

materials

Rooster Almerino DK, shade 204 Grape
Needle size: US 6 (4mm)

instructions

Cast on 37 sts.
Row 1 (right side) P2, *k5, p2; rep from * to end.
Row 2 K2, *p5, k2; rep from * to end.
Row 3 P2, *k2tog, yo, k1, yo, skpo, p2; rep from * to end.
Row 4 As Row 2.
Rep these four rows until work measures 6in. (15cm).
Bind (cast) off.

lace

A style of knitting that creates deliberate holes arranged in a decorative way, lace patterns have been in and out of fashion for centuries. Lace is traditionally made in fine yarn, but you can use any thickness. Lace knitting makes an elastic fabric that can stretch over time, but is a satisfying and challenging style for the experienced knitter.

lacy in the sky with diamonds

A lacy stitch in the shape of small repeating diamonds.

materials

Rowan Pure Wool DK, shade 005 Glacier
Needle size: US 6 (4mm)

special abbreviation

p2sso—pass 2 slipped sts over

instructions

Cast on 31 sts.
Row 1 (right side) *K1, k2tog, yo, k1, yo, k2tog tbl; rep from * to last st, k1.
Row 2 and every alt row Purl.
Row 3 K2tog, *yo, k3, yo, [sl 1] twice, k1, p2sso; rep from * to last 5 sts, yo, k3, yo, k2tog tbl.
Row 5 *K1, yo, k2tog tbl, k1, k2tog, yo; rep from * to last st, k1.
Row 7 K2, *yo, [sl 1] twice, k1, p2sso, yo, k3; rep from * to last 5 sts, yo, [sl 1] twice, k1, p2sso, yo, k2.
Row 8 Purl.
Rep these eight rows until work measures 6in. (15cm).
Bind (cast) off.

fir cone

If you put a border around a lace pattern, this will square it up. This seed (moss) stitch border sets off the lace really well and emphasizes the pattern.

materials

Rooster Almerino DK, shade 211
Brighton Rock
Needle size: US 6 (4mm)

instructions

Cast on 41 sts.
Knit 4 rows in seed (moss) stitch.
Cont as follows making a seed (moss) stitch border of 5 sts at the beginning and end of each row.
Row 5 (wrong side) Purl.
Row 6 K1, *Yo, k3, sl 1, k2tog, psso, k3, yo, k1; rep from * to end.
Rep these 2 rows 3 times more.
Row 13 Purl.
Row 14 K2tog, *k3, yo, k1, yo, k3, sl 1, k2tog, psso; rep from * to last 9 sts, k3, yo, k1, yo, k3, skpo.
Rep Rows 13–14 three more times.
Rep Rows 5–20 three more times.
Knit 4 rows in seed (moss) stitch.
Bind (cast) off.

crest of the wave pattern

A pretty delicate lace—if you've mastered this stitch in a light worsted (DK) yarn, try it in a fine, lace weight yarn to see its full potential.

materials

Rooster Almerino DK, shade 203
Strawberry Cream
Needle size: US 6 (4mm)

special abbreviation

Ssk (slip, slip, knit)—slip next 2 sts one at a time, insert left needle into fronts of slipped sts and knit tog

instructions

Cast on 34 sts.
Rows 1–4 Knit.
Row 5 K1, *k2tog twice, [yo, k1] 3 times, yo [ssk twice]; rep from * to end.
Row 6 Purl.
Rows 7, 9, 11 As Row 5.
Rows 8, 10, 12 As Row 6.
Rep these twelve rows twice more.
Knit 4 rows.
Bind (cast) off.

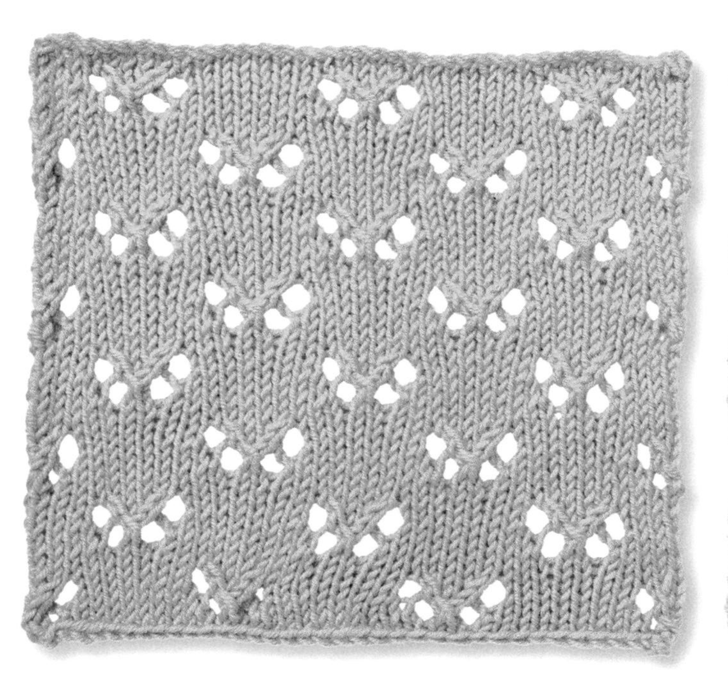

butterfly lace

If you turn this square upside down as shown here, the eyelets form the shapes of fluttering butterflies.

materials

Rooster Almerino DK, shade 210 Custard
Needle size: US 6 (4mm)

instructions

Cast on 37 sts.
Row 1 (right side) Knit.
Row 2 and every alt row Purl.
Row 3 K4, yo, skpo, k1, k2tog, yo, *k7, yo, skpo, k1, k2tog, yo; rep from * to last 4 sts, k4.
Row 5 K5, yo, sl 1, k2tog, psso, yo, *k9, yo, sl 1, k2tog, psso, yo; rep from * to last 5 sts, k5.
Row 7 Knit.
Row 9 K1, *k2tog, yo, k7, yo, skpo, k1; rep from * to end.
Row 11 K2tog, yo, k9, *yo, sl 1, k2tog, psso, yo, k9; rep from * to last 2 sts, yo, skpo.
Row 12 Purl.
Rep these twelve rows until work until measures 6in. (15cm).
Bind (cast) off.

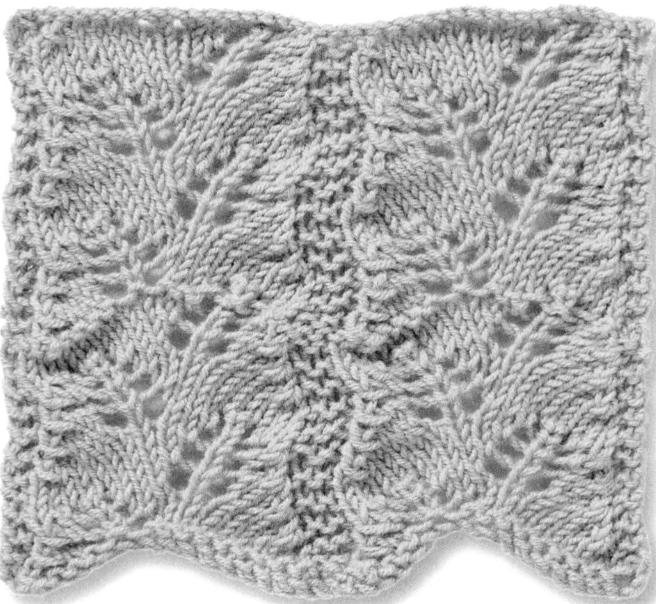

fern lace

Delicate little leaves seem to burst from this pattern. Lots of movement, but in a very satisfying design.

materials

Rooster Almerino DK, shade 203 Strawberry Cream
Needle size: US 6 (4mm)

instructions

Cast on 38 sts.
Row 1 and all WS rows Purl.
Row 2 P2, *k9, yo, k1, yo, k3, sl 1, k2tog, psso, p2; rep from * to end.
Row 4 P2, *k10, yo, k1, yo, k2, sl 1 k2tog, psso, p2; rep from * to end.
Row 6 P2, *k3tog, k4, yo, k1, yo, k3, [yo, k1] twice, sl 1, k2tog, psso, p2; rep from * to end.
Row 8 P2, *k3tog, k3, yo, k1, yo, k9, p2; rep from * to end.
Row 10 P2, *k3tog, k2, yo, k1, yo, k10, p2; rep from * to end.
Row 12 P2, *k3tog, [k1, yo] twice, k3, yo, k1, yo, k4, sl 1, k2tog, psso, p2; rep from * to end
Rep Rows 1–12 three more times.
Bind (cast) off.

seashell lace

When making the cluster for this stitch, take care not to snag the wool. Count the stitches regularly to make sure you have not picked up any extra loops.

materials

Rooster Almerino DK, shade 208 Ocean
Needle size: US 6 (4mm)

special abbreviation

Cluster 5—pass next 5 sts onto rh needle dropping extra loops, pass these 5 sts back onto lh needle, [k1, p1, k1, p1, k1] into all 5 sts tog, wrapping yarn twice around needle for each st

instructions

Cast on 31 sts.
Row 1 Knit.
Row 2 P1, *p5 wrapping yarn twice around needle for each st, p1; rep from * to end.
Row 3 K1, *Cluster 5, k1; rep from * to end.
Pass these 5 sts back onto left hand needle.
Row 4 P1, *k5 dropping extra loops, p1; rep from * to end.
Row 5 Knit.
Row 6 P4, p5 wrapping yarn twice around needle for each st, *p1, p5 wrapping yarn twice around needle for each st; rep from * to last 4 sts, p4.
Row 7 K4, Cluster 5, *k1, Cluster 5; rep from * to last 4 sts, k4.
Row 8 P4, k5 dropping extra loops, *p1, k5 dropping extra loops; rep from * to last 4 sts, p4.
Rep these eight rows three times more.
Row 25 Knit.
Bind (cast) off.

ridged eyelet pattern

A bumpy lace that also has small eyelet holes as well as ridges.

materials

Yarn used: Rooster DK, shade 205 Glace
Needle size: US 6 (4mm)

instructions

Cast on 28 sts.
Rows 1–3 Purl.
Row 4 *Yrn, skpo; rep from * to end.
Rep these four rows until work measures 6in. (15cm).
Bind (cast) off.

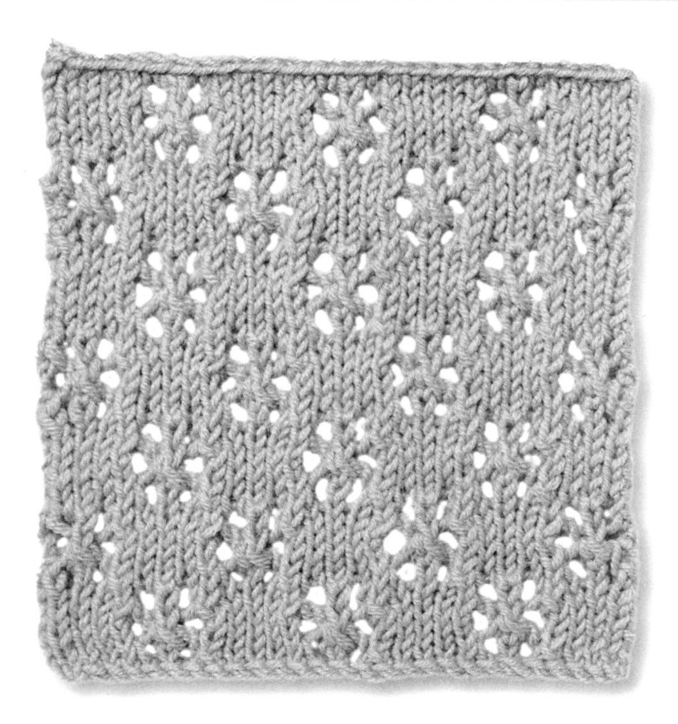

snowflake lace

Snowflake-shaped eyelets give a very feminine and delicate look to this square.

materials

Rooster Almerino DK, shade 203 Strawberry Cream
Needle size: US 6 (4mm)

special abbreviation

Ssk (slip, slip, knit)—slip next 2 sts one at a time, insert left needle into fronts of slipped sts and knit tog

instructions

Cast on 29 sts.
Row 1 and every alt row (wrong side) Purl.
Row 2 K4, *ssk, yo, k1, yo, k2tog, k3; rep from * to last st, k1.
Row 4 K5, *yo, sl 2, k1, p2sso, yo, k5; rep from * to end.
Row 6 As Row 2.
Row 8 Ssk, yo, k1, yo, k2tog, *k3, ssk, yo, k1, yo, k2tog; rep from * to end.
Row 10 K1, *yo, sl 2, k1, p2sso, yo, k5; rep from * to last st, k1.
Row 13 As Row 8.
Rep these twelve rows until work measures 6in. (15cm).
Bind (cast) off.

little shell

This pretty little textured pattern looks like lines of overlapping scallop shells.

materials

Rooster Almerino DK, shade 201 Cornish
Needle size: US 6 (4mm)

instructions

Cast on 44 sts.
Row 1 Knit.
Row 2 Purl.
Row 3 *K2, yrn, p1, p3 tog, p1, yrn; rep from * to last 2 sts, k2.
Row 4 Purl.
Rep these 4 rows until work measures 6in. (15cm).
Bind (cast) off.

petal lace leaf

This is part of the petal design that can be seen on the Lace Bed Throw on page 94.

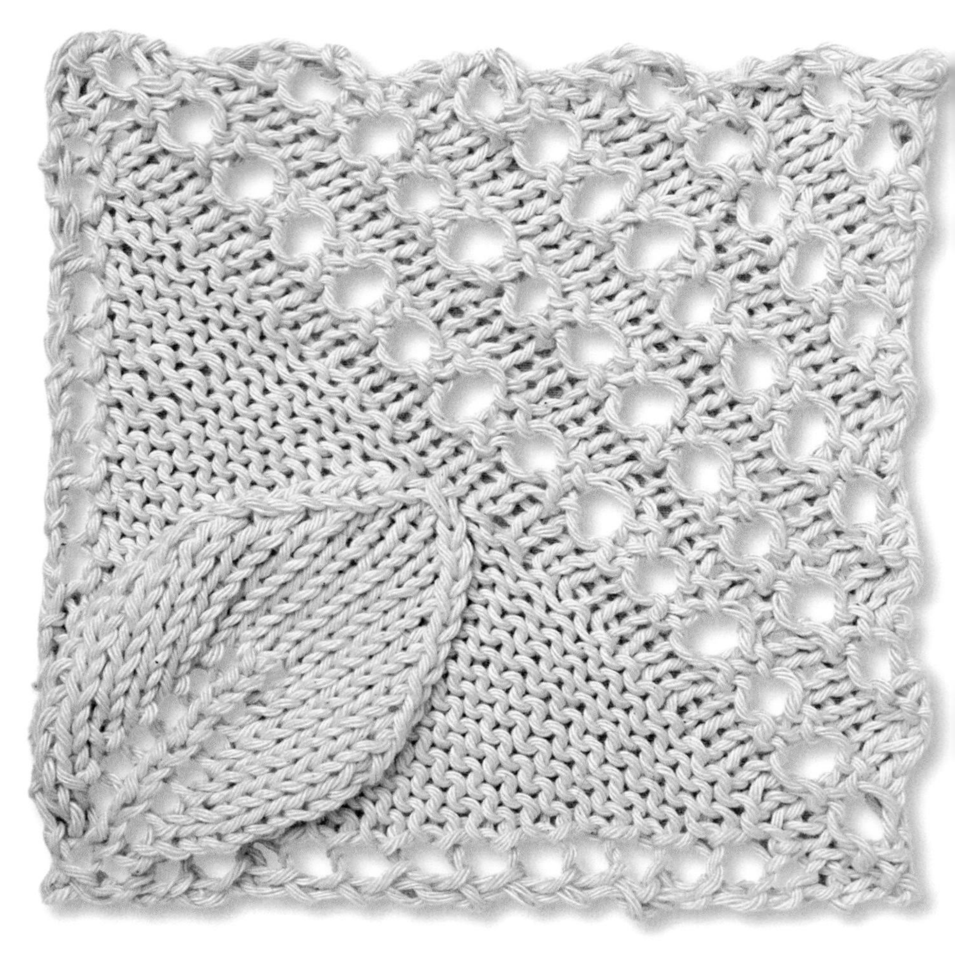

materials

Pegasus Craft Cotton, shade White
Needle size: US 8 (5mm)

instructions

Cast on 2 sts.
Row 1 (right side) K1, yo, k1.
Row 2 P3.
Row 3 [K1, yo] twice, k1.
Row 4 P5.
Row 5 [K1, yo] 4 times, k1.
Row 6 P9.
Row 7 K1, yfrn, p1, k2, yo, k1, yo, k2, p1, yon, k1.
Row 8 P2, k1, p7, k1, p2.
Row 9 K1, yfrn, p2, k3, yo, k1, yo, k3, p2, yon, k1.
Row 10 P2, k2, p9, k2, p2.
Row 11 K1, yfrn, p3, k4, yo, k1, yo, k4, p3, yon, k1.
Row 12 P2, k3, p11, k3, p2.
Row 13 K1, yfrn, p4, k5, yo, k1, yo, k5, p4, yon, k1.
Row 14 P2, k4, p13, k4, p2.
Row 15 K1 yfrn, p5, k6, yo, k1, yo, k6, p5, yon, k1.
Row 16 P2, k5, p15, k5, p2.
Row 17 K1, yfrn, p6, skpo, k11, k2tog, p6, yon, k1.
Row 18 P2, k6, p13, k6, p2.
Row 19 K1, yfrn, p7, skpo, k9, k2tog, p7, yon, k1.
Row 20 P2, k7, p11, k7, p2.
Row 21 K1, yfrn, p8, skpo, k7, k2tog, p8, yon, k1.
Row 22 P2, k8, p9, k8, p2.
Row 23 K1, yfrn, p9, skpo, k5, k2tog, p9, yon, k1.
Row 24 P2, k9, p7, k9, p2.
Row 25 K1, yfrn, p10, skpo, k3, k2tog, p10, yon, k1.
Row 26 P2, k10, p5, k10, p2.
Row 27 K1, yfrn, p11, skpo, k1, k2tog, p11, yon, k1.
Row 28 P2, k11, p3, k11, p2.
Row 29 K1, yfrn, p12, sl 1, k2tog, psso, p12, yon, k1.
Row 30 Purl. (29 sts)
Row 31 Inc in first st, k27, inc in last st. (31 sts)
Rows 32–33 Purl.
Row 34 [K2tog, yo] to last 3 sts, k3tog.
Row 35 Purl.
Row 36 P2tog, p to last 2 sts, p2tog.
Row 37 Knit.
Row 38 As Row 36.
Row 39 Purl.
Rep Rows 34–39 three times more then Rows 34–37 once.
Next row P3tog.
Bind (cast) off.

stripes & color

It's great to mix colors, and stripes and other color designs are easily created by changing color either at the end or in the middle of a row. Make sure you always sew the ends in after you finish, by threading them along the edges of the same color at the back of the work.

brighton beach

A bright, sunny square with memories of lazy, warm days on the sand of the beach at Brighton.

materials

Rowan Handknit Cotton, shade 315 Double Choc (A), shade 336 Sunflower (B), shade 313 Slick (C)
Needle size: US 6 (4mm)

instructions

Cast on 30 sts using A.
Row 1 Knit to end.
Row 2 Purl to end.
Row 3 As Row 1.
Change to B.
Row 4 Knit to end.
Row 5 Purl to end.
Change to A.
Rows 6–8 Work in st st.
Change to C.
Rows 9–14 Work in st st.
Change to A.
Rows 15–17 Work in st st.
Change to B.
Rows 18–19 Work in st st.
Change to A.
Rows 20–22 Work in st st.
Change to C.
Rows 23–28 Work in st st.
Change to A.
Rows 29–31 Work in st st.
Change to B.
Rows 32–33 Work in st st.
Change to A.
Rows 34–36 Work in st st.
Bind (cast) off.

nautical stripe

This is a great combination of colors to drop into a knitted patchwork that is based around a nautical theme.

materials

Rowan Pure Wool DK, shade 013 Enamel (A), shade 044 Frost (B), shade 010 Indigo (C)
Needle size: US 6 (4mm)

instructions

Cast on 34 sts using A.
Using in stockinette (stocking) stitch throughout, work 4 rows in A, change to B, work 4 rows in B, change to C, work 4 rows in C. Cont in this way changing color in the same sequence every four rows for a total of 44 rows or until work measures 6in. (15cm).
Bind (cast) off.

battenberg cake

Delicious and pretty, the colors in this square really do look good enough to eat.

materials

Rooster Almerino DK, shade 201 Cornish (A), shade 203 Strawberry Cream (B), shade 210 Custard (C)
Needle size: US 6 (4mm)

instructions

Cast on 34 sts using A.
Work 42 rows in stockinette (stocking) stitch, following the chart.
Bind (cast) off.

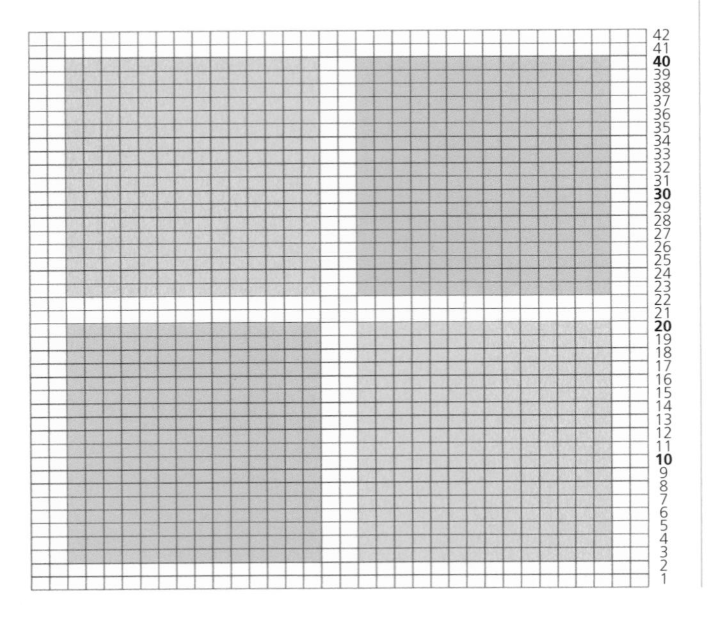

two-row stripe

Great nautical colors in a summer cotton, but these simple stripes would look great in any combination of colors.

materials

Debbie Bliss Cotton DK, shade 39 Mid Blue (A) and shade 02 Cream (B)
Needle size: US 6 (4mm)

instructions

Cast on 32 sts using A.
Using in stockinette (stocking) stitch throughout, work 2 rows in A, change to B, work 2 rows in B.
Cont in this way changing color in the same sequence every two rows for a total of 44 rows or until work measures 6in. (15cm).
Bind (cast) off.

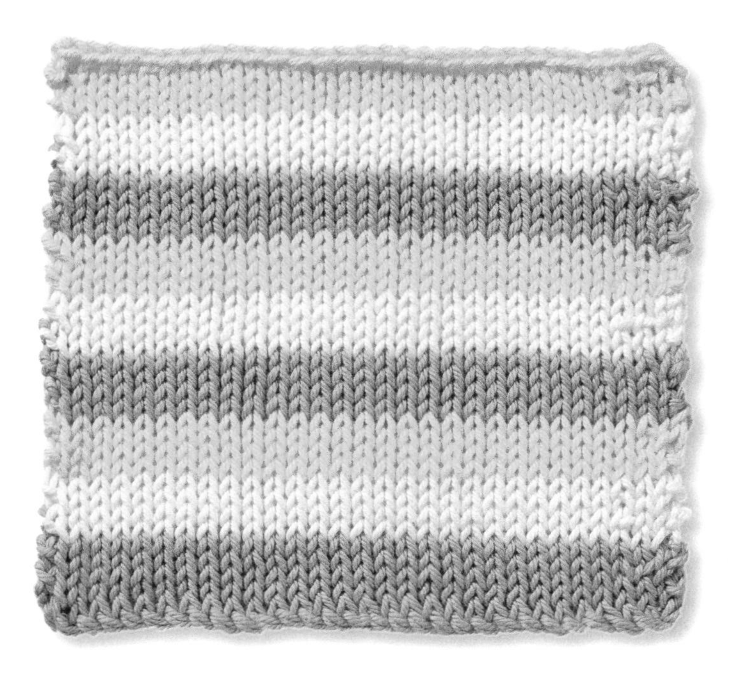

candy cane

A bright, candy-colored square in a series of simple 4-row stripes.

materials

Rowan Handknit Cotton, shade 303 Sugar (A), shade 251 Ecru (B), shade 336 Sunflower (C)
Needle size: US 6 (4mm)

instructions

Cast on 30 sts using A.
Using stockinette (stocking) stitch throughout, work 4 rows in A, change to B, work 4 rows in B, change to C, work 4 rows in C.
Cont in this way until work measures 6in. (15cm).
Bind (cast) off.

basket stripes

This basket stitch is a very traditional stitch that replicates the look of a wicker basket. It works well on its own with one single color, or in warm multicolors as here.

materials

Rooster Almerino DK, shade 201 Cornish (A), shade 203 Strawberry Cream (B), shade 213 Cherry (C)
Needle size: US 6 (4mm)

instructions

Cast on 36 sts using A.
Row 1 *K4, p4; rep from * to last 4 sts, k4.
Row 2 *P4, k4; rep from * to last 4 sts, p4.
Row 3 As Row 1.
Row 4 As Row 2.
Change to B.
Rows 5, 7 As Row 2.
Rows 6, 8 As Row 1.
Change to C.
Rows 9, 11 As Row 1.
Rows 10, 12 As Row 2.
Change to A.
Rows 13, 15 As Row 2.
Rows 14, 16 As Row 1.
Change to Col B.
Rows 17, 19 As Row 1.
Rows 18, 20 As Row 2.
Change to C.
Rows 21, 23 As Row 2.
Rows 22, 24 As Row 1.
Change to A.
Rows 25, 27 As Row 1.
Rows 26, 28 As Row 2.
Change to B.
Rows 29, 31 As Row 2.
Rows 30, 32 As Row 1.
Change to C.
Rows 33, 35 As Row 1.
Rows 34, 36 As Row 2.
Change to A.
Rows 37, 39 As Row 2.
Rows 38, 40 As Row 1.
Change to B.
Rows 41, 43 As Row 1.
Rows 42, 44 As Row 2.
Change to C
Rows 45, 47 As Row 2.
Rows 46, 48 As Row 1.
Bind (cast) off.

quarter master

This quick and easy garter stitch block uses four different colors, one in each quadrant.

materials

Rooster Almerino DK, shade 207 Gooseberry (A), shade 205 Glace (B), shade 203 Strawberry Cream (C), shade 201 Cornish (D)
Needle size: US 6 (4mm)

instructions

Cast on 16 sts using A, then 16 sts in B.
Using garter stitch throughout, cont in these colors as set until the work measures 3in. (7.5cm).
Change A to C, and B to D.
Cont in these colors as set until work measures 6in. (15cm).
Bind (cast) off.

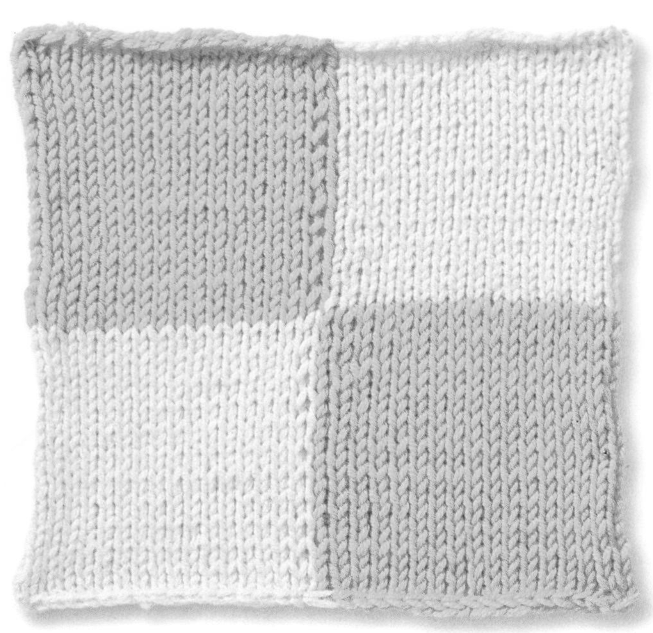

block quarters

Making simple color blocks is a great introduction to using color. Use the intarsia method of twisting the two colors of yarn together to bind them together at the join.

materials

Rooster Almerino DK 210 Custard (A), 201 Cornish (B)
Needle size: US 6 (4mm)

instructions

Cast on 17 sts using A, then 17 sts in B.
Using in stockinette (stocking) stitch throughout, cont in these two colors for 22 rows or until work measures 3in. (7.5cm).
Alternate colors and work another 22 rows or until work measures 6in. (15cm).
Bind (cast) off.

garter stitch stripes

Garter stitch is the easiest stitch and these random stripes make an interesting color combination. This square is knitted in an Aran weight yarn because I love the Rooster Almerino Aran palette.

materials

Rooster Almerino Aran, shade 305 Custard (A), shade 304 Mushroom (B), shade 306 Gooseberry (C), shade 302 Sugared Almond (D), shade 310 Rooster (E), shade 309 Ocean (F), shade 301 Cornish (G), shade 308 Spiced Plum (H), shade 303 Strawberry Cream (I)
Needle size: US 6 (4mm)

instructions

Cast on 30 sts using A.
Work in garter stitch (all rows knit) throughout as follows:
2 rows in A.
2 rows in B.
6 rows in C.
2 rows in D.
6 rows in E.
4 rows in F.
2 rows in G.
8 rows in H.
4 rows in I.
4 rows in G.
2 rows in B.
6 rows in D
3 rows in C.
Bind (cast) off.

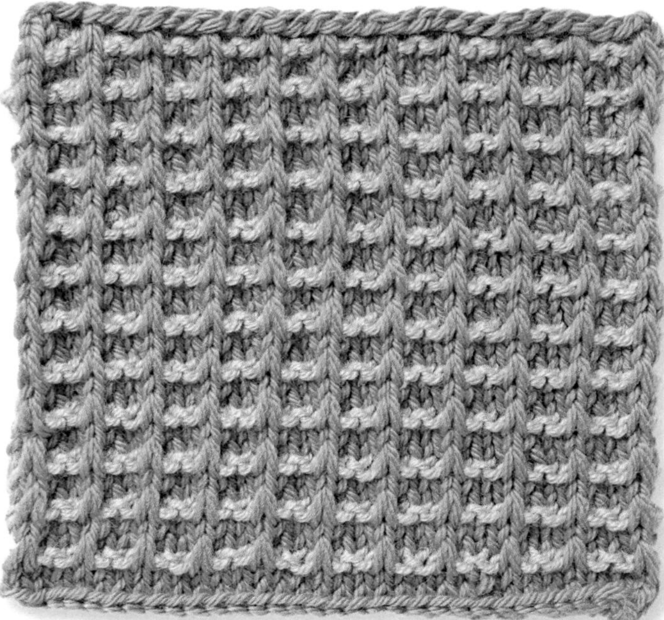

slip stitch tweed

Slipping stitches is an easy and effective way of working with color. Slip all stitches purlwise. Carry the colors not in use up the side of your work.

materials

Rooster Almerino DK, shade 207 Gooseberry (A), shade 203 Strawberry Cream (B)
Needle size: US 6 (4mm)

instructions

Cast on 39 sts using A.
Row 1 Using A, knit.
Row 2 Purl.
Change to B.
Row 3 K1, sl 1, *k2, sl 1; rep from * to last st, k1.
Row 4 K1, *yarn to front, sl 1 purlwise, yarn to back, k2; rep from * to last 2 sts, yarn to front, sl 1 purlwise, yarn to back, k1.
Rep these four rows fourteen times more, ending with Row 4.
Using A, rep Rows 1–2.
Bind (cast) off.

mosaics

For a blanket, alternate colors to give a multicolor, random mosaic effect.

materials

BLOCK 1: HEATHERS
Cascade 220 DK, shade 2419 Aster Heather (A), shade 2429 Irelande (B), shade 8901 Groseille (C), shade 8912 Lilac Mist (D), shade 9478 Candy Pink (E)

BLOCK 2: TEXTURED
Rooster Almerino DK, shade 210 Custard (E), shade 204 Grape (F), shade 207 Gooseberry (G), shade 203 Strawberry Cream (H), shade 205 Glace (I), shade 209 Smoothie (J), shade 214 Damson (K), shade 201 Cornish (L), shade 206 Ocean (M)
Needle size: US 6 (4mm)

instructions

BLOCK 1: HEATHERS
Cast on 10 sts using A, then 10 sts in B, then a further 10 sts in C.
Using stockinette (stocking) stitch throughout, work 12 rows in each color block. Follow the chart for color changes and work for a total of 36 rows.
Bind (cast) off.

BLOCK 2: TEXTURED
Cast on 10 sts using E, then 10 sts in F, then a further 10 sts in G.
Row 1 Using E, [k1, pl] for 10 sts, change to F, [k1, pl] for 10 sts, change to G, [k1, pl] to end.
Row 2 Using G, [pl, k1] for 10 sts, change to F, [pl, k1] for 10 sts, change to E, [pl, k1] to end.
Rep Rows 1–2 seven more times until block measures 2in. (5cm).
Change colors.
Row 17 As Row 1, using H, I and J.
Row 18 As Row 2, using J, I and H.
Rep Rows 17–18 seven more times until color block measures 2in. (5cm).
Change colors.
Row 33 As Row 1, using K, L and M.
Row 34 As Row 2, using M, L and K.
Rep Rows 33–34 seven more times until color block measures 2in. (5cm).
Bind (cast) off.

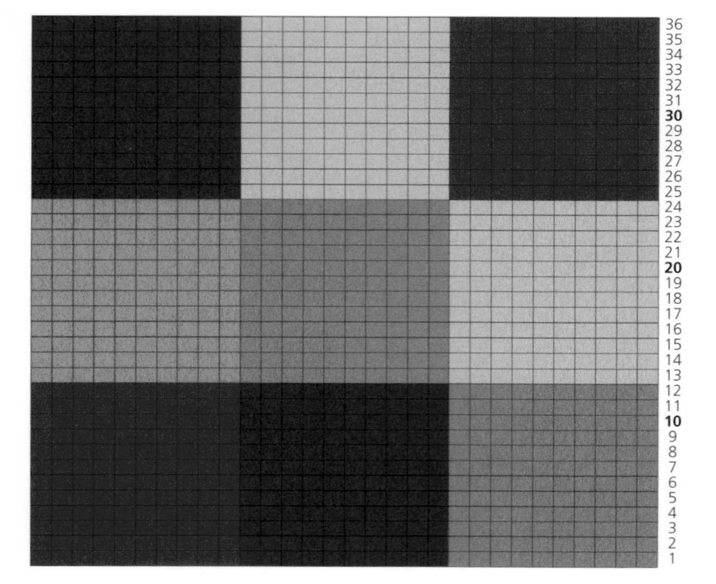

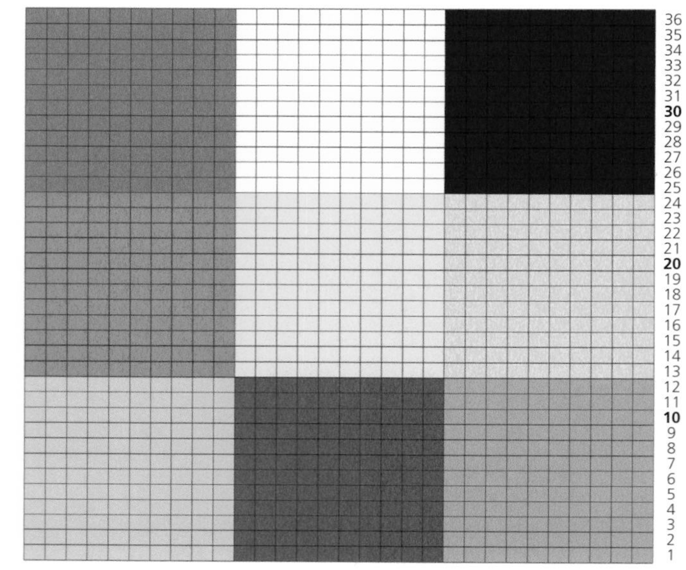

jazzy

This square is made up using little blocks of stockinette (stocking) stitch and seed (moss) stitch. The stockinette (stocking) stitch tends to bring your knitting in slightly smaller than the seed (moss) stitch, so when working stockinette (stocking) stitch, make the gauge (tension) a little looser to make the square even.

materials

Rooster Almerino DK, shade 203 Strawberry Cream (A), shade 206 Caviar (B), shade 211 Brighton Rock (C)
Rowan Pure Wool DK, shade 042 Dahlia (D)
Needle size: US 6 (4mm)

instructions

Cast on 18 sts using A, then 18 sts in B.
Row 1 Using B, k16, change to A, k1, p1 to end. (36 sts)
Row 2 Using A, p1, k1 for 16 sts, change to B, purl to end.
Rep Rows 1–2 until work measures 3in. (7.5cm) ending with a Row 2.
Next row Using C, k1, P1 for 16 sts, change to D, k to end.
Next row Using D, p16, change to C, p1, k1 to end.
Rep these two rows until work measures 6in. (15cm).
Bind (cast) off.

humbug

A favorite at the candy store, these stripes evoke memories of the humbugs of my childhood.

materials

Debbie Bliss, Rialto DK, shade 03 Black (A), shade 02 Off White (B)
Needle size: US 6 (4mm)

instructions

Cast on 35 sts using A.
Using stockinette (stocking) stitch throughout, knit 2 rows in A and 3 rows in B. Alternate this color sequence for 45 rows or until work measures 6in. (15cm).
Bind (cast) off.

sherbet fizz

All the fizzy colors of sherbet will just bounce off your knitting needles.

materials

Rooster Almerino DK, shade 211 Brighton Rock (A)
Cascade 220 DK, shade 2419 Aster Heather (B)
Rooster Almerino DK, shade 210 Custard (C)
Cascade 220 DK, shade 8912 Lilac Mist (D)
Needle size: US 6 (4mm)

instructions

Cast on 32 sts using A.
Work in seed (moss) stitch as follows:
Row 1 K1, p1 to end.
Row 2 P1, k1 to end.
Change color.
Rep Rows 1–2 for 50 rows, alternating colors every 2 rows.
Bind (cast) off.

---

dotty

A really fun and colorful textured stitch, which would look great on a cardigan or in a blanket.

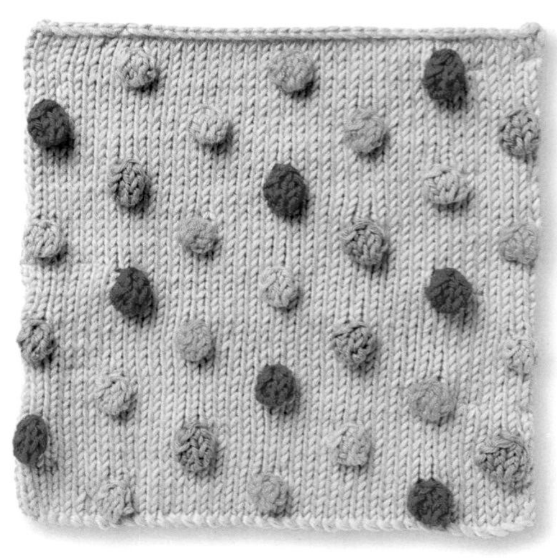

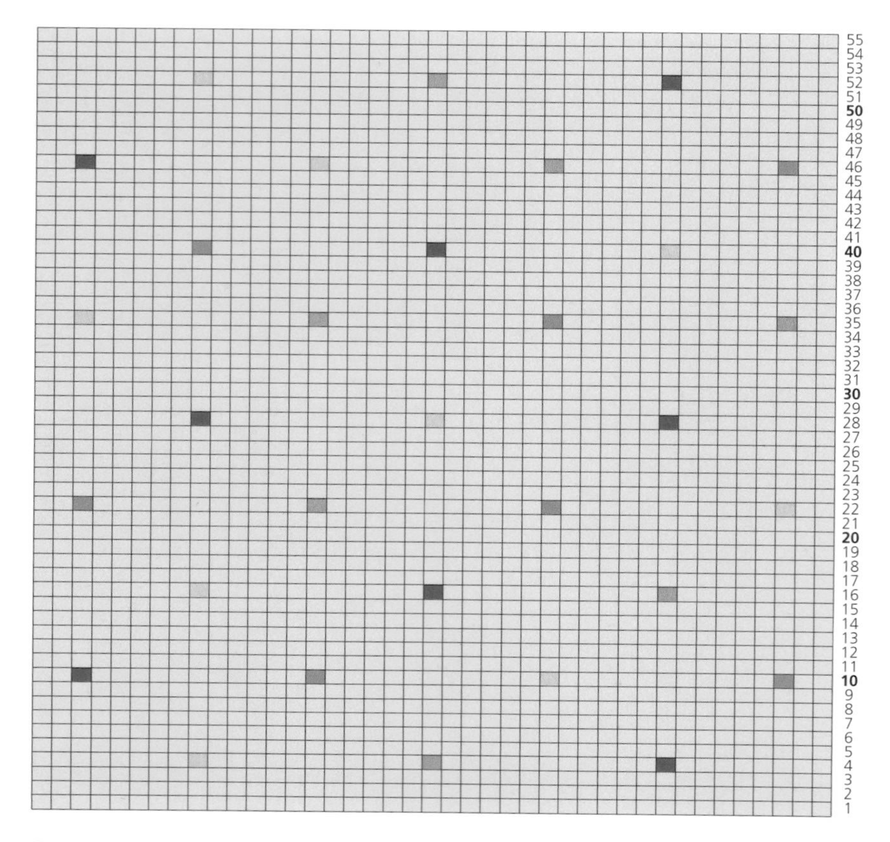

materials

Rowan Classic Bamboo Soft, shade 103 (A)
Rowan Cotton Glace, shade 812 Ivy (B), shade 741 Poppy (C), shade 826 Carnation (D), shade 832 Persimmon (E)
Needle size: US 3 (3.25mm)

instructions

Cast on 41 sts using A.
Using stockinette (stocking) stitch work 55 rows, following the chart for positioning of contrast colored bobbles.

BOBBLE
Using B, C, D, or E, k1, p1, k1, p1, k1 into next st, turn, p5, turn, k5, turn, p2tog, p1, p2tog, turn, sl 1, k2tog, psso. Break off yarn. Continue working in A until next bobble.
Bind (cast) off.

intarsia

The great thing about intarsia knitting is that you can make pictures and motifs. Intarsia is a technique of using different colors in which the unused yarn is not carried along the back of the work. Here is a variety of gorgeous pictures and motifs; put them in a frame as artwork or incorporate into other knitting.

little speckled hen

This is a very cute hen pattern; try changing the color of the hen to the color of your choice.

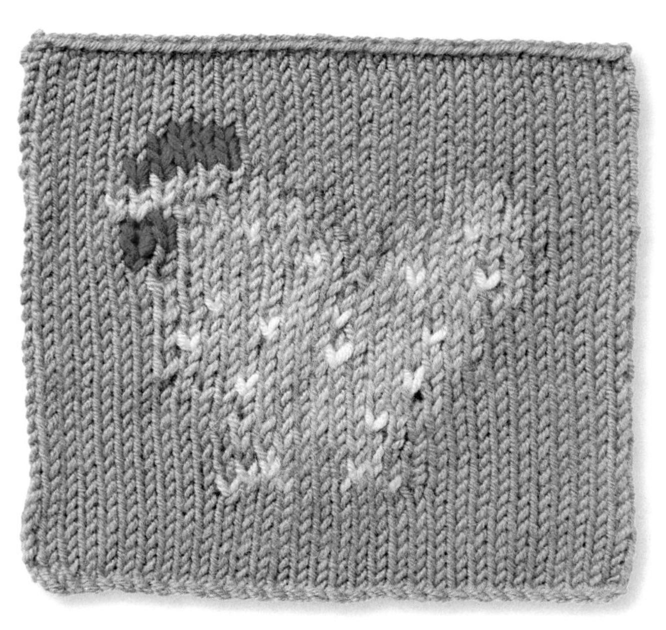

materials

Rooster Almerino DK, shade 207 Gooseberry (A), shade 202 Hazelnut (B), shade 203 Strawberry Cream (C), shade 201 Cornish (D), shade 213 Cherry (E), shade 210 Custard (F)
Needle size: US 6 (4mm)

instructions

Cast on 32 sts.
Work 42 rows in stockinette (stocking) stitch following the chart.
Bind (cast) off.

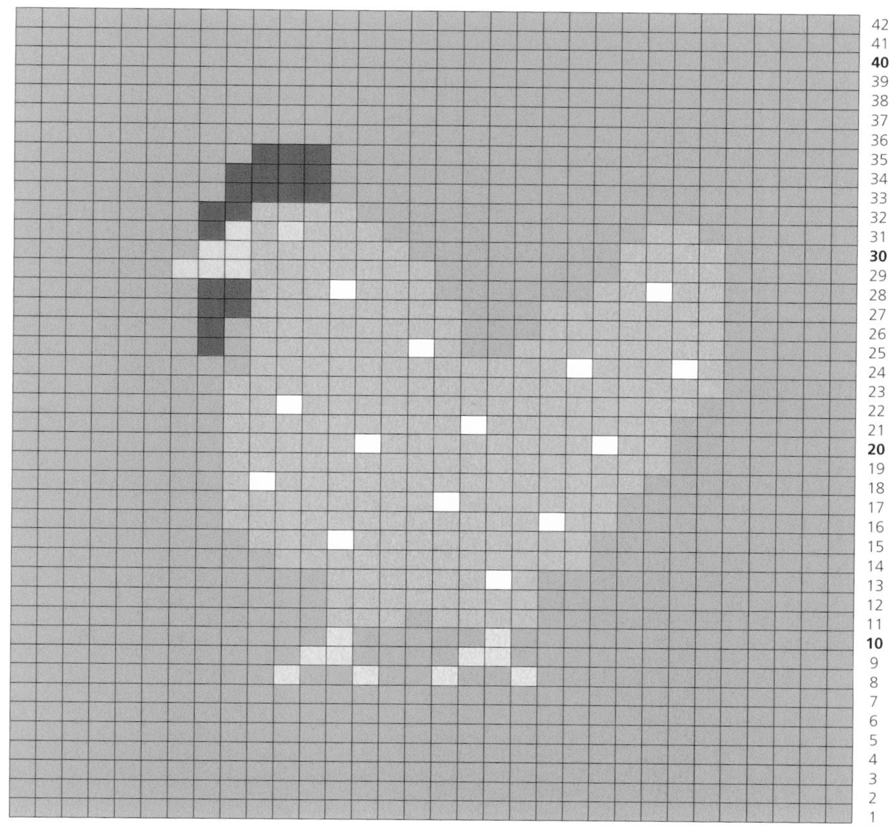

house

Knit your own house! Change the colors to match those of your own home and frame the square when you have finished it.

materials

Rooster Almerino DK, shade 205 Glace (A), shade 204 Grape (B), shade 206 Caviar (C), shade 201 Cornish (D), shade 207 Gooseberry (E), shade 202 Hazelnut (F), shade 210 Custard (G), shade 203 Strawberry Cream (H)
Needle size: US 6 (4mm)

instructions

Cast on 32 sts.
Work 42 rows in stockinette (stocking) stitch following the chart.
Knit the roof in seed (moss) stitch.
Bind (cast) off.

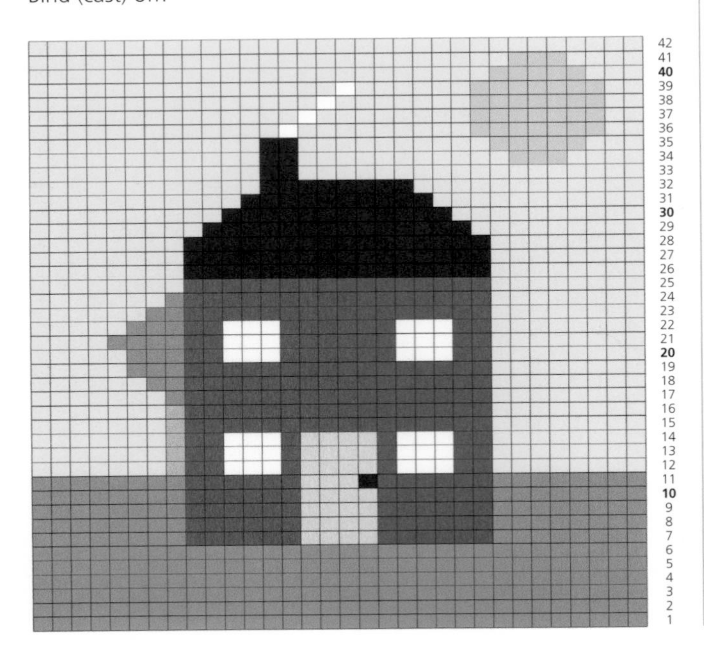

bunny rabbit

This cute little rabbit would look great in a blanket with other different colored bunnies.

materials

Rooster Almerino DK, shade 202 Hazelnut (A), shade 201 Cornish (B), shade 203 Strawberry Cream (C), shade 205 Glace (D)
Needle size: US 6 (4mm)

instructions

Cast on 32 sts.
Work 42 rows in stockinette (stocking) stitch following the chart.
Bind (cast) off.

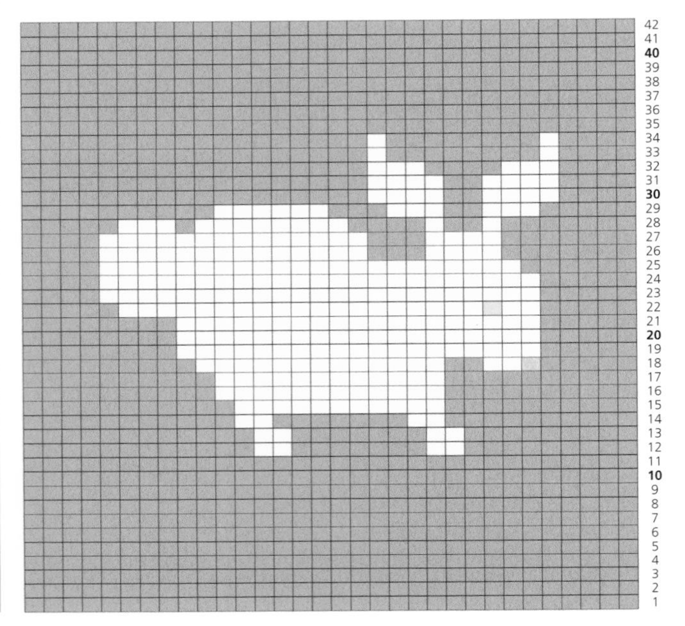

strawberry tea cozy

Such a lovely little teapot square featuring a very smart strawberry teapot cover.

materials

Rooster Almerino DK, shade 205 Glace (A)
Debbie Bliss Rialto DK, shade 12 Red (B), shade 02 Cream (C)
Rooster Almerino DK, shade 207 Gooseberry (D)
Needle size: US 6 (4mm)

instructions

Cast on 32 sts.
Work 42 rows in stockinette (stocking) stitch following the chart.
Bind (cast) off.

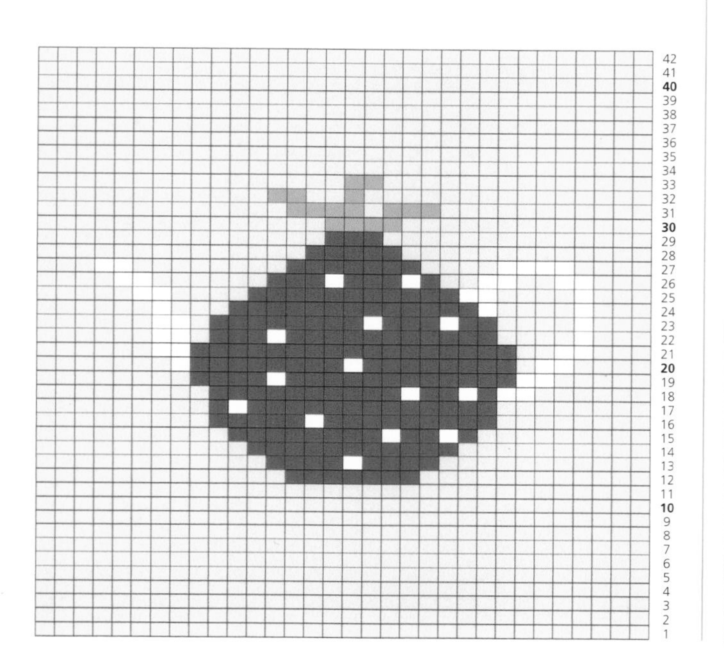

flower

A sunny, happy flower square.

materials

Rowan Pure Wool DK, shade 043 Flour (A)
Debbie Bliss Rialto, shade 32 Orange (B), shade 10 Green (C)
Needle size: US 6 (4mm)

instructions

Cast on 32 sts.
Work 40 rows in stockinette (stocking) stitch following the chart.
Bind (cast) off.

outlined spots

Big, colorful, outlined spots make a very striking design on squares.

materials

Cascade 220 DK, shade 8901 Groseille (A), shade 2429 Irelande (B), shade 8912 Lilac Mist (C)
Needle size: US 6 (4mm)

instructions

Cast on 32 sts.
Work 42 rows in stockinette (stocking) stitch following the chart.
Bind (cast) off.

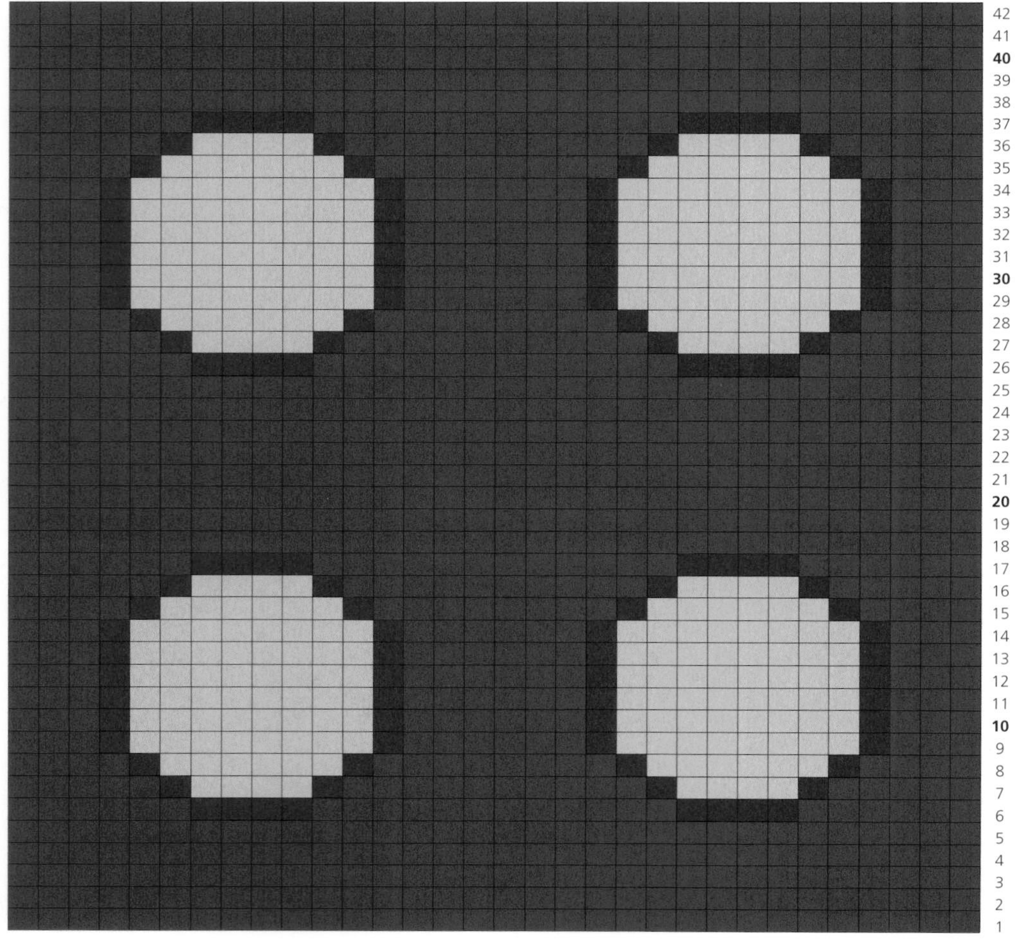

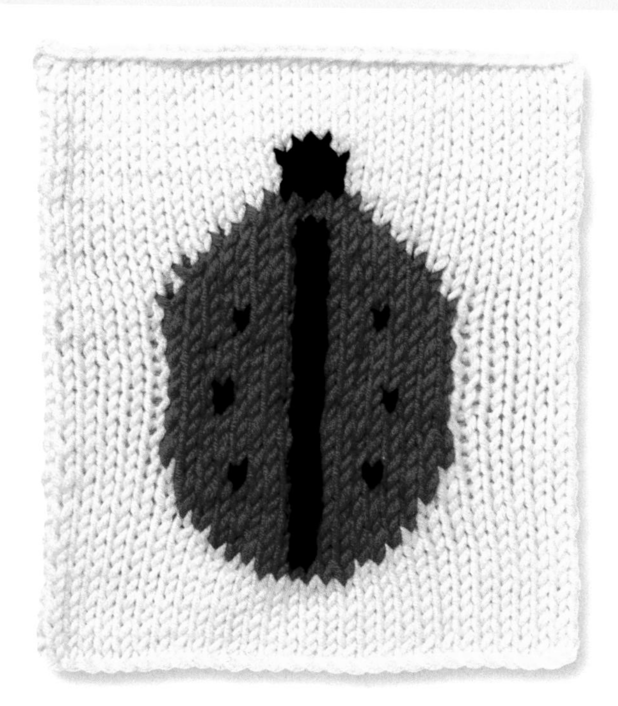

ladybug

These colorful insects are a firm favorite motif and can be used in all sorts of intarsia projects.

materials

Debbie Bliss Rialto, shade 02 Off White (A), shade 12 Red (B), shade 03 Black (C)
Needle size: US 6 (4mm)

instructions

Cast on 30 sts.
Work 42 rows in stockinette (stocking) stitch following the chart.
Bind (cast) off.

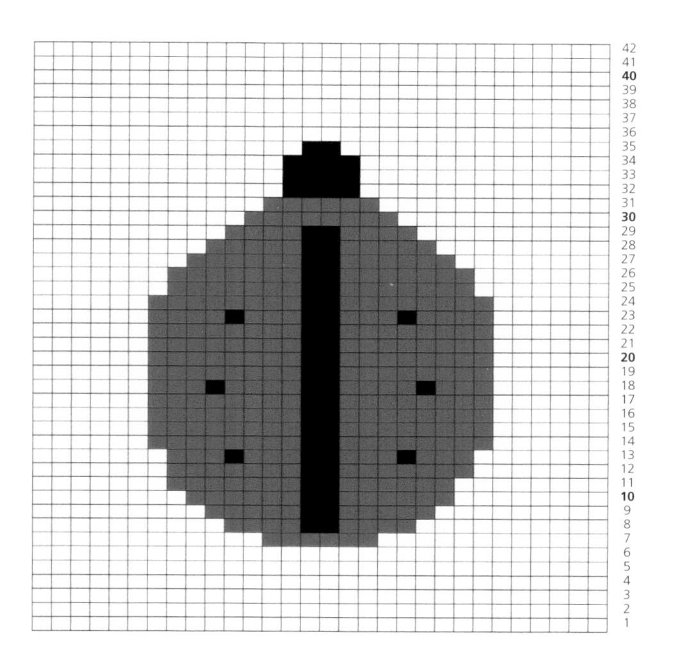

love heart

A heart shape is great on blankets and bibs—or for the Heart Lavender Pillow on page 124.

materials

Rowan Pure Wool DK, shade 043 Flour (A)
Debbie Bliss Rialto DK, shade 12 Red (B)
Needle size: US 6 (4mm)

instructions

Cast on 32 sts.
Work 42 rows in stockinette (stocking) stitch following the chart.
Bind (cast) off.

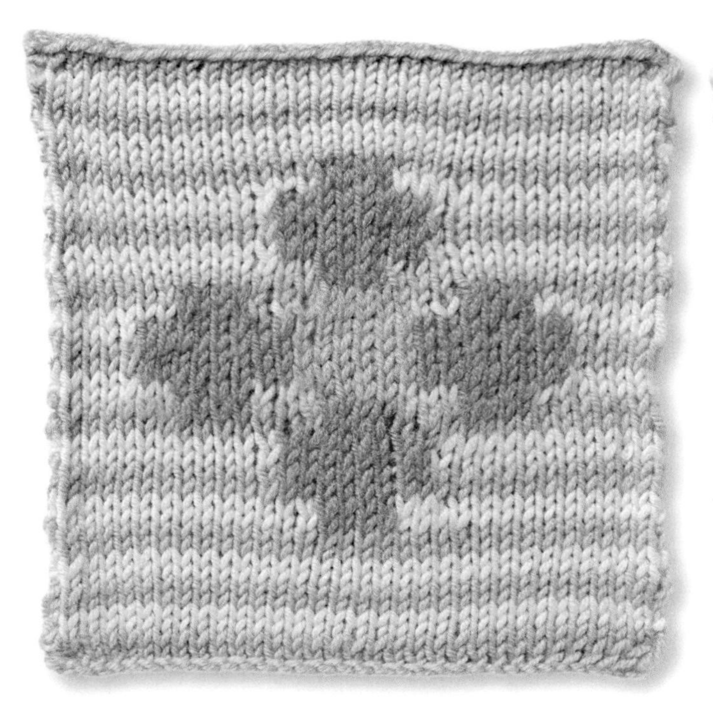

striped flower

Soft stripes and a bright flower make a striking square block.

materials

Rooster Almerino DK, shade 205 Glace (A), shade 201 Cornish (B), shade 203 Strawberry Cream (C), shade 211 Brighton Rock (D)
Needle size: US 6 (4mm)

instructions

Cast on 32 sts.
Work 42 rows in stockinette (stocking) stitch following the chart.
Bind (cast) off.

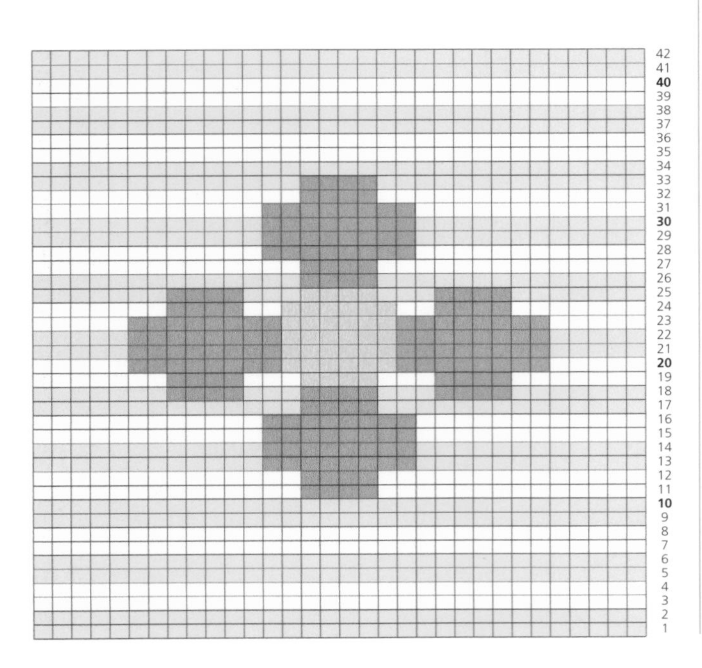

tulip

Try making a variety of these squares, changing the colors of the tulip.

materials

Debbie Bliss Rialto DK, shade 02 Cream (A), shade 07 Yellow (B)
Rowan Pure Wool DK, shade 020 Parsley (C)
Needle size: US 6 (4mm)

instructions

Cast on 32 sts.
Work 42 rows in stockinette (stocking) stitch following the chart.
Bind (cast) off.

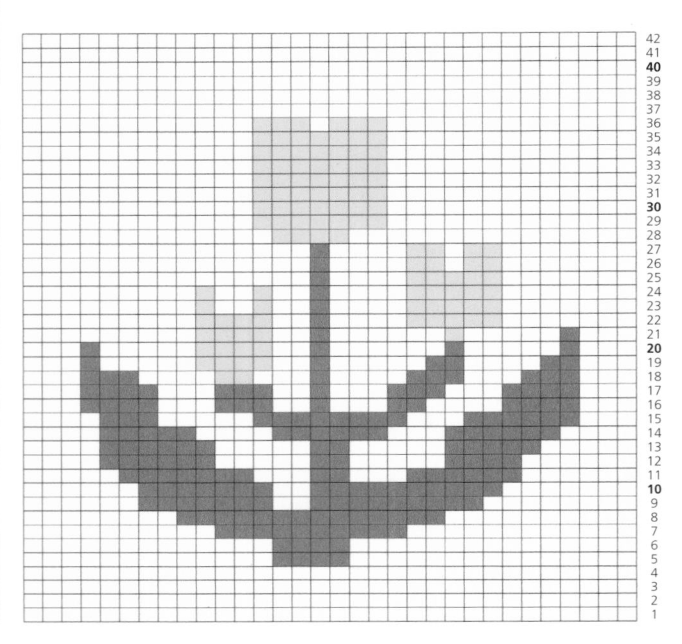

star

The background color of this square makes it the perfect foil to let the star really stand out.

materials

Rooster Almerino DK, shade 206 Caviar (A), shade 201 Cornish (B)
Needle size: US 6 (4mm)

instructions

Cast on 32 sts.
Work 42 rows in stockinette (stocking) stitch following the chart.
Bind (cast) off.

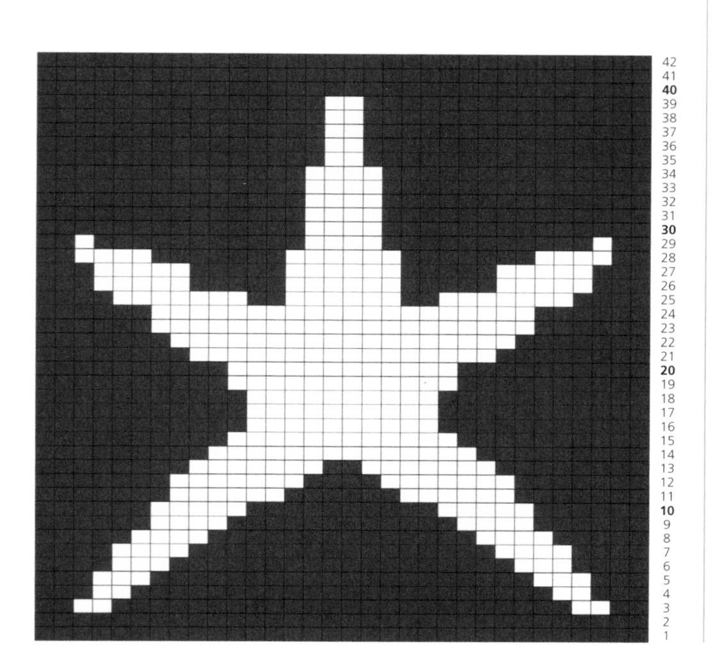

strawberry surprise

A great square to mix together with a mixture of other colors that look good enough to eat—try combining it with Sherbet Fizz on page 44 or Candy Cane on page 39.

materials

Debbie Bliss Rialto DK, shade 02 Cream (A), shade 12 Red (B), shade 10 Green (C)
Needle size: US 6 (4mm)

instructions

Cast on 32 sts.
Work 42 rows in stockinette (stocking) stitch following the chart.
Bind (cast) off.

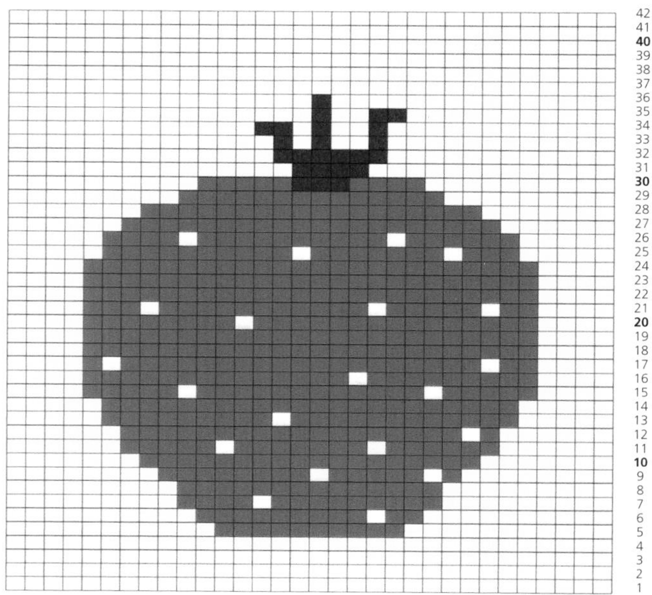

spots

These lovely pastel colors mix together beautifully.

materials

Rooster Almerino DK, shade 203 Strawberry Cream (A), shade 208 Ocean (B), shade 204 Grape (C), shade 201 Cornish (D), shade 205 Glace (E)
Needle size: US 6 (4mm)

instructions

Cast on 38 sts.
Work 42 rows in stockinette (stocking) stitch following the chart.
Bind (cast) off.

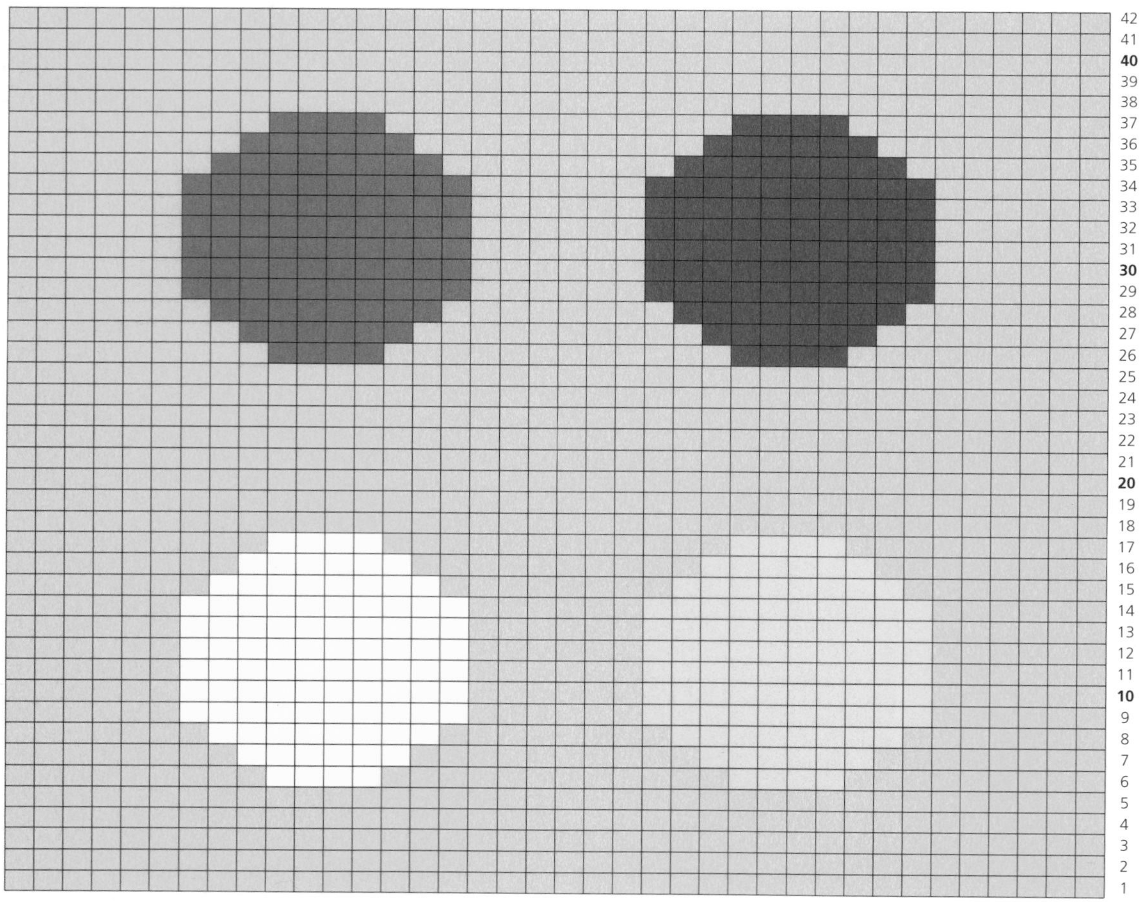

fair isle

This is my favorite form of color knitting, probably because I learnt it at an early age from my grandmother so carrying the yarn along the back of the work has become second nature. There are many designs and shapes to choose from; if you're a beginner, start with two colors and progress to more colorful designs later.

rhubarb & custard

This is the first Fair Isle pattern my grandmother taught me, when I was just a child.

materials

Rowan Pure Wool DK, shade 029 Pomegranate (A), shade 032 Gilt (B)
Needle size: US 6 (4mm)

instructions

Cast on 36 sts using A.
Work in stockinette (stocking) stitch, following the chart, for 44 rows or until the work measures 6in. (15cm).
Bind (cast) off.

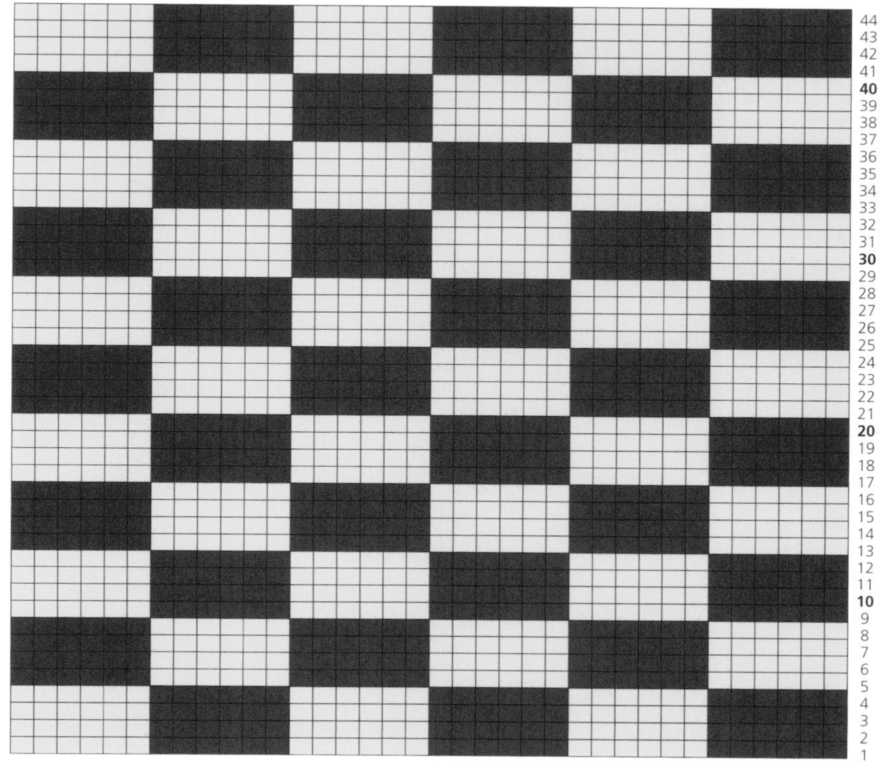

argyle

A very traditional Fair Isle pattern, popular for golfers' socks and with kilt-wearing Scotsmen.

materials

Rooster Almerino DK, shade 203 Strawberry Cream (A), shade 207 Gooseberry (B)
Needle size: US 6 (4mm)

instructions

Cast on 33 sts using A.
Work 42 rows in stockinette (stocking) stitch following the chart.
Bind (cast) off using A.

swiss check

A really easy slip stitch pattern—you don't have to carry the yarn along the back as the color pattern returns on the row of the same color. When stranding across the back of the three stitches, make sure you strand the yarn loosely.

materials

Rowan Pure Wool DK, shade 029 Pomegranate (A), shade 046 Tudor Rose (B)
Needle size: US 6 (4mm)

instructions

Cast on 37 sts using A.
Row 1 Using A, k1, purl to last st, k1.
Change to B.
Row 2 K1, sl 1, *k1, sl 3; rep from * ending k1 sl 1, k1.
Row 3 K1, *p3, sl 1; rep from * ending p3, k1.
Change to A.
Row 4 K2, *sl 1, k3; rep from * ending sl 1, k2.
Row 5 Purl to last st, k1.
Change to B.
Row 6 K1, *sl 3, k1; rep from * to end.
Row 7 K1, pl, *sl 1, p3; rep from * ending sl 1, p1, k1.
Change to A.
Row 8 K4, *sl 1, k3; rep from * ending k1.
Rep these eight rows until work measures 6in. (15cm).
Bind (cast) off.

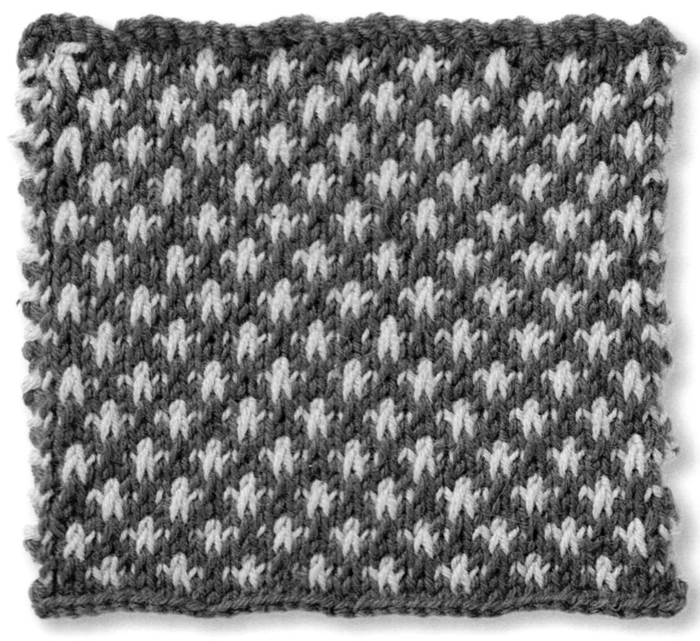

fair isle dreams

These diamond shapes are blended with and outlined in different colors, and make a beautiful design on their own or mixed with plain color squares.

materials

COLORWAY 1

Rooster Almerino DK, shade 207 Gooseberry (A), shade 201 Cornish (B), shade 213 Cherry (C), shade 210 Custard (D), shade 206 Caviar (E)

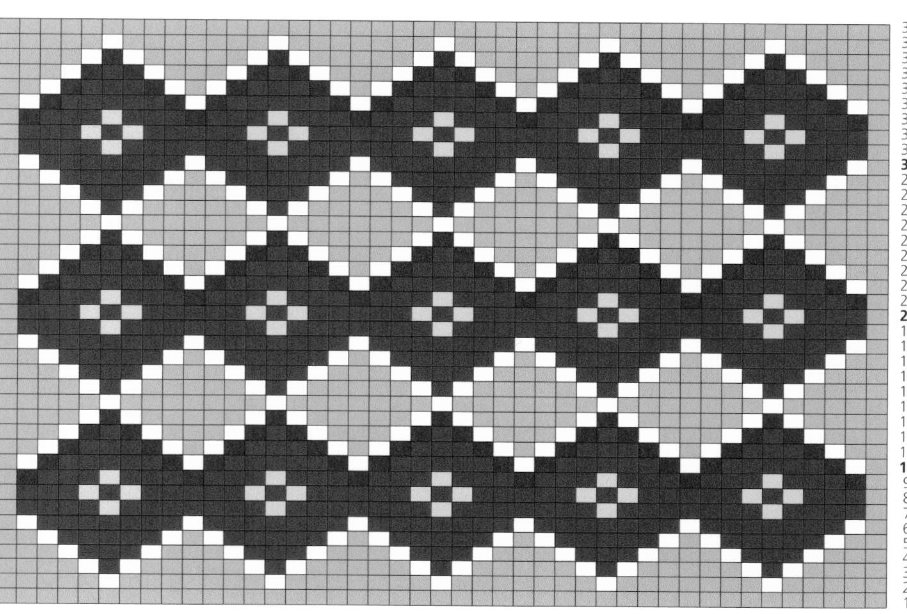

COLORWAY 2

Rooster Almerino DK, shade 208 Ocean (A), shade 203 Strawberry Cream (B)

Rowan Pure Wool DK, shade 042 Dahlia (C)

Debbie Bliss Rialto DK, shade 07 Yellow (D)

Cascade 220 DK, shade 9478 Candy Pink (E)

Needle size: US 6 (4mm)

instructions

Cast on 43 sts using A.

Work 39 rows in stockinette (stocking) stitch following the chart.

Bind (cast) off.

fleck

A great starter Fair Isle pattern—it's very simple and you don't need a chart.

materials

Rooster Almerino DK, shade 201
Cornish (A)
Rowan Pure Wool DK, shade 036 Kiss (B)
Needle size: US 6 (4mm)

instructions

Cast on 38 sts using A.
Work 2 sts in A, then 2 sts in B to end.
Rep using alt colors on each row until work measures 6in. (15cm).
Bind (cast) off.

little hearts

This makes a pretty design for a child's blanket or garment.

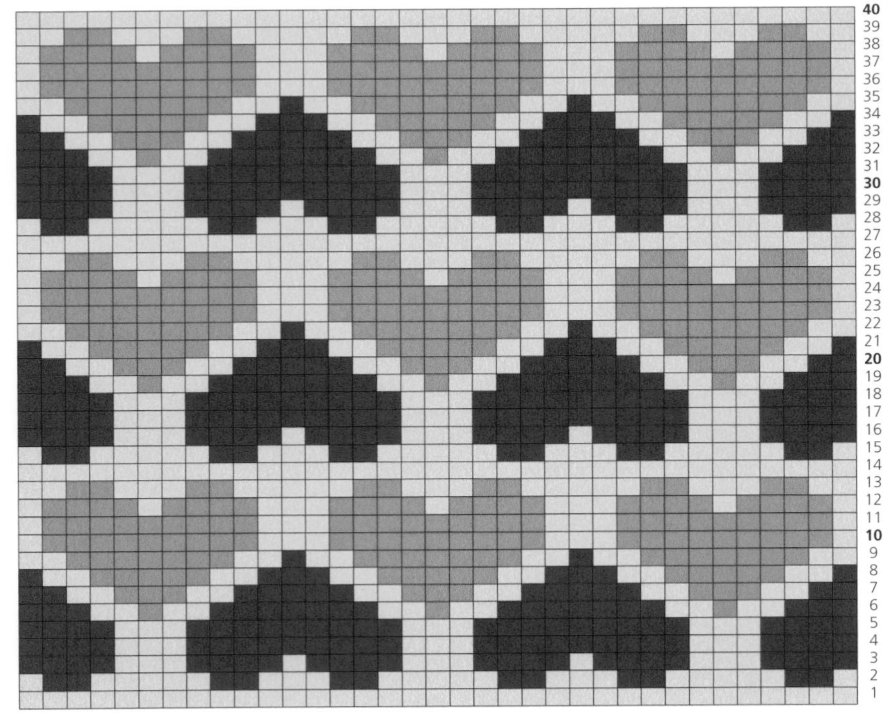

materials

Rooster Almerino DK, shade 203, Strawberry Cream (A)
Cascade 220 DK, shade 8901 Groseille (B), shade 9478 Candy Pink (C)
Needle size: US 6 (4mm)

instructions

Cast on 35 sts.
Work 40 rows in stockinette (stocking) stitch following the chart.
Bind (cast) off.

fair isle party

This is my favorite type of Fair Isle, with lots of lovely colors and a simple design. You can have fun with this pattern by changing the colors.

materials

Rowan Pure Wool DK, shade 029 Pomegranate (A)
Rooster Almerino DK, shade 203 Strawberry Cream (B)
Debbie Bliss Rialto DK, shade 32 Burnt Orange (C)
Rowan Pure Wool DK, shade 042 Dahlia (D)
Rooster Almerino DK, shade 208 Ocean (E), shade 207 Gooseberry (F), shade 201 Cornish (G)
Needle size: US 6 (4mm)

instructions

Cast on 37 sts using A.
Work 42 rows in stockinette (stocking) stitch following the chart.
Bind (cast) off.

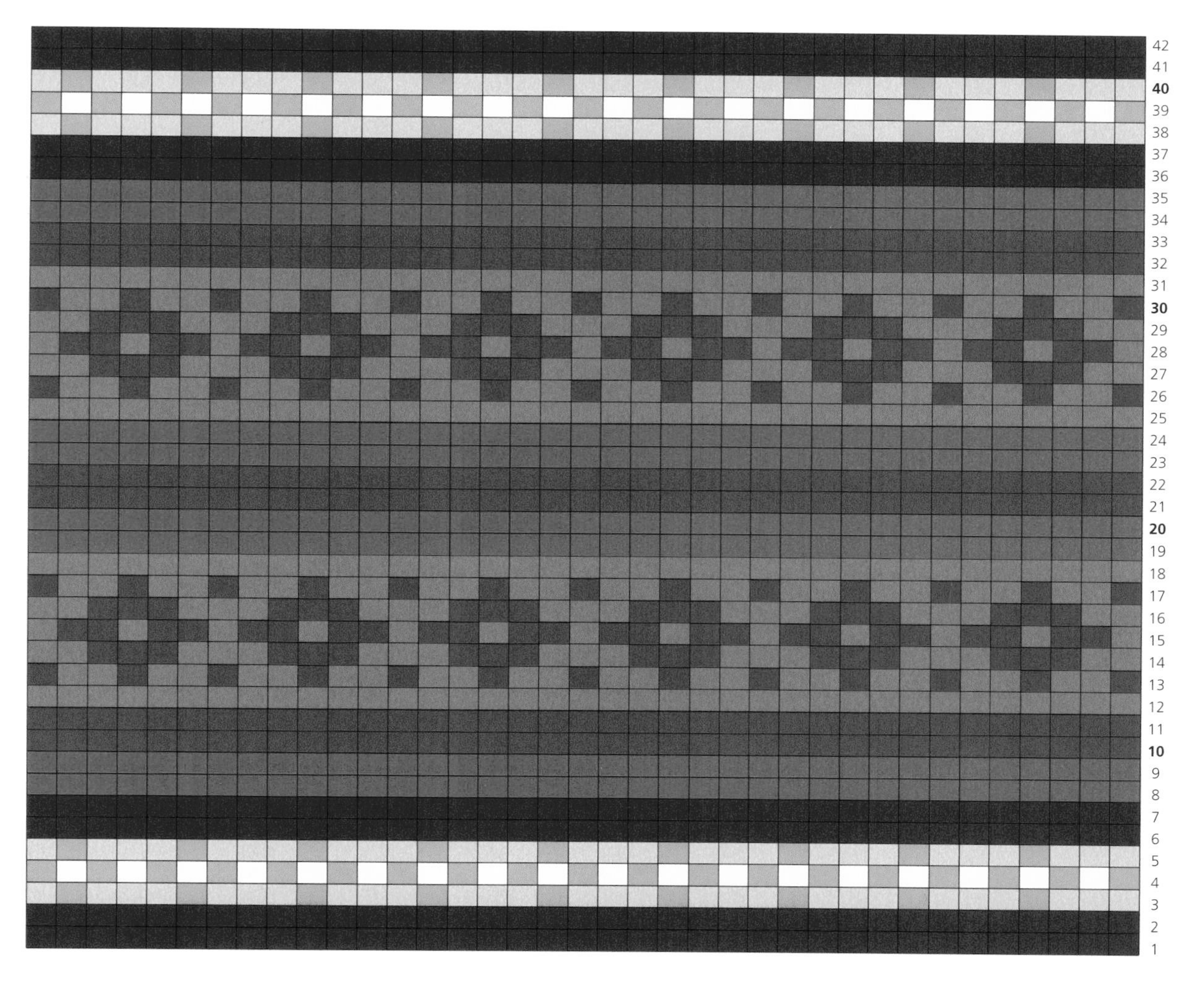

butterfly

This is the most pretty Fair Isle with a design that resembles butterflies and works really well in these gorgeous colors.

materials

Rooster Almerino DK, shade 203
Strawberry Cream (A), shade 207
Gooseberry (B), shade 201 Cornish (C)
Rowan Pure Wool DK, shade 029
Pomegranate (D)
Needle size: US 6 (4mm)

instructions

Cast on 37 sts using A.
Work 37 rows in stockinette (stocking) stitch, following the chart.
Bind (cast) off.

striped fair isle

A more masculine-looking Fair Isle design in tones of soft gray.

materials

Sublime Cashmere Merino Silk DK, shade 10 Sea Pearl (A)
Sublime Extra Fine Merino DK, shade 18 Dusted Grey (B)
Needle size: US 6 (4mm)

instructions

Cast on 32 sts using A.
Work 42 rows in stockinette (stocking) stitch, following the chart.
Bind (cast) off.

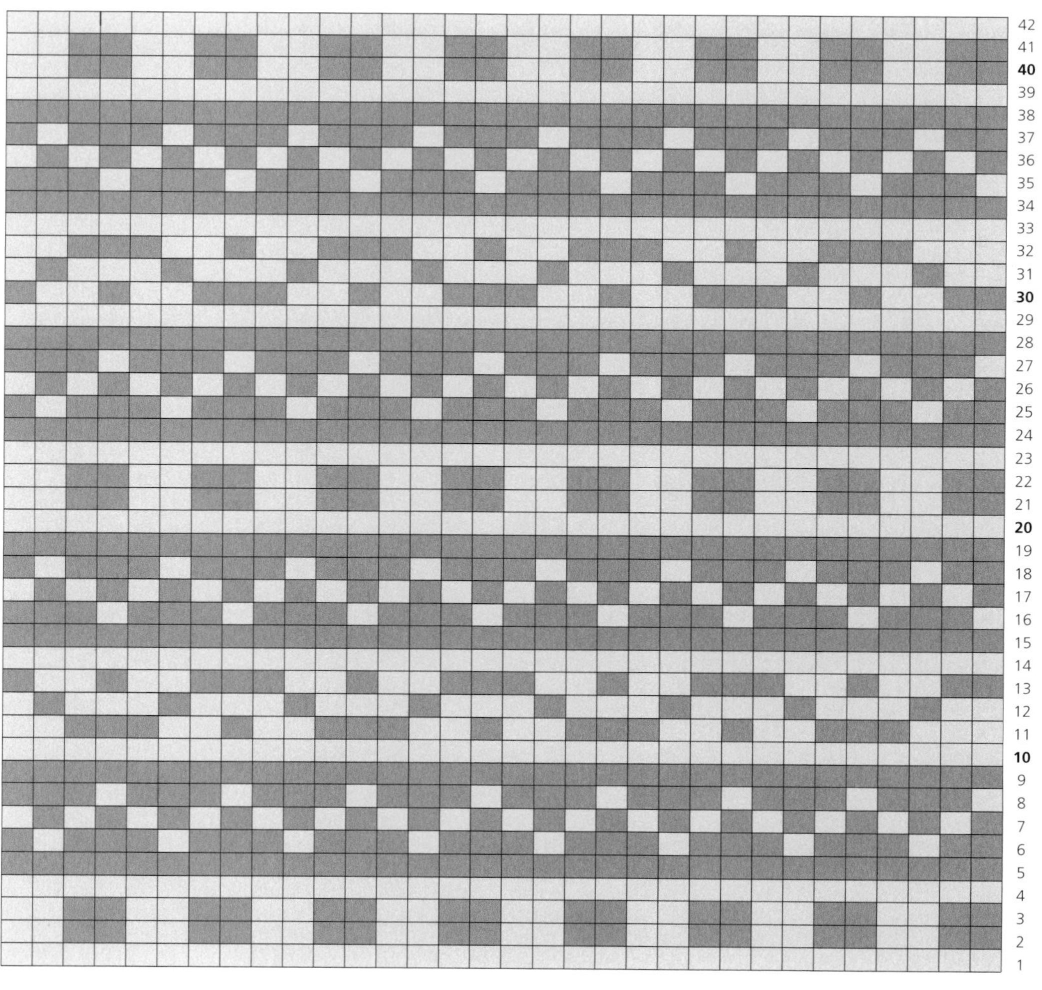

checkered diamonds fair isle

Bold diamond shapes in a subtle green-blue, outlined in soft pink.

materials

Sublime Organic Merino DK, shade 112 Chalk (A), shade 191 Laundry (B), shade 188 Tulle (C)
Needle size: US 6 (4mm)

instructions

Cast on 32 sts using A.
Work 42 rows in stockinette (stocking) stitch following the chart.
Bind (cast) off.

classic

This design uses the very classic Fair Isle shapes of crosses, diamonds, and squares.

materials

Rooster Almerino DK, shade 201 Cornish (A), shade 205 Glace (B)
Sublime Extra Fine Merino DK, shade 11 Clove (C), shade 106 Egg Nog (D)
Sublime Cashmere Merino Silk DK, shade 08 Sage (E)
Needle size: US 6 (4mm)

instructions

Cast on 37 sts using A.
Work 41 rows in stockinette (stocking) stitch, following the chart.
Bind (cast) off.

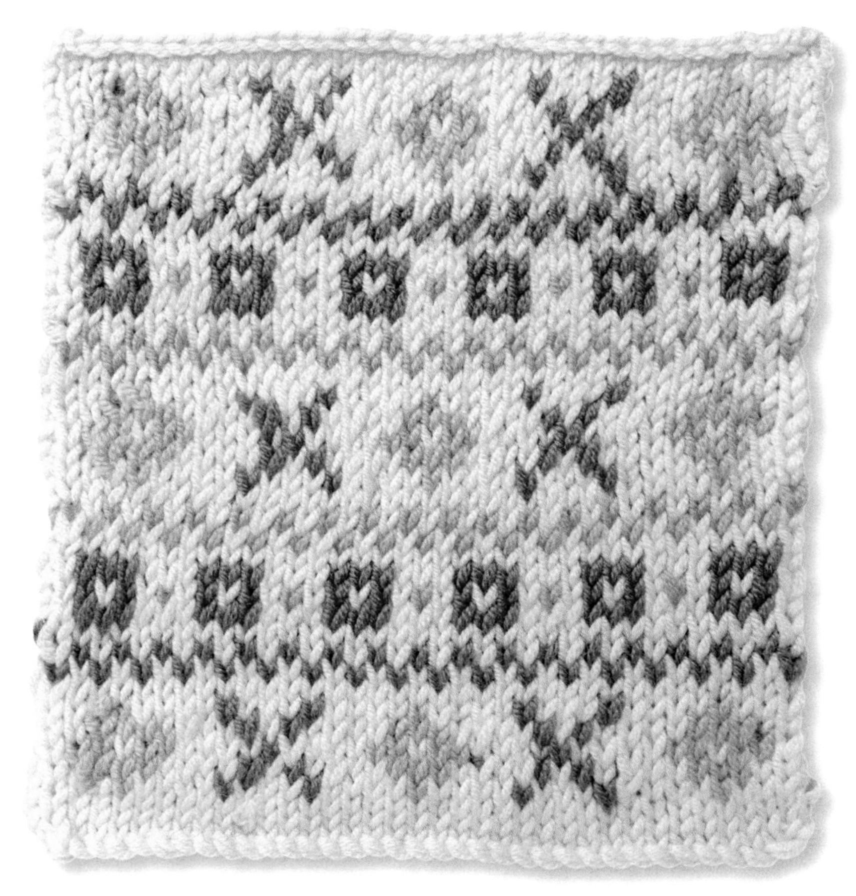

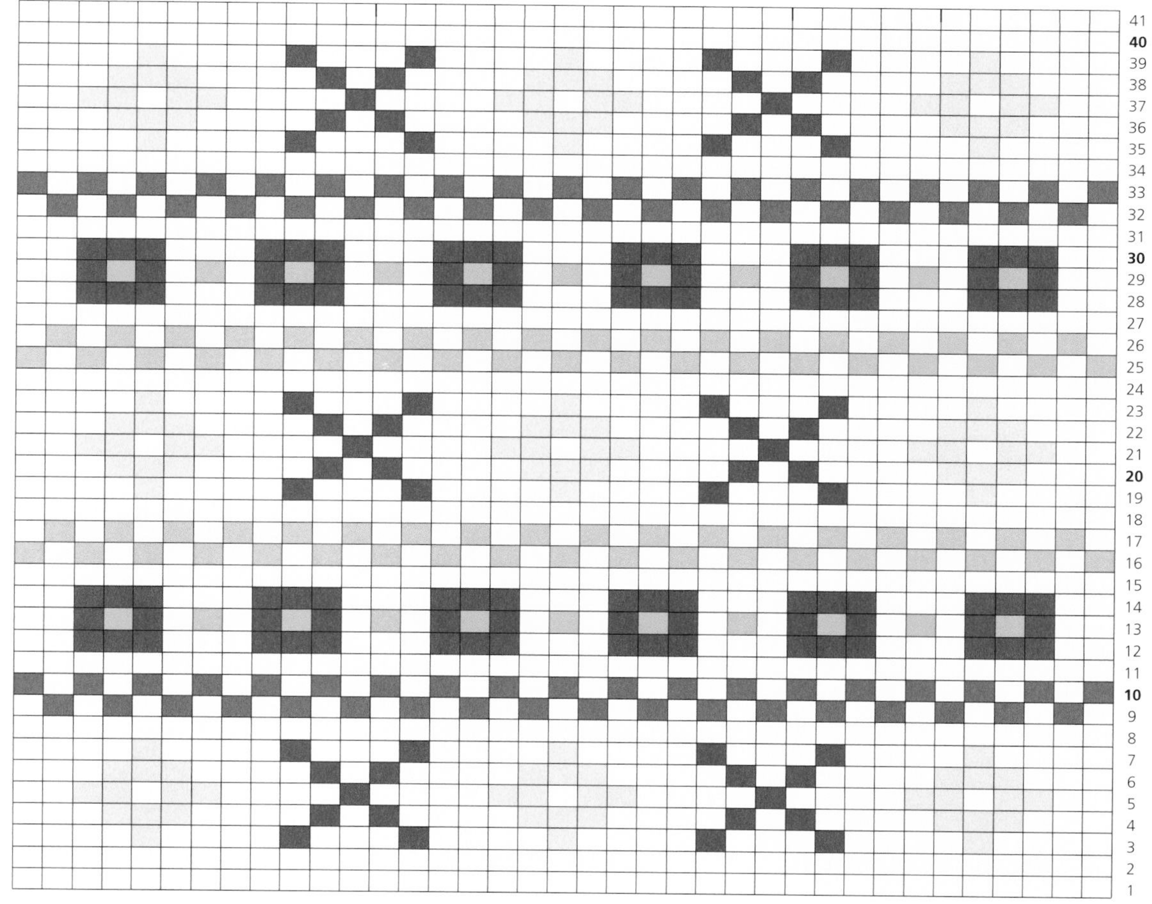

star fair isle

This is a very jolly and colorful Fair Isle star pattern.

materials

Rooster Almerino DK, shade 201 Cornish (A)
Sublime Extra Fine Merino DK, shade 11 Clove (B), shade 106 Egg Nog (C)
Rooster Almerino DK, shade 42 Dahlia (D), shade 207 Gooseberry (E)
Needle size: US 6 (4mm)

instructions

Cast on 37 sts.
Work 41 rows in stockinette (stocking) stitch following the chart.
Bind (cast) off.

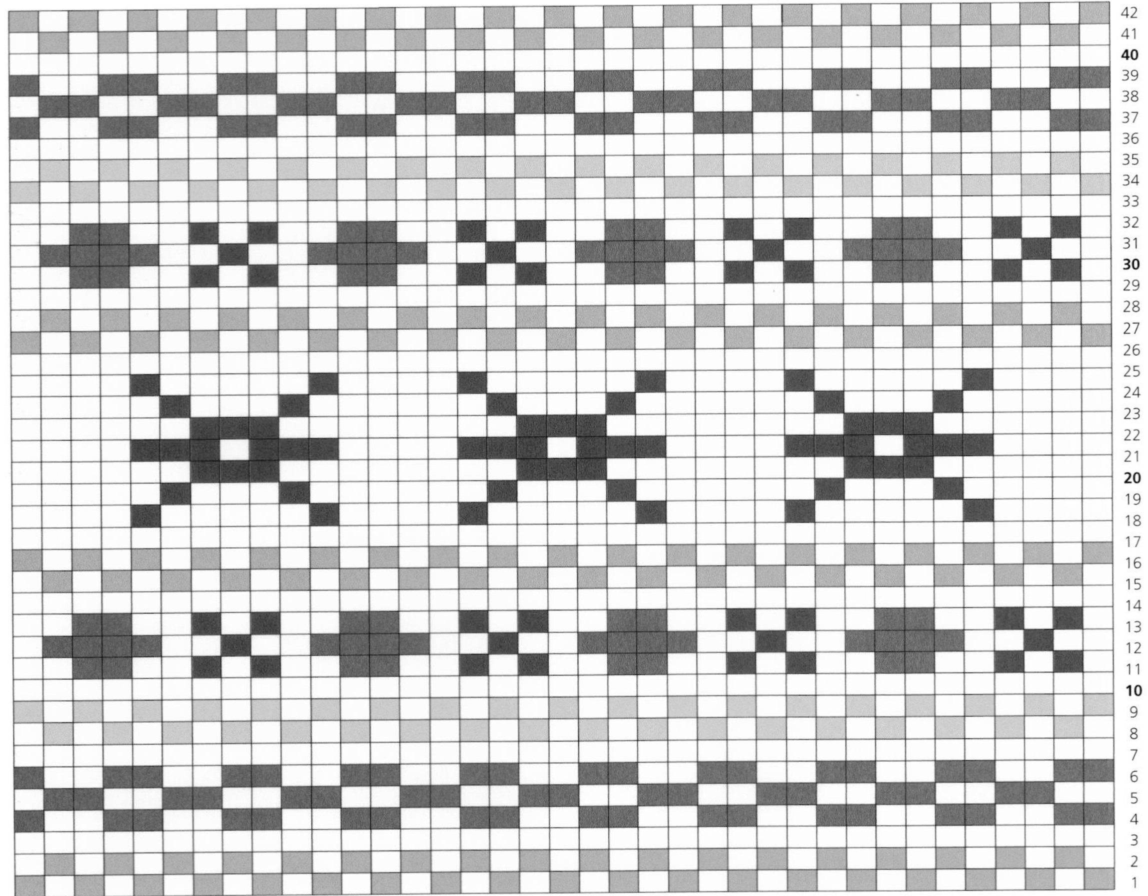

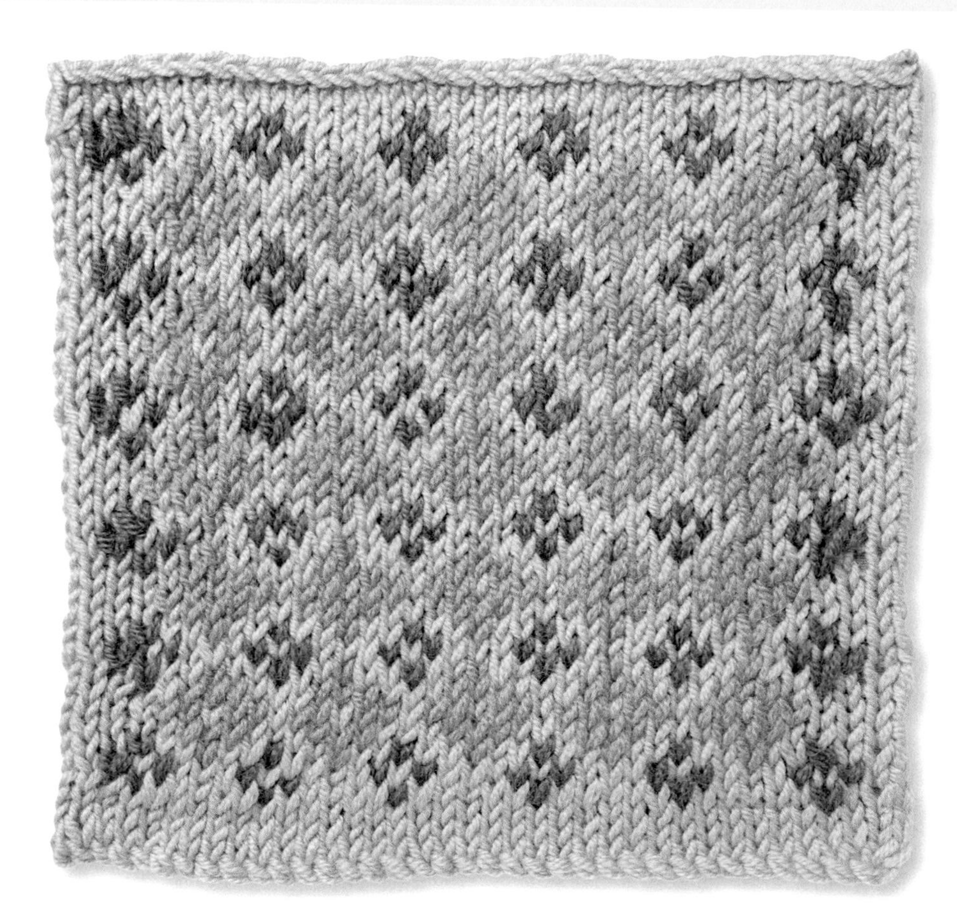

blossom fair isle

The color combinations on this traditional Fair Isle pattern give it a more contemporary feel.

materials

Rooster Almerino DK, shade 205 Glace (A), shade 208 Ocean (B), shade 211 Brighton Rock (C)
Needle size: US 6 (4mm)

instructions

Cast on 37 sts.
Work 37 rows in stockinette (stocking) stitch following the chart.
Bind (cast) off.

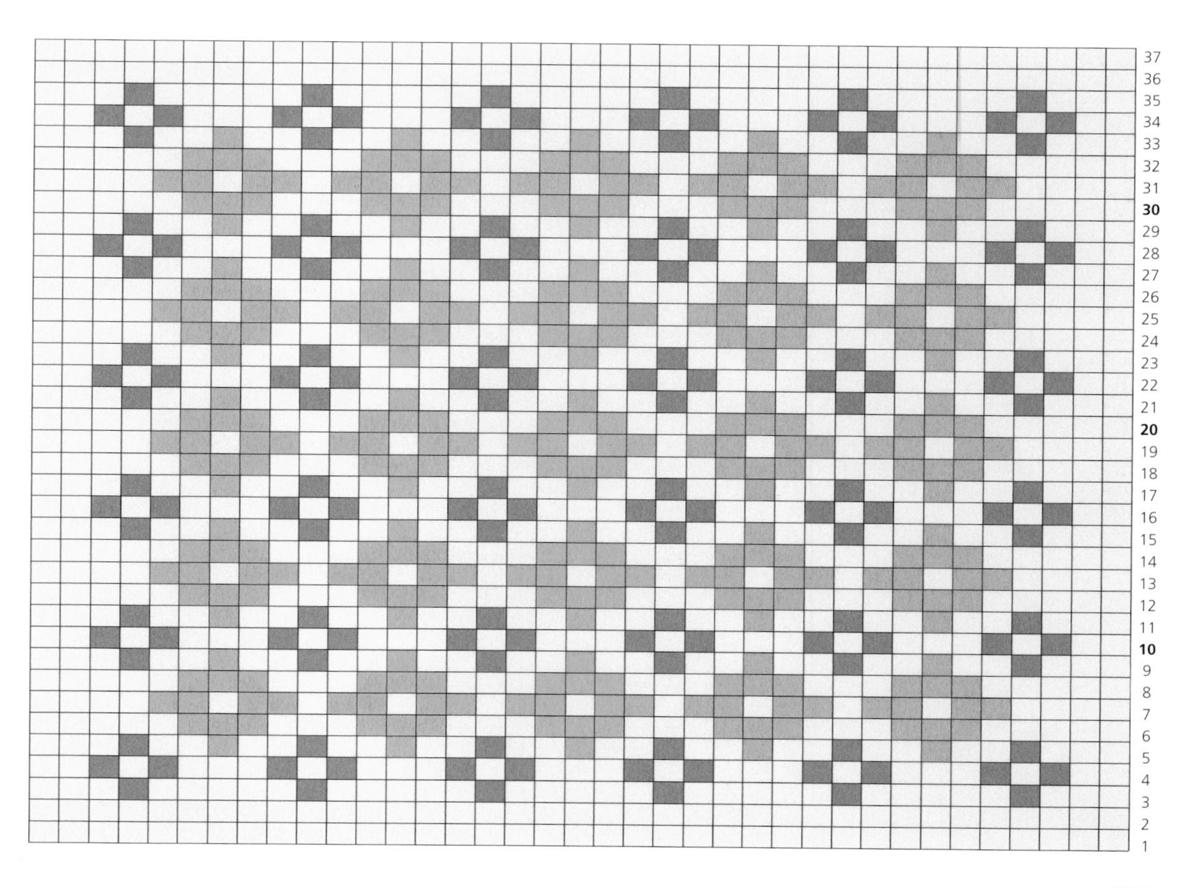

ripples

These are series of great designs created using colorful little waves and different textures. Ripples have an uneven edge so they are difficult to join together as blocks, but are great for using on the edges of projects.

wave

This ripple stitch has a curved bottom edge. It's a great way to finish off along the edge of a blanket or scarf.

materials

Rowan Pure Wool DK, shade 012 Snow (A), shade 005 Glacier (B), shade 044 Frost (C), shade 006 Pier (D), shade 007 Cypress (E)
Needle size: US 6 (4mm)

special abbreviation

kfb—knit into front and back of next st on RS rows

instructions

Cast on 33 sts using A.
Row 1 Knit.
Row 2 K1, p to last st, k1.
Row 3 [p2tog] twice, [m1, k1] 3 times, m1, * [p2tog] 4 times, [m1, k1] three times, m1; rep from * once, [p2tog] twice.
Row 4 K1, p to last st, k1.
Change color.
Rep these 4 rows, changing color after every 4th row.
Row 17 Cont knitting in E until work measures approx. 6in. (15cm).
Bind (cast) off.

atlantic storm

This pattern has lots of movement—just like thrashing waves—and is knitted in a variegated hand-dyed yarn.

materials

Fyberspates Scrumptious DK, Blue Lagoon
Needle size: US 6 (4mm)

instructions

Cast on 40 sts.
Row 1 and every alt row K1, p to last st, k1.
Row 2 K3, *yo, k2, skpo, k2tog, k2, yo, k1; rep from * to last st, k1.
Row 4 K2, *yo, k2, skpo, k2tog, k2, yo, k1; rep from * to last 2 sts, k2.
Rep these two rows until work measures 6in. (15cm).
Bind (cast) off.

fan tail ripple

This pattern has charming waves and ripples and resembles the feathers of a bird's tail.

materials

Cascade 220, shade 8912 Lilac Mist (A)
Debbie Bliss Alpaca Silk, shade 07 Green (B)
Rooster Almerino DK, shade 210 Custard (C)
Cascade 220, shade 2419 Aster Heather (D)
Needle size: US 6 (4mm)

special abbreviation

Ssk (slip, slip, knit)—slip next 2 sts one at a time, insert left needle into fronts of slipped sts and knit tog

instructions

Cast on 41 sts using A.
Work the foll rows, changing color every 2 rows in the foll sequence:
A, B, A, C, A, C, A, D, A, B, A, B, A, C, A, D, A, D, A, B, A, C
Row 1 K1, *ssk, k9, k2tog; rep from * to last st, k1.
Row 2 K1, p to last st, k1.
Change color.
Row 3 K1, *ssk, k7, k2tog; rep from * to last st, k1.
Row 4 As Row 2.
Change color.
Row 5 K1, *ssk, [yo, k1] five times, yo, k2tog; rep from * to last st, k1.
Row 6 Knit.
Change color.
Rep Rows 1–6 until you have completed 44 rows.
Bind (cast) off using A.

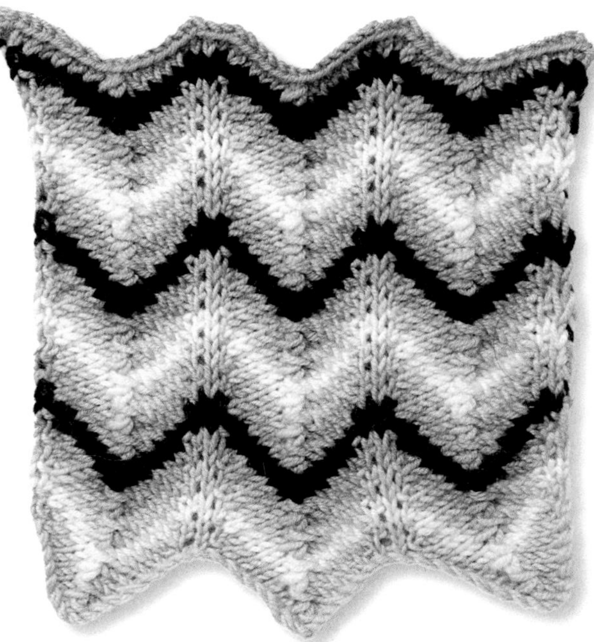

rock face

A design in the colors of a Cornish rockface. The green yarn is slightly finer than the others but was chosen for its color—another light worsted (DK) yarn would work just as well.

materials

Rooster Baby, shade 409 Pistachio (A)
Rooster Almerino DK, shade 201 Cornish (B), shade 202 Hazelnut (C)
Debbie Bliss Rialto DK, shade 05 Brown (D)
Needle size: US 6 (4mm)

special abbreviations

kfb—knit into front and back of next st on RS rows
pfb—purl into front and back of next st on WS rows

instructions

Cast on 49 sts using A.
Work the foll rows, changing color every 2 rows in the foll sequence:
A, B, A, C, D, C
Row 1 (right side) K1, *kfb, k5, sl 1 knitwise, k2tog, psso, k5, kfb, k1; rep from * to end.
Row 2 P1, *pfb, p5, sl 1 purlwise, p2tog, psso, p5, pfb, p1; rep from * to end.
Change color.
Rep Rows 1–2, ending with a Row 2, until work measures 6in. (15cm).
Bind (cast) off.

embroidery

Embroidery onto a knitted piece can look very pretty and elegant. You can embroider any number of designs, but in these blocks I've concentrated mainly on putting little bunches of flowers together on a plain stockinette (stocking) stitch background.

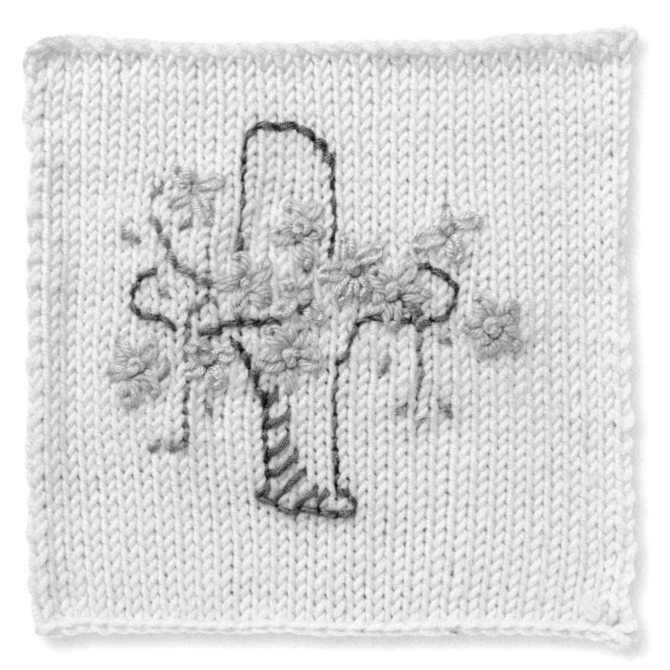

basket

A delightful vintage-style design using delicate pastel colors.

materials

BASIC SQUARE
Debbie Bliss Rialto DK, shade 02 Off White

EMBROIDERY
Rooster Almerino DK, shade 203 Strawberry Cream (Pale pink), shade 210 Custard (Yellow), shade 207 Gooseberry (Green)
Debbie Bliss Pure Silk, shade 02 (Silver)
Rowan Bamboo Soft DK, 110 Pompadour (Purple)
Needle size: US 6 (4mm)
Tapestry needle

instructions

Cast on 33 sts.
Work in stockinette (stocking) stitch for 45 rows or until the work measures 6in. (15cm).
Bind (cast) off.

EMBROIDERY
Split the wool and use only one strand, as you would with embroidery floss (thread).
Thread the tapestry needle and follow the template to embroider the design.

summer

Daisies look simple and fresh in green, white, and yellow.

materials

BASIC SQUARE
Debbie Bliss Rialto DK, shade 02 Off White

EMBROIDERY
Rowan Pure Wool DK, shade 020 Parsley (Green)
Rooster Almerino DK, shade 210 Custard (Yellow)
Debbie Bliss Pure Silk, shade 02 (Silver)
Needle size: US 6 (4mm)
Tapestry needle

instructions

Cast on 33 sts.
Work in stockinette (stocking) stitch for 45 rows or until the work measures 6in. (15cm).
Bind (cast) off.

EMBROIDERY
Split the wool and use only one strand, as you would with embroidery floss (thread).
Thread the tapestry needle and follow the template to embroider the design.

forget-me-not

A heart combined with delicate forget-me-nots is the ultimate romantic symbol.

materials

BASIC SQUARE
Debbie Bliss Rialto DK, shade 02 Off White

EMBROIDERY
Debbie Bliss Baby Cashmerino, shade 204 (Mid blue)
Debbie Bliss Rialto Aran, shade 04 (Pink)
Rooster Almerino DK, 207 Gooseberry (Green)
Debbie Bliss Pure Silk, shade 02 (Silver)
Needle size: US 6 (4mm)
Tapestry needle

instructions

Cast on 33 sts.
Work in stockinette (stocking) stitch for 45 rows or until the work measures 6in. (15cm).
Bind (cast) off.

EMBROIDERY
Split the wool and use only one strand, as you would with embroidery floss (thread).
Thread the tapestry needle and follow the template to embroider the design.

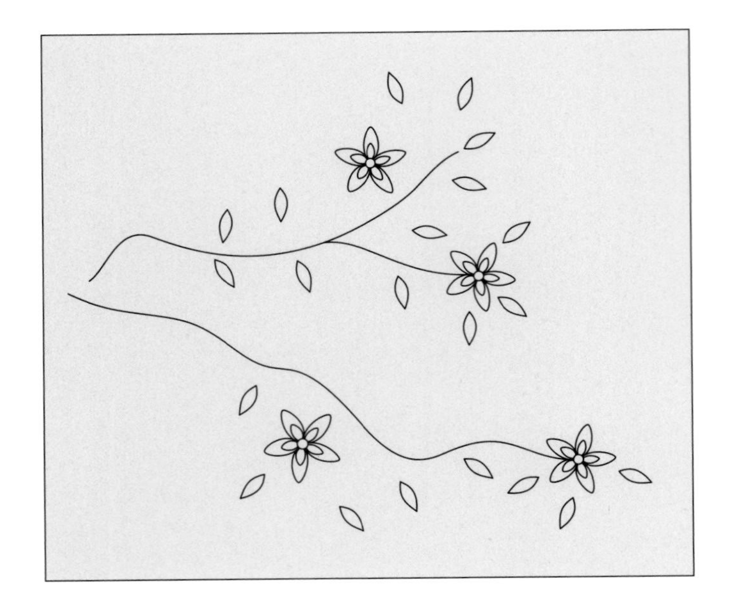

blossom

This charming spray of spring blossom is sophisticated in purple and silver with touches of green.

materials

BASIC SQUARE

Debbie Bliss Rialto DK, shade 02 Off White

EMBROIDERY

Rooster Almerino Aran, shade 308 Spiced Plum (Dark plum)
Rowan Pure Wool DK, shade 020 Parsley (Green)
Debbie Bliss Pure Silk, shade 02 (Silver)
Cascade 220 DK, shade 2419 Aster Heather (Mid purple)
Needle size: US 6 (4mm)
Tapestry needle

instructions

Cast on 33 sts.
Work in stockinette (stocking) stitch for 45 rows or until the work measures 6in. (15cm).
Bind (cast) off.

EMBROIDERY

Split the wool and use only one strand, as you would with embroidery floss (thread).
Thread the tapestry needle and follow the template to embroider the design.

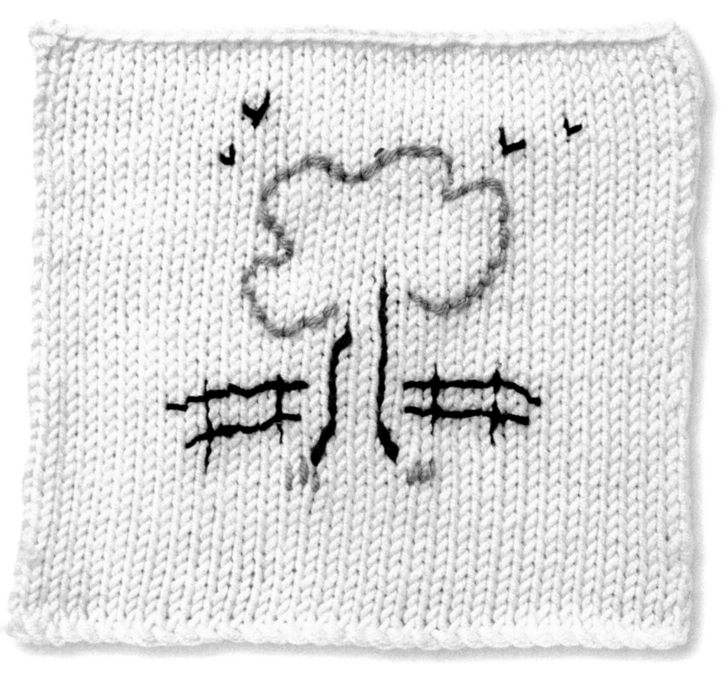

tree

A design that evokes sunny English meadows with birds wheeling above the trees.

materials

BASIC SQUARE
Debbie Bliss Rialto DK, shade 02 Off White

EMBROIDERY
Rooster Almerino Aran, shade 308 Spiced Plum (Dark plum), shade 207 Gooseberry (Green)
Debbie Bliss Rialto DK, shade 03 (Black)
Needle size: US 6 (4mm)
Tapestry needle

instructions

Cast on 33 sts.
Work in stockinette (stocking) stitch for 45 rows or until the work measures 6in. (15cm).
Bind (cast) off.

EMBROIDERY
Split the wool and use only one strand, as you would with embroidery floss (thread).
Thread the tapestry needle and follow the template to embroider the design.

bouquet

Pink, green, and silver combine to add a vintage charm to this bouquet of pretty flowers.

materials

BASIC SQUARE
Debbie Bliss Rialto DK, shade 02 Off White

EMBROIDERY
Rooster Almerino DK, shade 207 Gooseberry (Green), shade 203 Strawberry Cream (Pale pink)
Debbie Bliss Pure Silk, shade 02 (Silver)
Cascade 220 DK, shade 2419 Aster Heather (Mid purple)
Needle size: US 6 (4mm)
Tapestry needle

instructions

Cast on 33 sts.
Work in stockinette (stocking) stitch for 45 rows or until the work measures 6in. (15cm).
Bind (cast) off.

EMBROIDERY
Split the wool and use only one strand, as you would with embroidery floss (thread).
Thread the tapestry needle and follow the template to embroider the design.

beading

Once you start knitting with beads, it's difficult to stop; your knitting will look so pretty that beading will become addictive. Use beads to either etch out a motif or just to pretty up plain knitting. Once you get started it takes no time at all.

beaded diamond

A textured beaded diamond design brings sparkle and a touch of sophistication to this square.

materials

Rooster Almerino DK, shade 208 Ocean
Needle size: US 6 (4mm)
240 x Rowan beads J3001008

+ = add bead
◆ = knit on WS, purl on RS
☐ = knit on RS, purl on WS

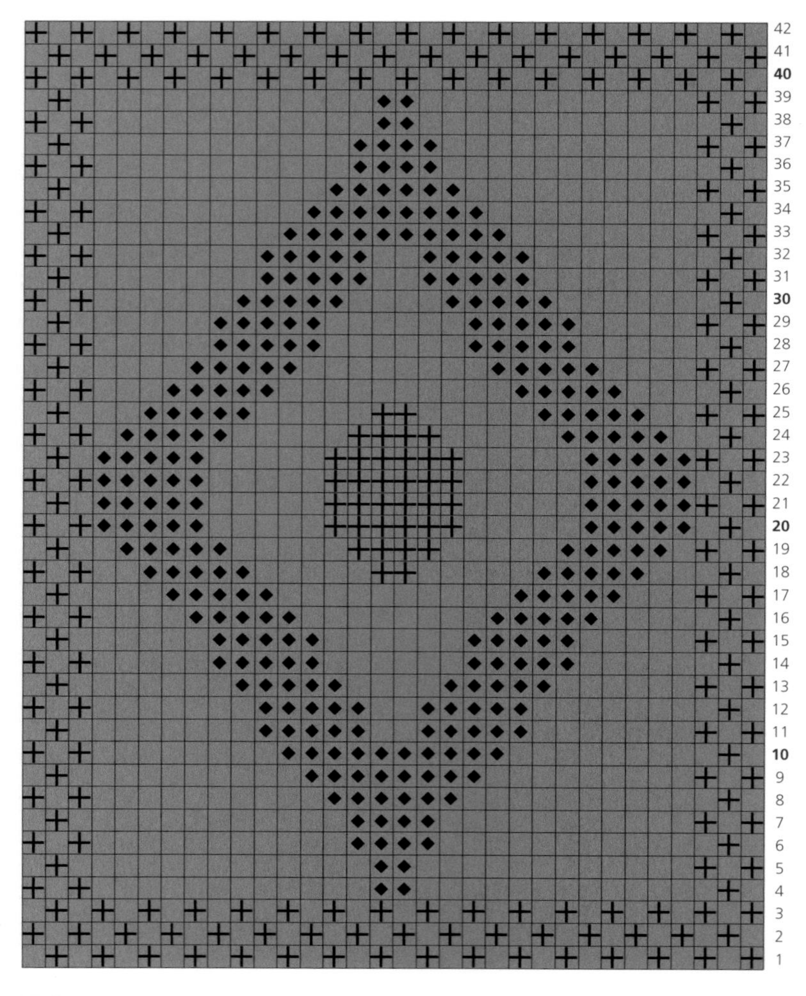

instructions

Cast on 31 sts.
Work as foll to form a stockinette (stocking) stitch square with a seed (moss) stitch border, following chart to place beads at the same time.
Row 1 K1, p1 to end.
Row 2 P1, k1 to end.
Row 3 K1, p1, knit next 27 sts, p1, k1.
Row 4 P1, k1, purl next 27 sts, k1, p1.
Rep Rows 3–4 until 40 rows have been completed.
Row 41 As Row 1.
Row 42 As Row 2.
Bind (cast) off.

beaded stripes

In order for the bead to be positioned exactly over the stripe, it needs to be placed when working the row above.

materials

Rooster Almerino DK, shade 208 Ocean (A), shade 205 Glace (B)
Needle size: US 6 (4mm)
80 x Rowan seed beads 01023

special abbreviation

Pb—place bead

instructions

Cast on 34 sts using A.
Work 44 rows in stockinette (stocking) stitch, as follows:
Rows 1, 3 Knit.
Rows 2, 4 Purl.
Change to B.
Row 5 As Row 1.
Change to A.
Row 6 P4, *wyib, sl 1 knitwise and Pb at back of work, wyif, p4; rep from * to end.
Row 7 As Row 1.
Row 8 As Row 2.
Row 9 As Row 1.
Change to B.
Row 10 As Row 2.

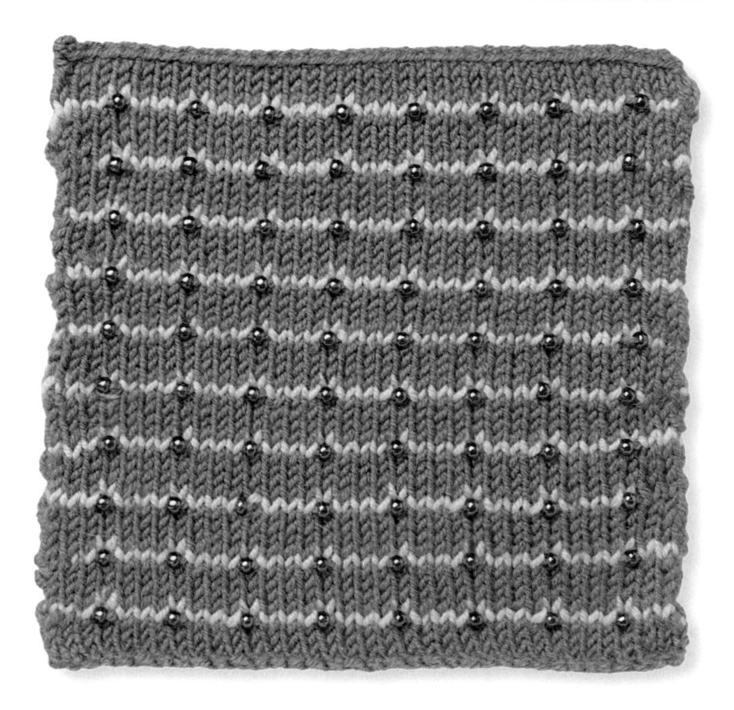

Change to A.
Row 11 K4, *wyif, sl purlwise and Pb at front of work, wyib, k4; rep from * to end.
Rep Rows 2–11 until work measures 6in. (15cm).
Bind (cast) off.

beaded seeded diamonds

The center of each diamond in this square alternates between a knit and purl row.

materials

Rooster Almerino DK, shade 204 Grape
Needle size: US 6 (4mm)
110 x iridescent pink seed beads

special abbreviation

Pb—place bead

instructions

Cast on 31 sts.
Row 1 (right side) K3, *p1, k5; rep from * to last 4 sts, p1, k3.
Row 2 P2, *k1, p1, k1, p3; rep from * to last 5 sts, k1, p1, k1, p2.
Row 3 K1, *p1, k3, p1, k1; rep from * to end.
Row 4 K1, *p2 [sl 1 knitwise and PB], p2, k1; rep from * to end.
Row 5 As Row 3.
Row 6 As Row 2.
Row 7 K3, *p1, k2 [Sl 1 purlwise and PB], k2; rep from * to last 4 sts, p1, k3.
Row 8 P2, *k1, p1, k1, p3; rep from * to last 5 sts, k1, p1, k1, p2.
Row 9 K1, *p1, k3, p1, k1; rep from * to end.
Row 10 K1, *p2 [sl 1 knitwise and PB] p2, k1; rep from * to end.
Row 11 As Row 3.

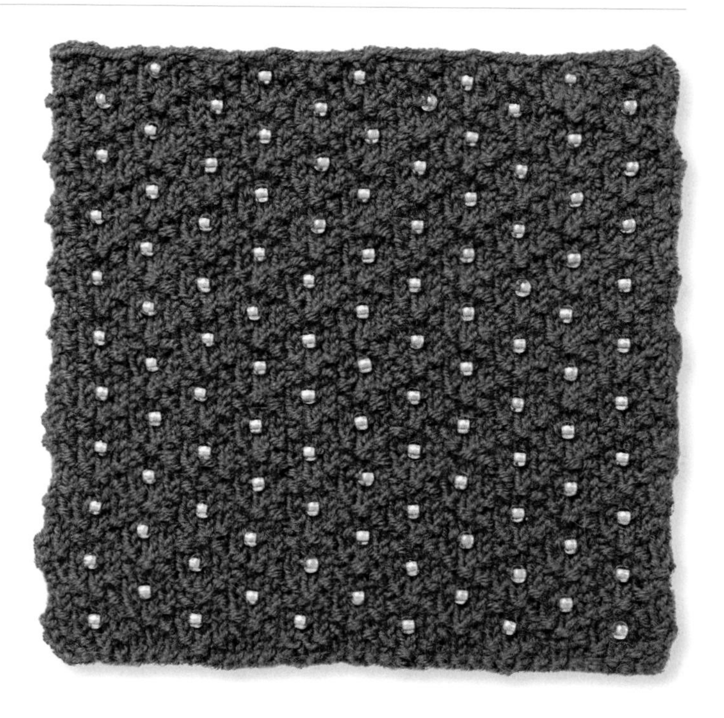

Row 12 As Row 2.
Rep Rows 7–12 until work measures 6in. (15cm).
Bind (cast) off.

beaded tulip

These pretty pink beads give a different dimension to this little tulip in a vase.

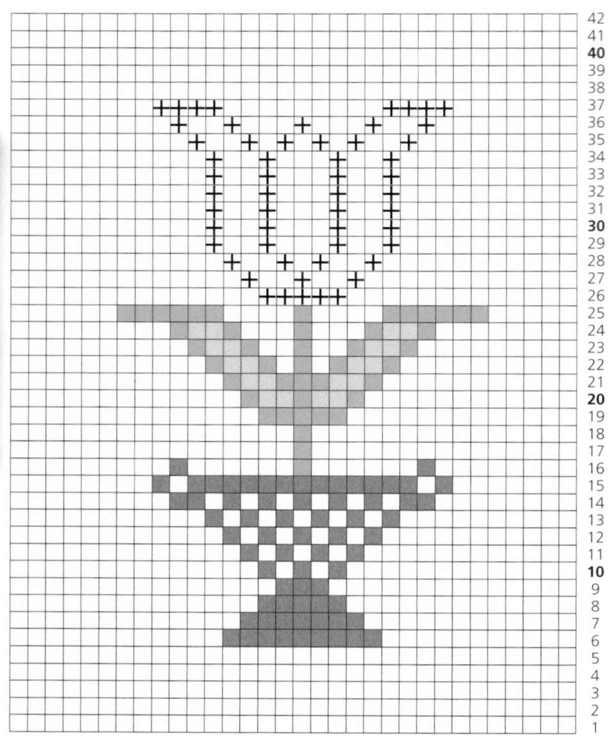

materials

Rooster Almerino DK, shade 201 Cornish (A), shade 210 Custard (B), shade 208 Ocean (C)
Needle size: US 6 (4mm)
55 x Rowan pink beads J3001015

instructions

Cast on 32 sts.
Work as foll to form a stockinette (stocking) stitch square with seed (moss) stitch border, following chart to place beads at the same time.

Row 1 K1, p1 to end.
Row 2 P1, k1 to end.
Rows 3, 5 K1, p1, knit next 28 sts, k1, p1.
Row 4 P1, k1, purl next 28 sts, k1, p1.
Continue working as set, foll chart for Rows 6–37.
Rows 38, 40 As Row 4.
Row 39 As Row 3.
Row 41 As Row 1.
Row 42 As Row 2.
Bind (cast) off.

+ = add bead

beaded snowflake

For more of a snowflake look, work this design in white, pale blue, and silver.

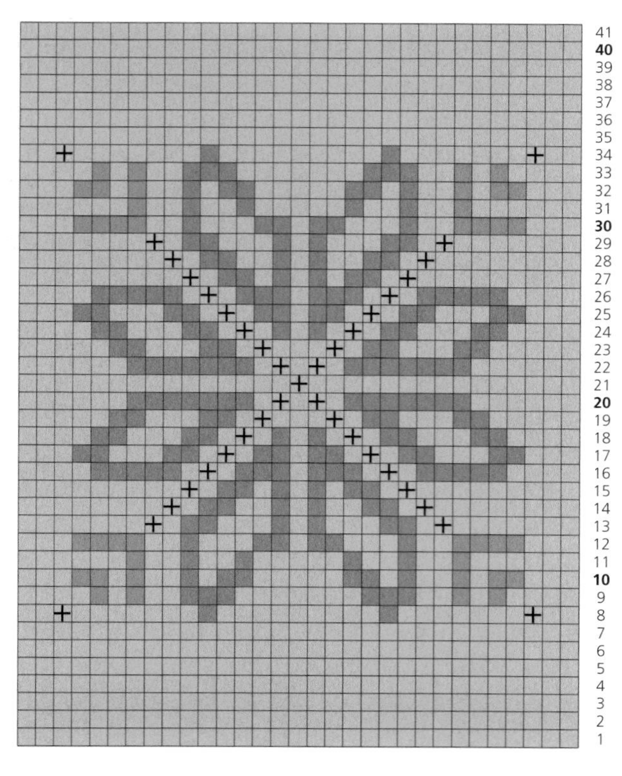

materials

Cascade 220 DK, shade 8912 Lilac Mist (A), shade 2419 Aster Heather (B), shade 9478 Candy Pink (C)
Needle size: US 6 (4mm)
37 x Rowan Pink Beads J3001015

instructions

Cast on 31 sts.

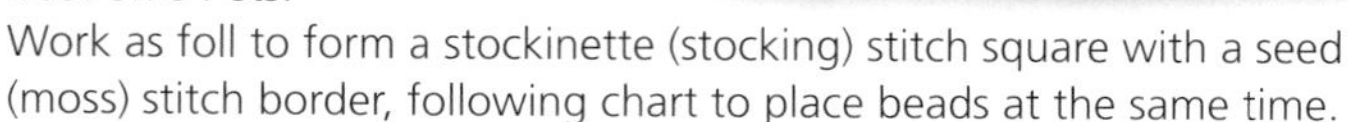

Work as foll to form a stockinette (stocking) stitch square with a seed (moss) stitch border, following chart to place beads at the same time.

Row 1 K1, p1 to end.
Row 2 P1, k1 to end.
Row 3 K1, p1, knit next 27 sts, p1, k1.
Row 4 P1, k1, purl next 27 sts, k1, p1.
Rep Rows 3–4 until 40 rows have been completed.
Row 41 As Row 1.
Row 42 As Row 2.
Bind (cast) off.

+ = add bead

beaded anchor

A very delicate motif, etched out with tiny pearl beads.

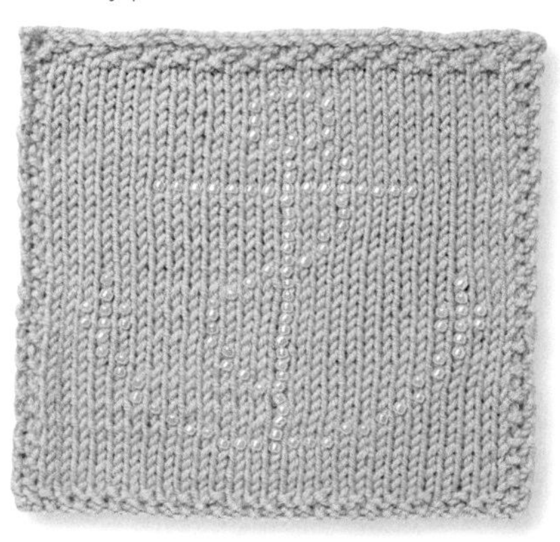

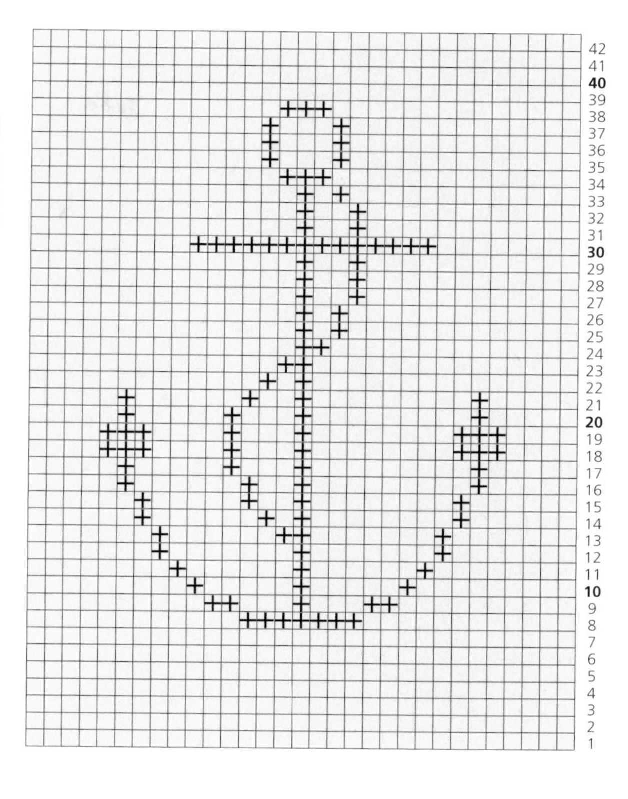

materials

Rooster Almerino DK, shade 205 Glace
Needle size: US 6 (4mm)
113 x Rowan pearl beads J3001016

instructions

Cast on 31 sts.
Work as foll to form a stockinette (stocking) stitch square with a seed (moss) stitch border, following the chart to place beads at the same time.
Row 1 K1, p1 to end.
Row 2 P1, k1 to end.
Row 3 K1, p1, knit next 27 sts, p1, k1.
Row 4 P1, k1, purl next 27 sts, k1, p1.
Rep Rows 3–4 until 40 rows have been completed.
Row 41 As Row 1.
Row 42 As Row 2.
Bind (cast) off.

+ = add bead

beaded flower

This is a great example how beads can brighten up a motif for a more sophisticated look.

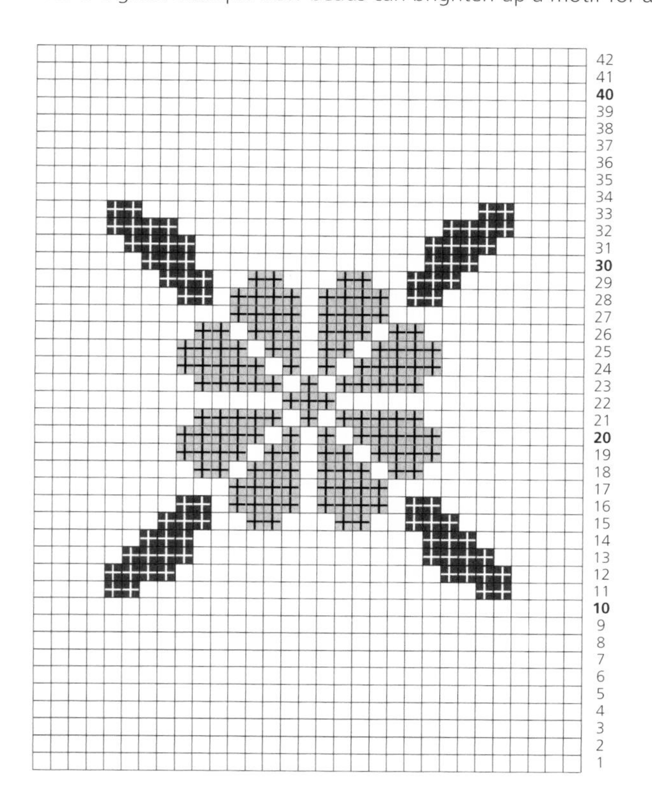

materials

Debbie Bliss Rialto DK, shade 02 Cream (A)
Cascade 220 DK, shade 8912 Lilac Mist (B), shade 2429 Groseille (C)
Needle size: US 6 (4mm)
205 x Rowan Pearl Beads J3001016

instructions

Cast on 31 sts.
Work as foll to form a stockinette (stocking) stitch square with a seed (moss) stitch border, following the chart to place beads at the same time.
Row 1 K1, p1 to end.
Row 2 P1, k1 to end.
Row 3 K1, p1, knit next 27 sts, p1, k1.
Row 4 P1, k1, purl next 27 sts, k1, p1.
Rep Rows 3–4 until 40 rows have been completed.
Row 41 As Row 1.
Row 42 As Row 2.
Bind (cast) off.

+ = add bead

alphabet

Use the alphabet blocks either as initials in a blanket or to spell out words or names, or join rows of letters to make a hanging garland. In this section the full alphabet is shown in capital letters in a variety of different bright colors. Use the intarsia method when making these blocks.

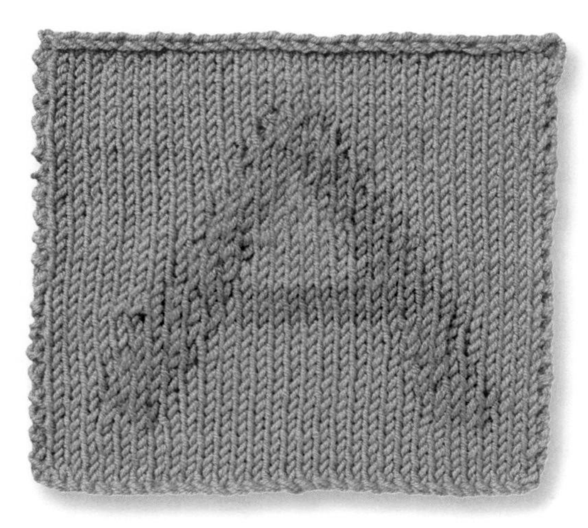

materials

BACKGROUND
Rooster Almerino DK, shade 211 Brighton Rock

LETTER
Rooster Almerino DK, shade 207 Gooseberry
Needle size: US 6 (4mm)

instructions

Cast on 32 sts using background color.
Work in stockinette (stocking) stitch for 40 rows following the chart to create a 6in. (15cm) square.
Bind (cast) off.

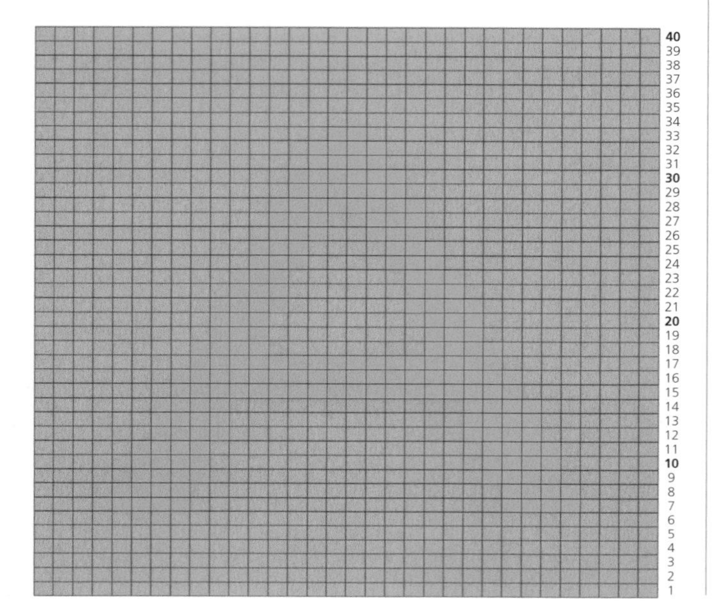

materials

BACKGROUND
Rooster Almerino DK, shade 203 Strawberry Cream

LETTER
Rowan Pure Wool DK, shade 10 Indigo
Needle size: US 6 (4mm)

instructions

Cast on 32 sts using background color.
Work in stockinette (stocking) stitch for 40 rows following the chart to create a 6in. (15cm) square.
Bind (cast) off.

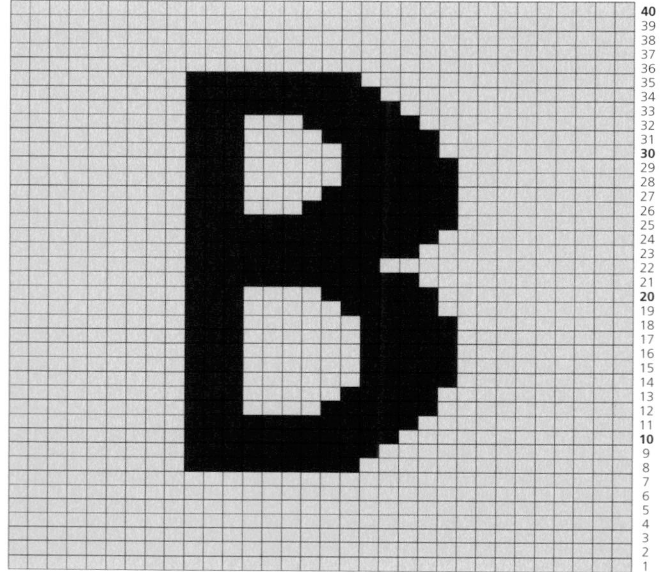

materials

BACKGROUND

Rooster Almerino DK, shade 208 Ocean

LETTER

Debbie Bliss Rialto DK, shade 12 Red

Needle size: US 6 (4mm)

instructions

Cast on 32 sts using background color.

Work in stockinette (stocking) stitch for 40 rows following the chart to create a 6in. (15cm) square.

Bind (cast) off.

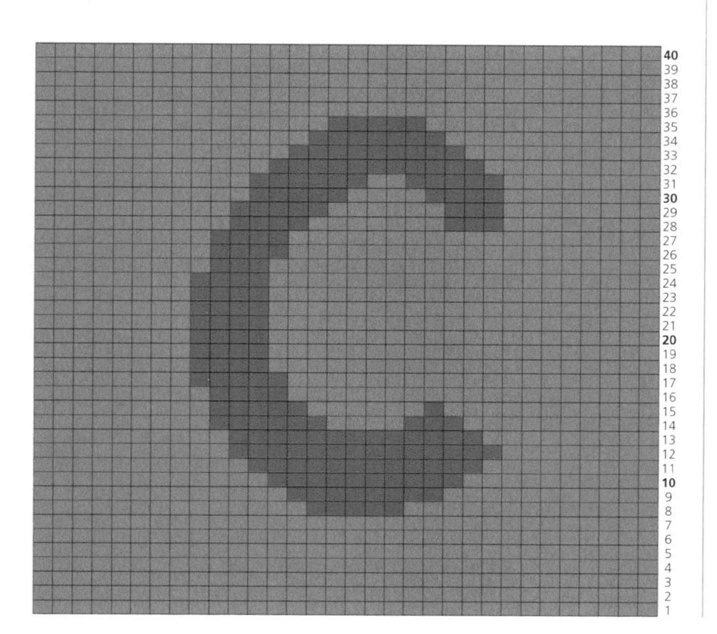

materials

BACKGROUND

Debbie Bliss Rialto DK, shade 12 Red

LETTER

Rooster Almerino DK, shade 201 Cornish

Needle size: US 6 (4mm)

instructions

Cast on 32 sts using background color.

Work in stockinette (stocking) stitch for 40 rows following the chart to create a 6in. (15cm) square.

Bind (cast) off.

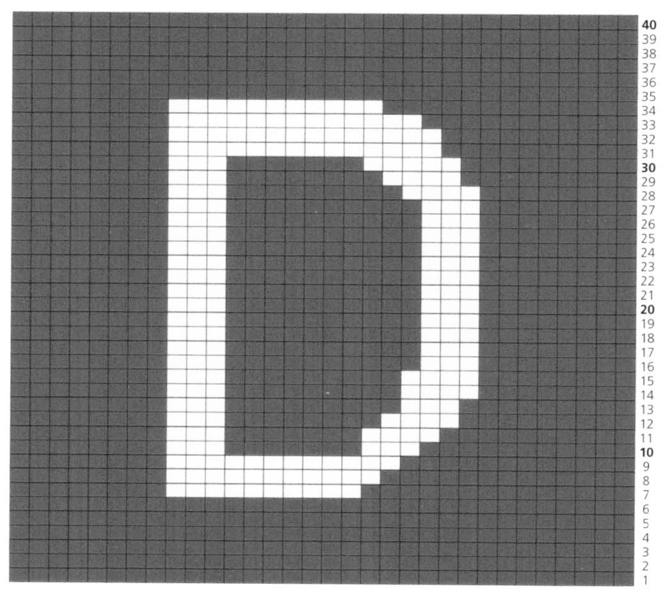

materials

BACKGROUND
Rowan Pure Wool DK, shade 037 Port

LETTER
Rowan Pure Wool DK, shade 031 Platinum Yellow
Needle size: US 6 (4mm)

instructions

Cast on 32 sts using background color.
Work in stockinette (stocking) stitch for 40 rows following the chart to create a 6in. (15cm) square.
Bind (cast) off.

materials

BACKGROUND
Rowan Pure Wool DK, shade 027 Hydrangea

LETTER
Rowan Pure Wool DK, shade 005 Glacier
Needle size: US 6 (4mm)

instructions

Cast on 32 sts using background color.
Work in stockinette (stocking) stitch for 40 rows following the chart to create a 6in. (15cm) square.
Bind (cast) off.

materials

BACKGROUND
Rooster Almerino DK, shade 207 Gooseberry

LETTER
Rowan Pure Wool DK, shade 033 Honey
Needle size: US 6 (4mm)

instructions

Cast on 32 sts using background color.
Work in stockinette (stocking) stitch for 40 rows following the chart to create a 6in. (15cm) square.
Bind (cast) off.

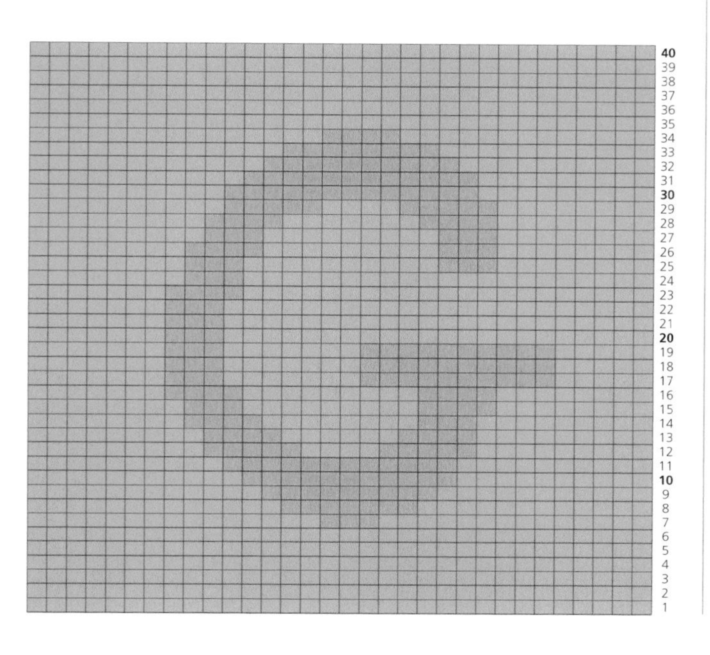

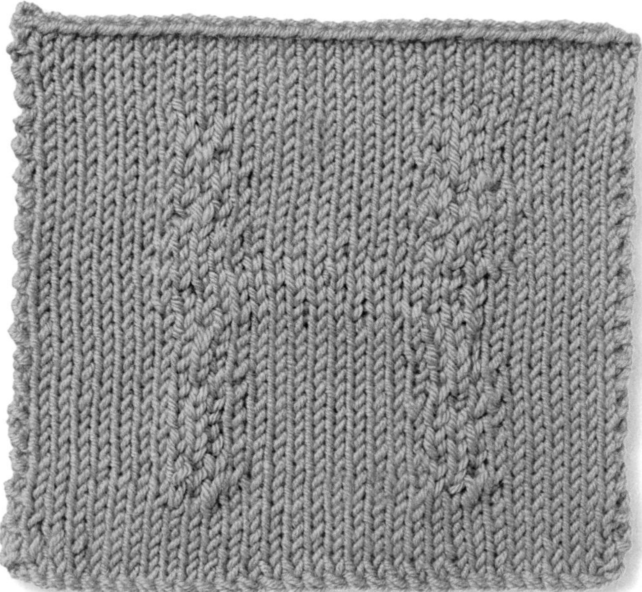

materials

BACKGROUND
Rooster Almerino DK, shade 211 Brighton Rock

LETTER
Rooster Almerino DK, shade 207 Gooseberry
Needle size: US 6 (4mm)

instructions

Cast on 32 sts using background color.
Work in stockinette (stocking) stitch for 40 rows following the chart to create a 6in. (15cm) square.
Bind (cast) off.

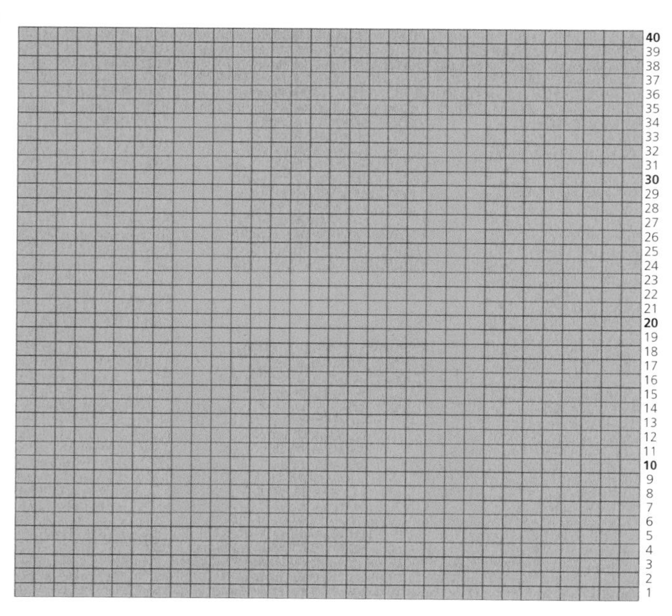

materials

BACKGROUND
Rowan Pure Wool DK, shade 005 Glacier

LETTER
Rowan Pure Wool DK, shade 042 Dahlia
Needle size: US 6 (4mm)

instructions

Cast on 32 sts using background color.
Work in stockinette (stocking) stitch for 40 rows following the chart to create a 6in. (15cm) square.
Bind (cast) off.

materials

BACKGROUND
Cascade 220 DK, shade 2419 Aster Heather

LETTER
Debbie Bliss Cashmerino DK, shade 17 Lilac
Needle size: US 6 (4mm)

instructions

Cast on 32 sts using background color.
Work in stockinette (stocking) stitch for 40 rows following the chart to create a 6in. (15cm) square.
Bind (cast) off.

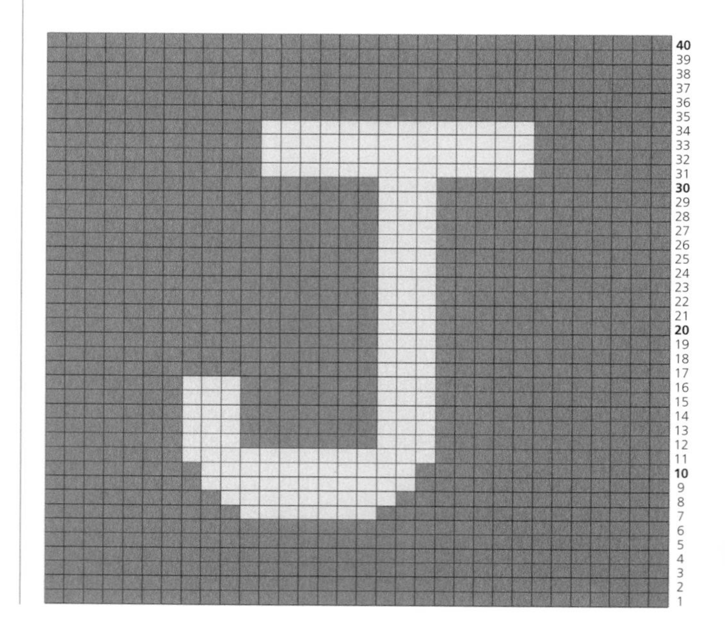

materials

BACKGROUND
Rooster Almerino DK, shade 202 Hazelnut

LETTER
Debbie Bliss Rialto DK, shade 12 Red
Needle size: US 6 (4mm)

instructions

Cast on 32 sts using background color.
Work in stockinette (stocking) stitch for 40 rows following the chart to create a 6in. (15cm) square.
Bind (cast) off.

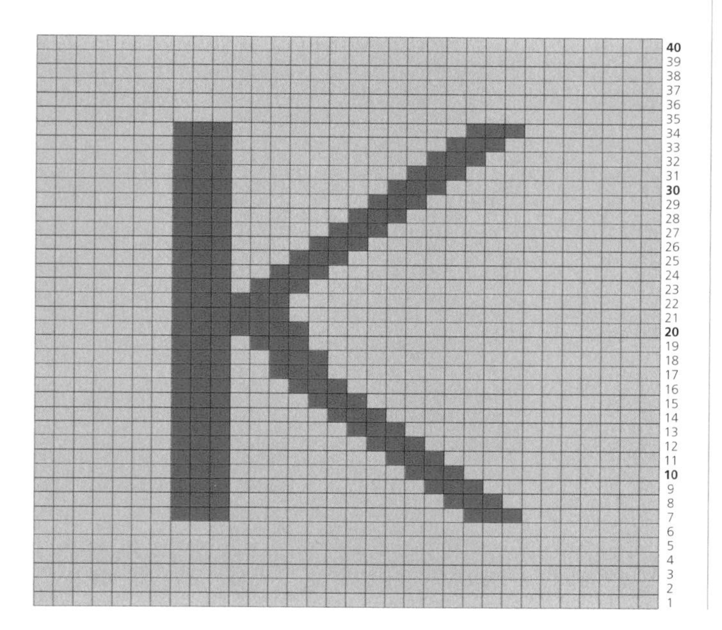

materials

BACKGROUND
Rooster Almerino DK, shade 209 Smoothie

LETTER
Rowan Pure Wool DK, shade 034 Spice
Needle size: US 6 (4mm)

instructions

Cast on 32 sts using background color.
Work in stockinette (stocking) stitch for 40 rows following the chart to create a 6in. (15cm) square.
Bind (cast) off.

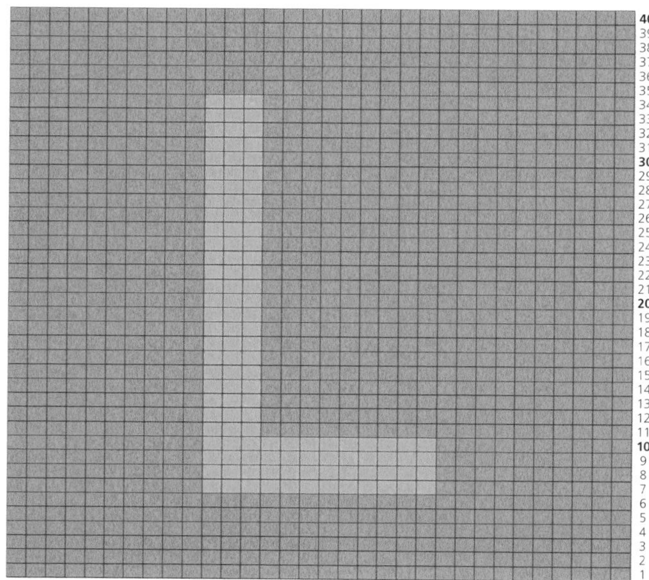

materials

BACKGROUND
Rowan Pure Wool DK, shade 010 Indigo

LETTER
Rowan Pure Wool DK, shade 031 Platinum Yellow
Needle size: US 6 (4mm)

instructions

Cast on 32 sts using background color.
Work in stockinette (stocking) stitch for 40 rows following the chart to create a 6in. (15cm) square.
Bind (cast) off.

materials

BACKGROUND
Debbie Bliss Cashmerino DK, shade 17 Lilac

LETTER
Rooster Almerino DK, shade 214 Damson
Needle size: US 6 (4mm)

instructions

Cast on 32 sts using background color.
Work in stockinette (stocking) stitch for 40 rows following the chart to create a 6in. (15cm) square.
Bind (cast) off.

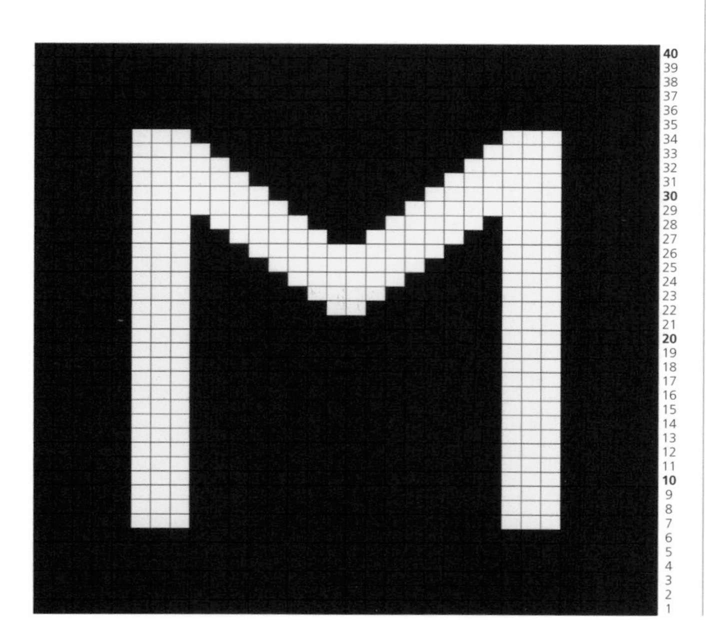

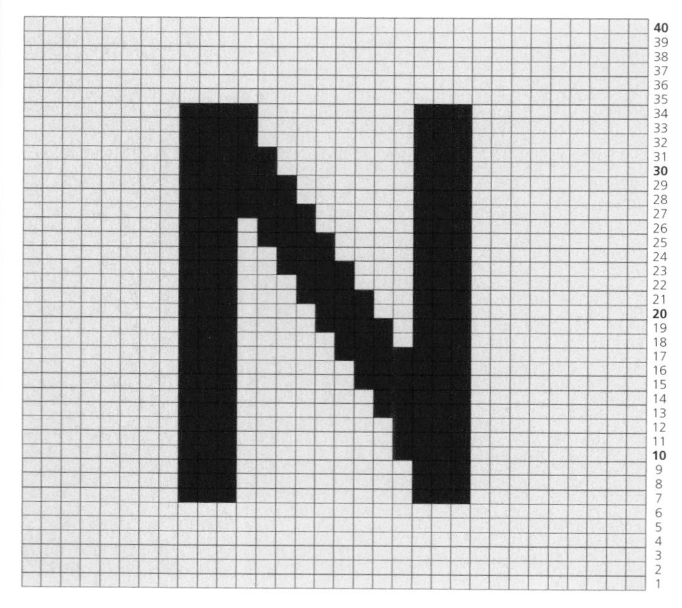

materials

BACKGROUND
Rooster Almerino DK, shade 204 Grape

LETTER
Rowan Pure Wool DK, shade 031 Platinum Yellow
Needle size: US 6 (4mm)

instructions

Cast on 32 sts using background color.
Work in stockinette (stocking) stitch for 40 rows following the chart to create a 6in. (15cm) square.
Bind (cast) off.

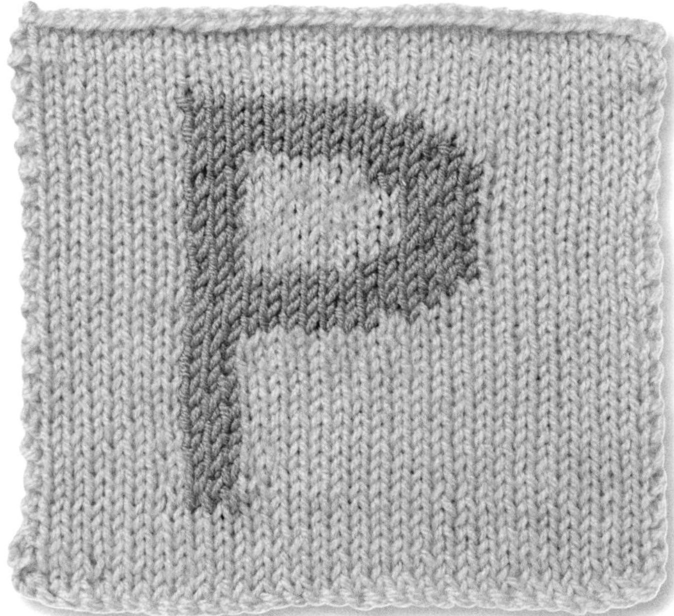

materials

BACKGROUND
Rowan Pure Wool DK, shade 044 Frost

LETTER
Rooster Almerino DK, shade 211 Brighton Rock
Needle size: US 6 (4mm)

instructions

Cast on 32 sts using background color.
Work in stockinette (stocking) stitch for 40 rows following the chart to create a 6in. (15cm) square.
Bind (cast) off.

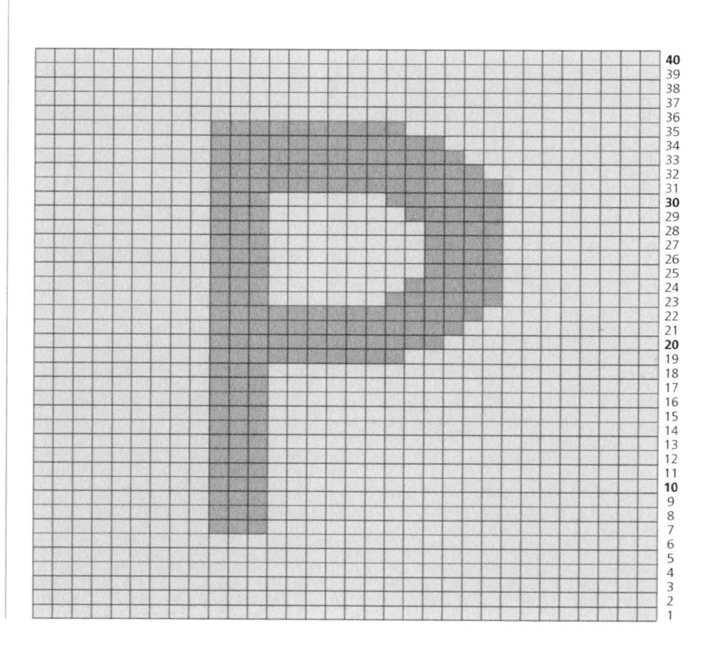

materials

BACKGROUND
Rowan Pure Wool DK, shade 029 Pomegranate

LETTER
Rooster Almerino DK, shade 202 Hazelnut
Needle size: US 6 (4mm)

instructions

Cast on 32 sts using background color.
Work in stockinette (stocking) stitch for 40 rows following the chart to create a 6in. (15cm) square.
Bind (cast) off.

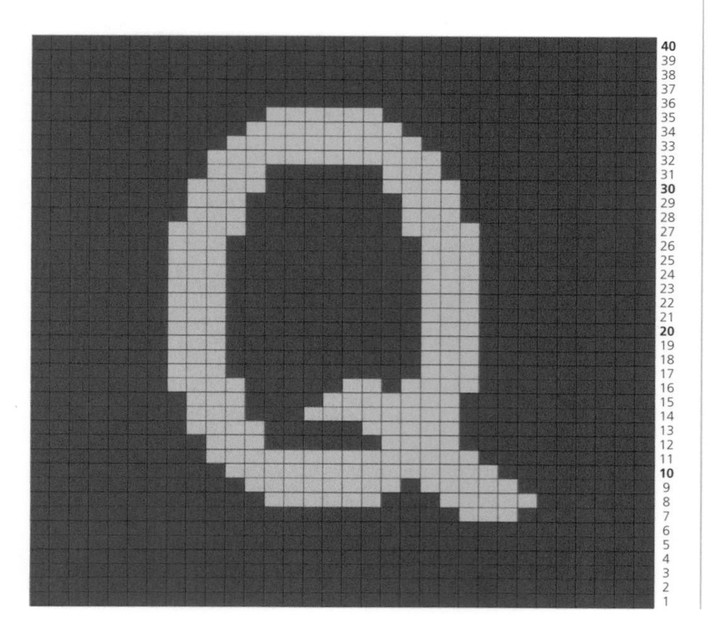

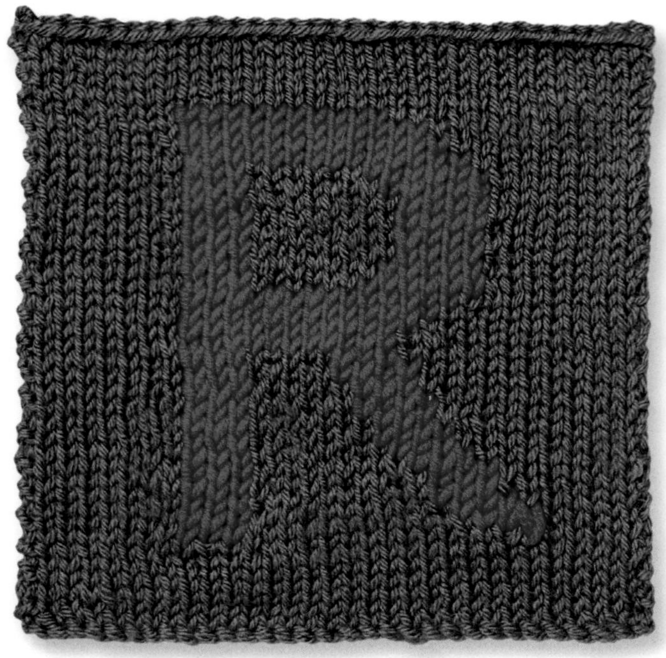

materials

BACKGROUND
Rowan Pure Wool DK, shade 021 Glade

LETTER
Debbie Bliss Rialto DK, shade 12 Red
Needle size: US 6 (4mm)

instructions

Cast on 32 sts using background color.
Work in stockinette (stocking) stitch for 40 rows following the chart to create a 6in. (15cm) square.
Bind (cast) off.

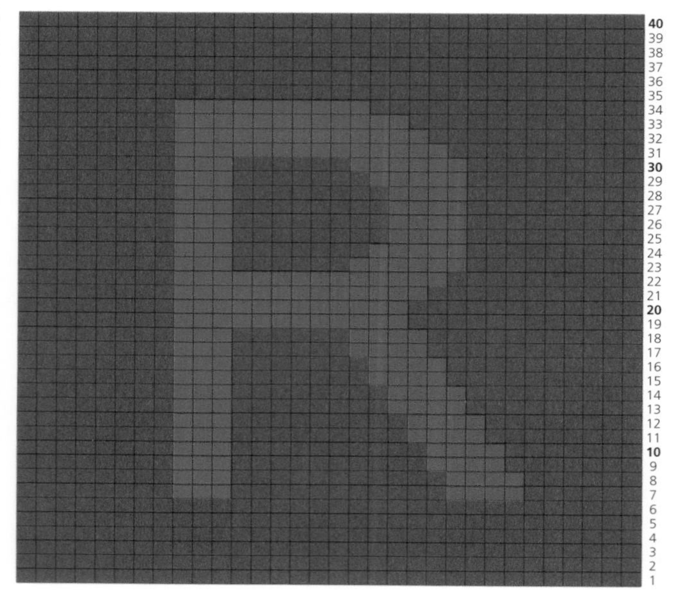

materials

BACKGROUND
Debbie Bliss Rialto DK, shade 12 Red

LETTER
Rowan Pure Wool DK, shade 044 Frost
Needle size: US 6 (4mm)

instructions

Cast on 32 sts using background color.
Work in stockinette (stocking) stitch for 40 rows following the chart to create a 6in. (15cm) square.
Bind (cast) off.

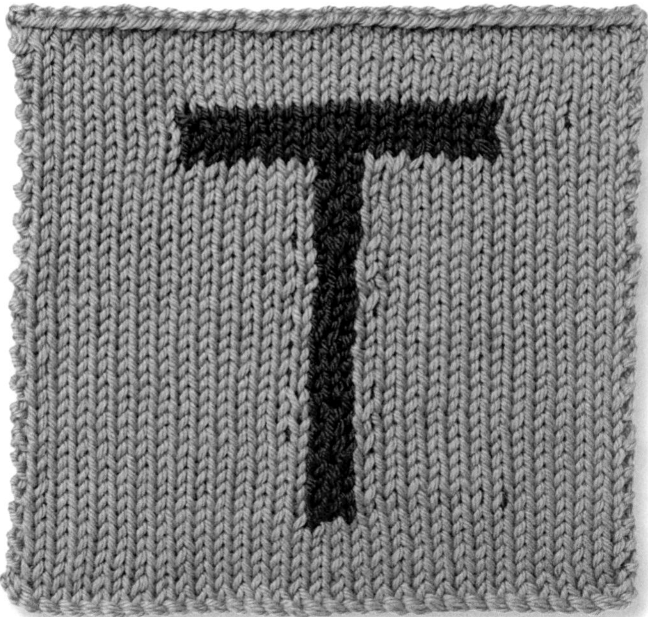

materials

BACKGROUND
Rowan Pure Wool DK, shade 046 Tudor Rose

LETTER
Rowan Pure Wool DK, shade 027 Hydrangea
Needle size: US 6 (4mm)

instructions

Cast on 32 sts using background color.
Work in stockinette (stocking) stitch for 40 rows following the chart to create a 6in. (15cm) square.
Bind (cast) off.

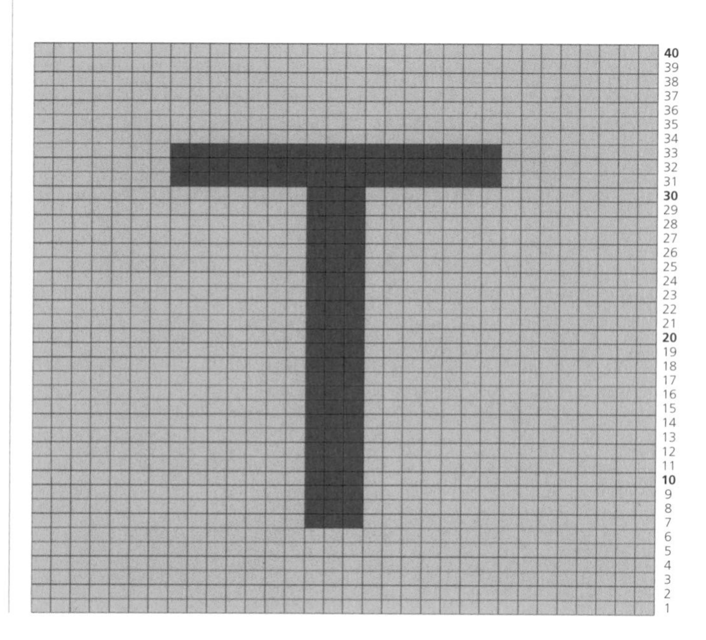

materials

BACKGROUND
Rowan Pure Wool DK, shade 023 Shamrock

LETTER
Rowan Pure Wool DK, shade 033 Honey
Needle size: US 6 (4mm)

instructions

Cast on 32 sts using background color.
Work in stockinette (stocking) stitch for 40 rows following the chart to create a 6in. (15cm) square.
Bind (cast) off.

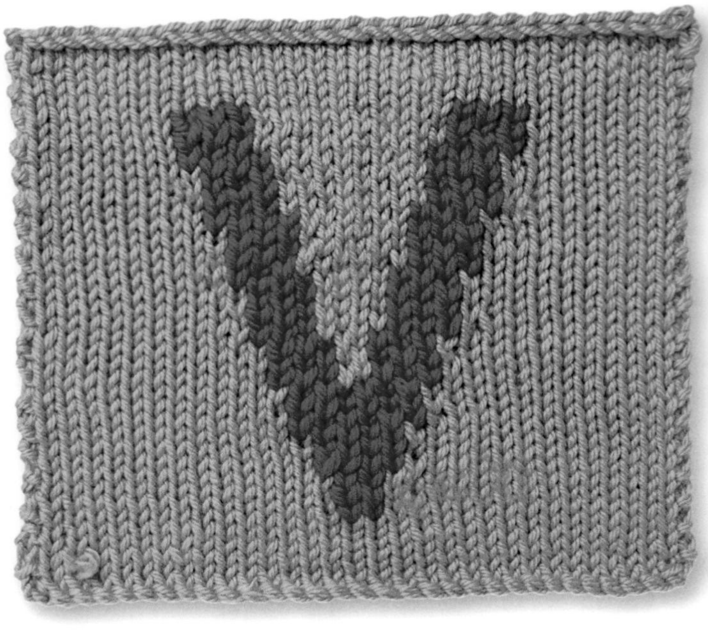

materials

BACKGROUND
Rooster Almerino DK, shade 207 Gooseberry

LETTER
Debbie Bliss Rialto DK, shade 12 Red
Needle size: US 6 (4mm)

instructions

Cast on 32 sts using background color.
Work in stockinette (stocking) stitch for 40 rows following the chart to create a 6in. (15cm) square.
Bind (cast) off.

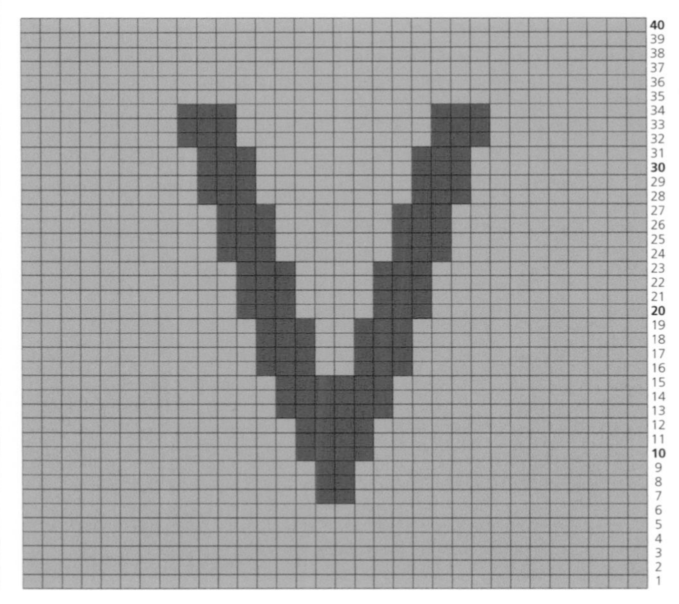

materials

BACKGROUND
Sirdar Country Style DK, shade 602 Soft Teal

LETTER
Rowan Pure Wool DK, shade 031 Platinum Yellow
Needle size: US 6 (4mm)

instructions

Cast on 32 sts using background color.
Work in stockinette (stocking) stitch for 40 rows following the chart to create a 6in. (15cm) square.
Bind (cast) off.

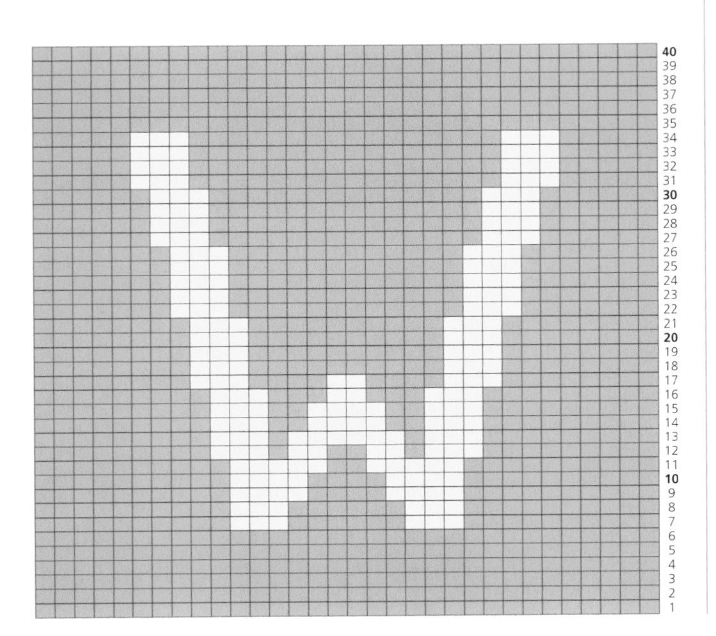

materials

BACKGROUND
Rooster Almerino DK, shade 208 Ocean

LETTER
Rooster Almerino DK, shade 202 Hazelnut
Needle size: US 6 (4mm)

instructions

Cast on 32 sts using background color.
Work in stockinette (stocking) stitch for 40 rows following the chart to create a 6in. (15cm) square.
Bind (cast) off.

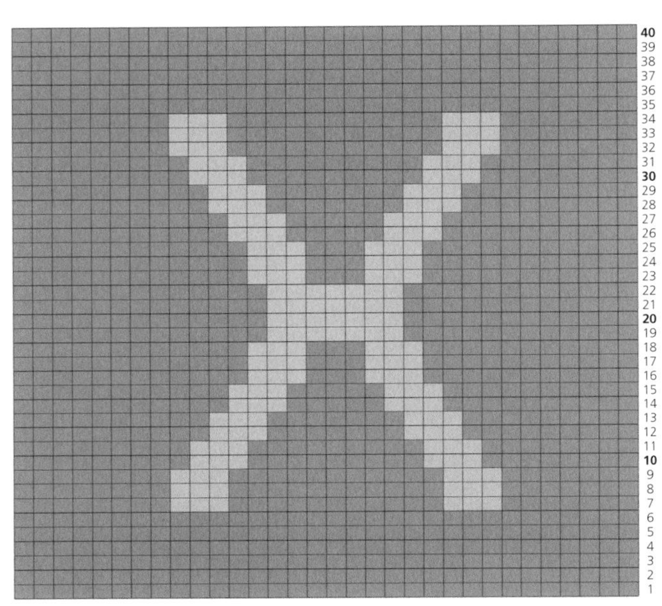

materials

BACKGROUND
Rooster Almerino DK, shade 204 Grape

LETTER
Debbie Bliss Rialto DK, shade 12 Red
Needle size: US 6 (4mm)

instructions

Cast on 32 sts using background color.
Work in stockinette (stocking) stitch for 40 rows following the chart to create a 6in. (15cm) square.
Bind (cast) off.

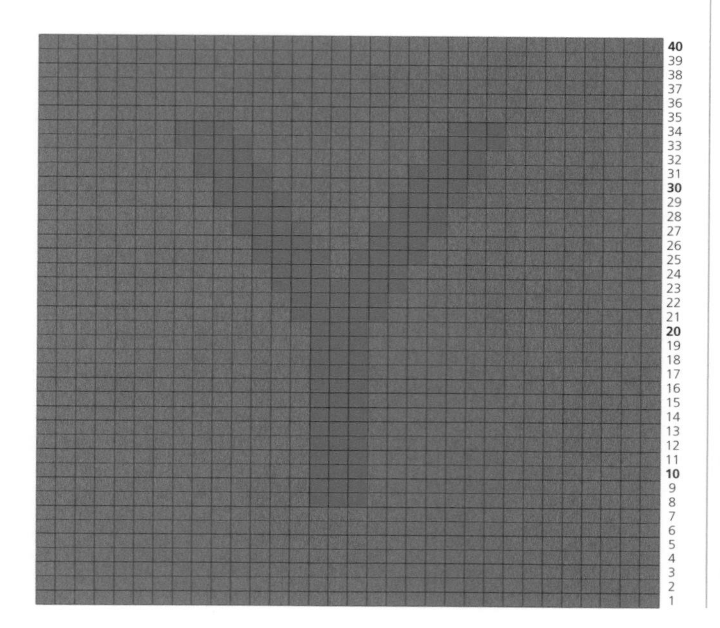

materials

BACKGROUND
Rowan Pure Wool DK, shade 033 Honey

LETTER
Rooster Almerino DK, shade 208 Ocean
Needle size: US 6 (4mm)

instructions

Cast on 32 sts using background color.
Work in stockinette (stocking) stitch for 40 rows following the chart to create a 6in. (15cm) square.
Bind (cast) off.

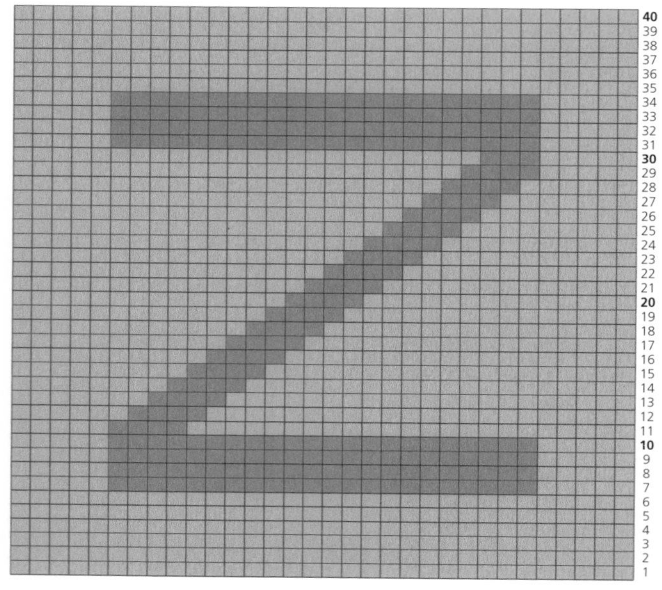

numbers

Another set of blocks utilizing the intarsia technique. Knitted blocks are a lovely way to teach a child to count—if you back a set of these with fabric they could make a lovely wall hanging, or try incorporating them into a blanket.

materials

BACKGROUND

Sirdar Country Style DK, shade 602, Soft Teal

NUMBER

Rowan Pure Wool DK, shade 025 Tea Rose

Needle size: US 6 (4mm)

instructions

Cast on 32 sts using background color.

Work in stockinette (stocking) stitch for 40 rows following the chart to create a 6in. (15cm) square.

Bind (cast) off.

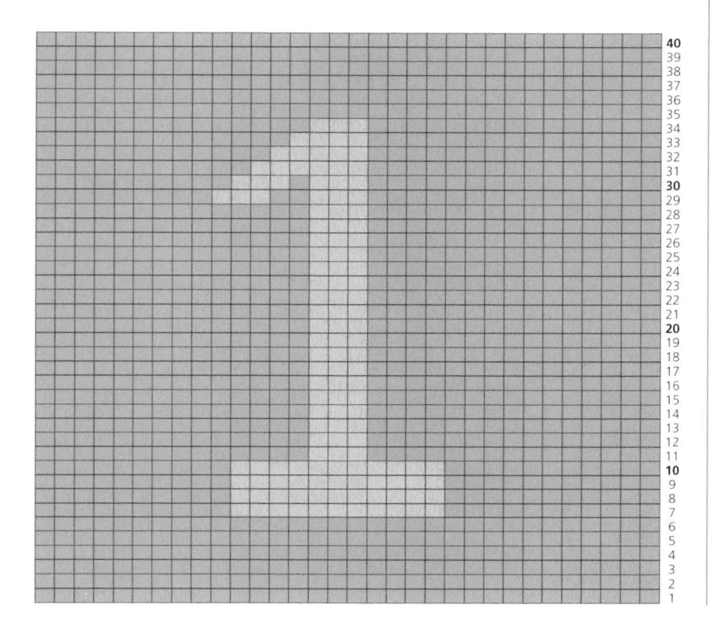

materials

BACKGROUND

Rooster Almerino DK, shade 202 Hazelnut

NUMBER

Rowan Pure Wool DK, shade 037 Port

Needle size: US 6 (4mm)

instructions

Cast on 32 sts using background color.

Work in stockinette (stocking) stitch for 40 rows following the chart to create a 6in. (15cm) square.

Bind (cast) off.

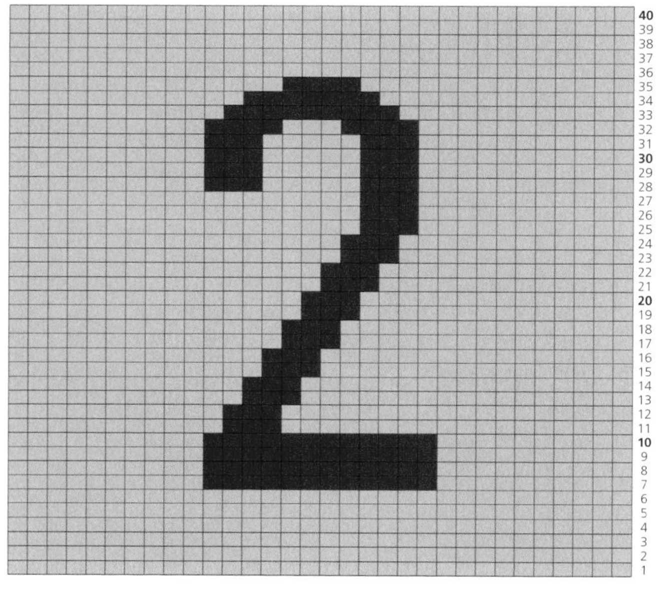

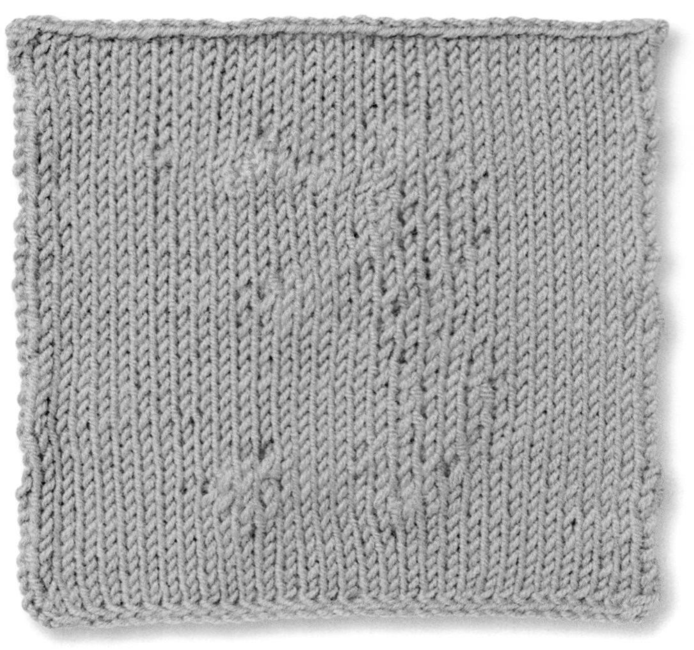

materials

BACKGROUND

Debbie Bliss Cashmerino DK, shade 17 Lilac

NUMBER

Rooster Almerino DK, shade 210 Custard

Needle size: US 6 (4mm)

instructions

Cast on 32 sts using background color.

Work in stockinette (stocking) stitch for 40 rows following the chart to create a 6in. (15cm) square.

Bind (cast) off.

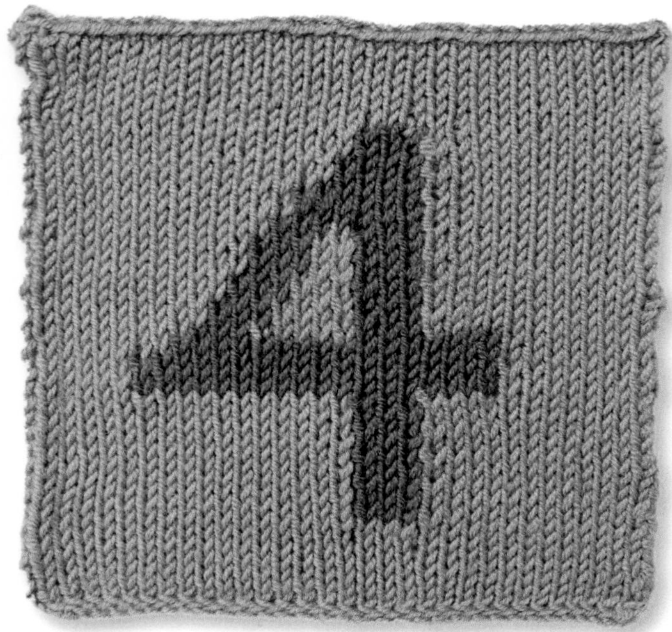

materials

BACKGROUND

Rooster Almerino DK, shade 202 Hazelnut

NUMBER

Rooster Almerino DK, shade 208 Ocean

Needle size: US 6 (4mm)

instructions

Cast on 32 sts using background color.

Work in stockinette (stocking) stitch for 40 rows following the chart to create a 6in. (15cm) square.

Bind (cast) off.

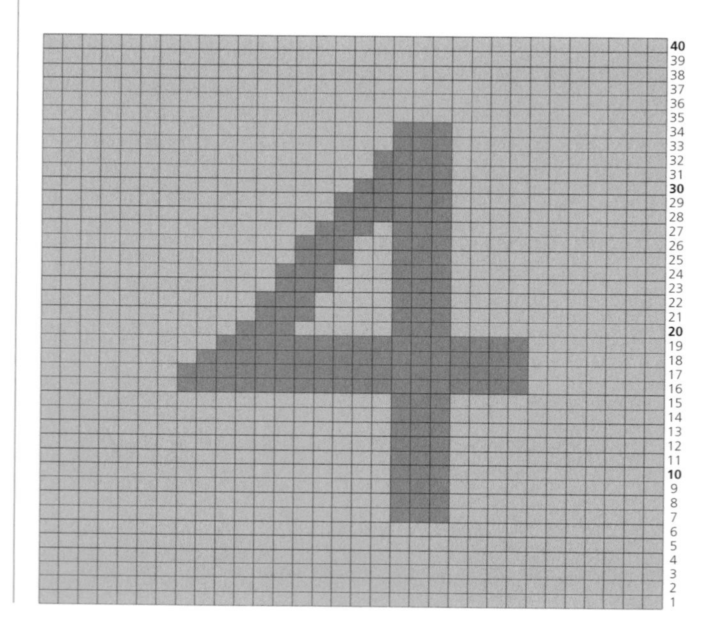

materials

BACKGROUND
Rowan Pure Wool DK, shade 005 Glacier

NUMBER
Debbie Bliss Rialto DK, shade 35 Navy Blue
Needle size: US 6 (4mm)

instructions

Cast on 32 sts using background color.
Work in stockinette (stocking) stitch for 40 rows following the chart to create a 6in. (15cm) square.
Bind (cast) off.

materials

BACKGROUND
Rooster Almerino DK, shade 202 Hazelnut

NUMBER
Rooster Almerino DK, shade 205 Glace
Needle size: US 6 (4mm)

instructions

Cast on 32 sts using background color.
Work in stockinette (stocking) stitch for 40 rows following the chart to create a 6in. (15cm) square.
Bind (cast) off.

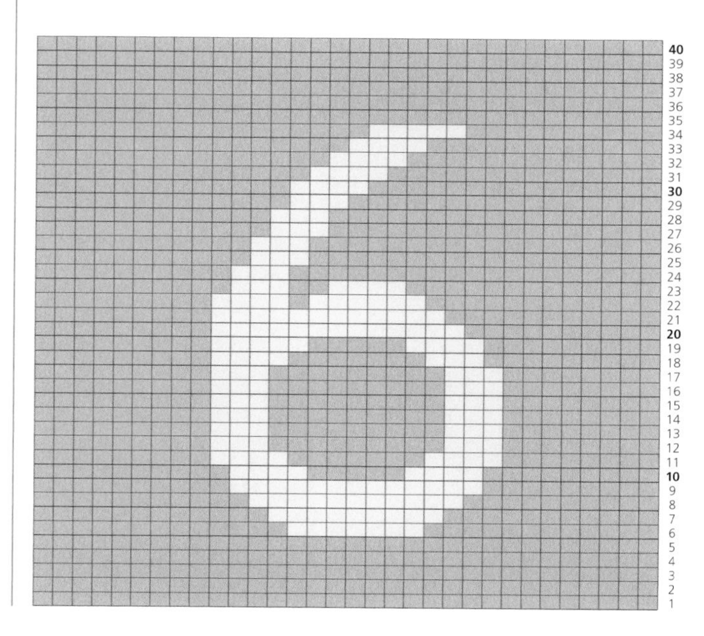

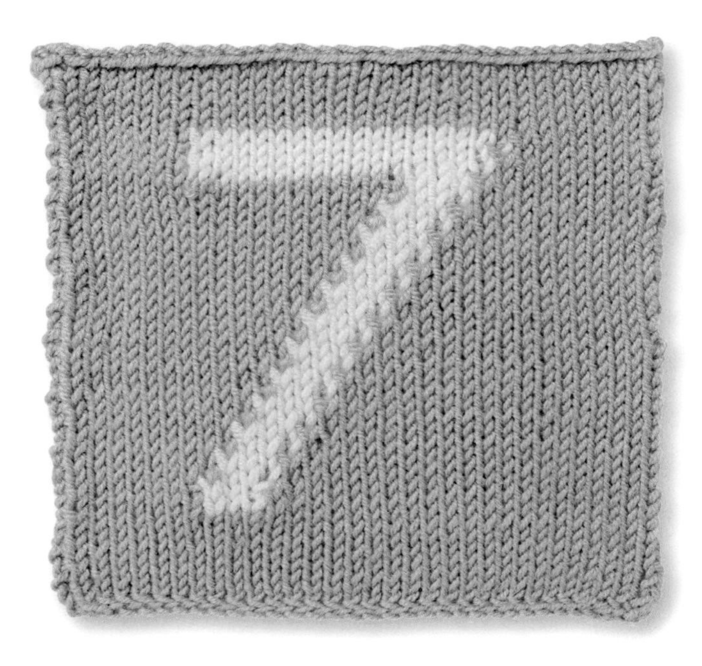

materials

BACKGROUND
Rowan Pure Wool DK, shade 005 Glacier

NUMBER
Rooster Almerino DK, shade 201 Cornish
Needle size: US 6 (4mm)

instructions

Cast on 32 sts using background color.
Work in stockinette (stocking) stitch for 40 rows following the chart to create a 6in. (15cm) square.
Bind (cast) off.

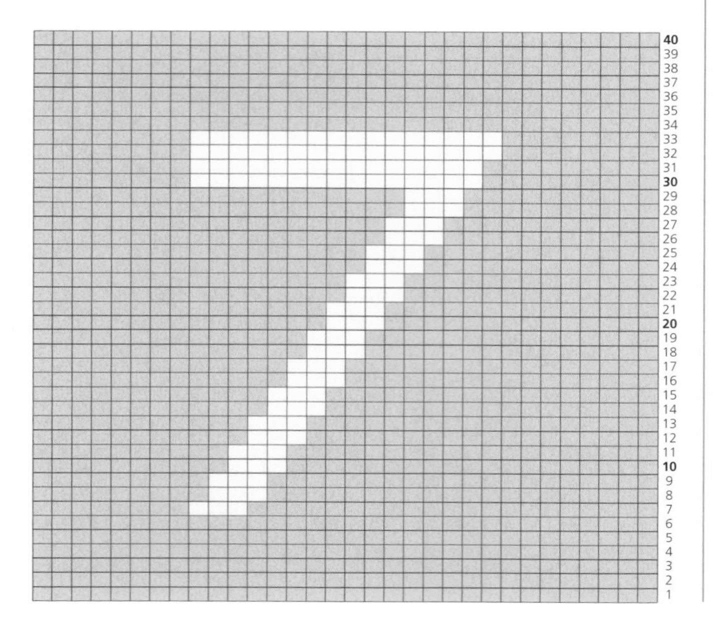

materials

BACKGROUND
Debbie Bliss Cashmerino DK, shade 17 Lilac

NUMBER
Rooster Almerino DK, shade 204 Grape
Needle size: US 6 (4mm)

instructions

Cast on 32 sts using background color.
Work in stockinette (stocking) stitch for 40 rows following the chart to create a 6in. (15cm) square.
Bind (cast) off.

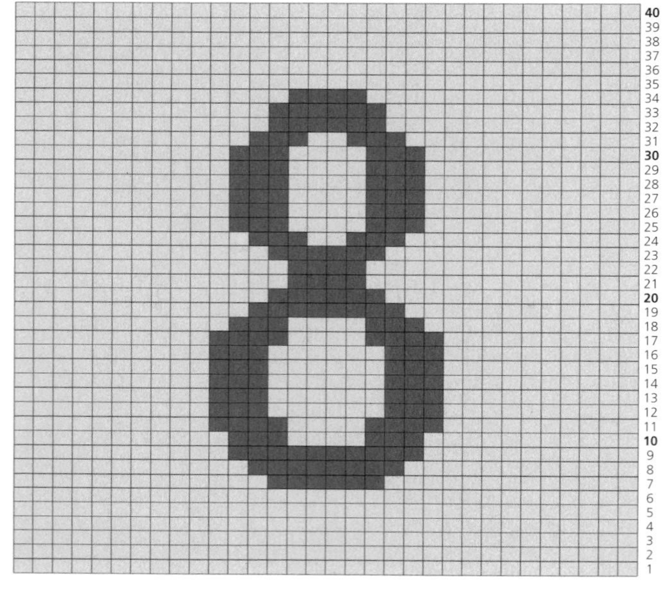

materials

BACKGROUND
Debbie Bliss Cashmerino DK, shade 17 Lilac

NUMBER
Rooster Almerino DK, shade 207 Gooseberry
Needle size: US 6 (4mm)

instructions

Cast on 32 sts using background color.
Work in stockinette (stocking) stitch for 40 rows following the chart to create a 6in. (15cm) square.
Bind (cast) off.

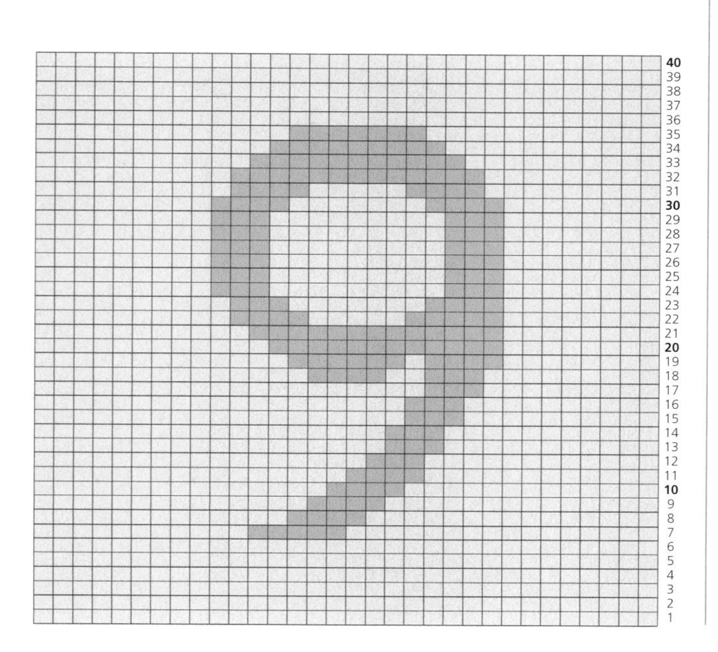

materials

BACKGROUND
Rooster Almerino DK, shade 202 Hazelnut

NUMBER
Rowan Pure Wool DK, shade 030 Damson
Needle size: US 6 (4mm)

instructions

Cast on 32 sts using background color.
Work in stockinette (stocking) stitch for 40 rows following the chart to create a 6in. (15cm) square.
Bind (cast) off.

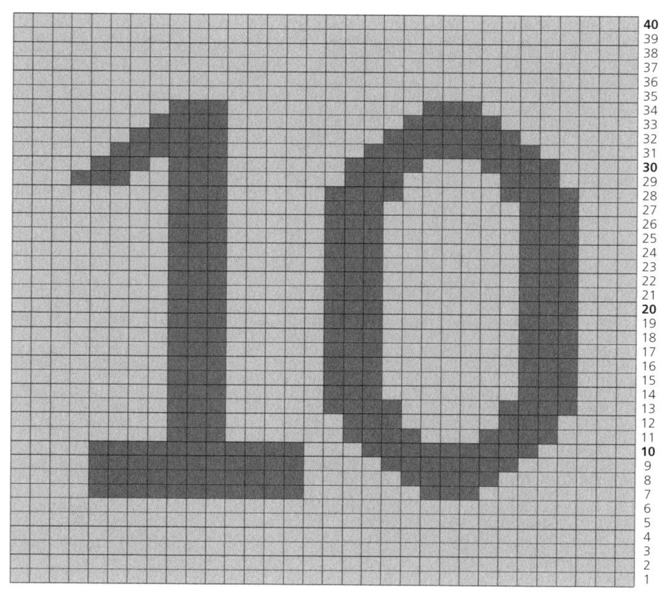

part two

projects

These projects use many of the techniques and designs in the blocks section, but also include some additional ideas. On some of them you could also utilize the basic design idea but substitute different blocks of your choice—don't be afraid to experiment and mix and match.

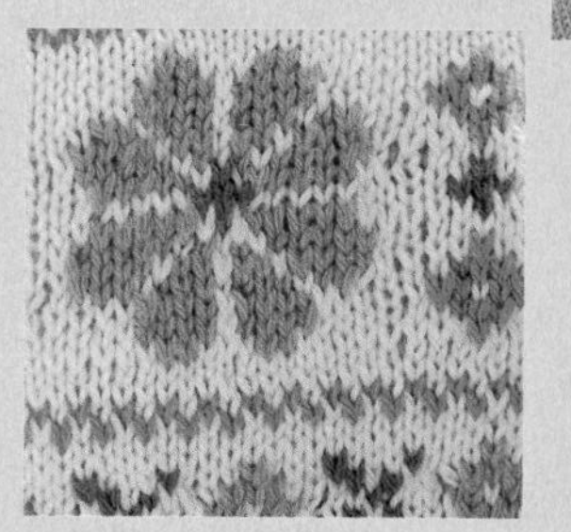

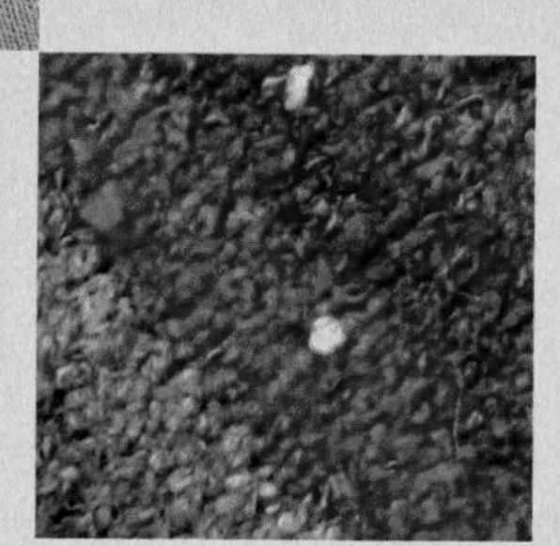

lace bed throw

This is a very cozy and homely throw that is a major project and a labor of love. My mother originally made two of these, one each for my sister and me, which were stored in a bag in the attic until we both had homes of our own. Now our own daughters are all demanding one!

size

Single: approx. 87 x 62in. (218 x 157cm), excluding fringing
Double: approx. 87 x 74in. (218 x 185cm), excluding fringing
Each large square (4 motifs together): approx. 12in. (30cm) square

materials

100 percent cotton yarn, such as Pegasus Craft Cotton/Dishcloth cotton

SINGLE
40 x 3½oz (100g) balls—approx. 6400yd (5920m)—of white

DOUBLE
45 x 3½oz (100g) balls—approx. 7200yd (6660m)—of white
Needle size: US 8 (5mm)
Yarn sewing needle

gauge (tension)

19 sts and 28 rows over 4in. (10cm) square using stockinette (stocking) stitch. Change needle size if necessary to achieve the required gauge (tension).

MOTIF (MAKE 4 FOR EACH SQUARE)
Cast on 2 sts.
Row 1 (right side) k1, yo, k1. (3 sts)
Row 2 Purl.
Row 3 [K1, yo] twice, k1. (5 sts)
Row 4 Purl.
Row 5 [K1, yo] 4 times, k1. (9 sts)
Row 6 Purl.
Row 7 K1, yfrn, p1, k2, yo, k1, yo, k2, p1, yon, k1. (13 sts)
Row 8 P2, k1, p7, k1, p2.
Row 9 K1, yfrn, p2, k3, yo, k1, yo, k3, p2, yon, k1. (17 sts)
Row 10 P2, k2, p9, k2, p2.
Row 11 K1, yfrn, p3, k4, yo, k1, yo, k4, p3, yon, k1. (21 sts)
Row 12 P2, k3, p11, k3, p2.
Row 13 K1, yfrn, p4, k5, yo, k1, yo, k5, p4, yon, k1. (25 sts)
Row 14 P2, k4, p13, k4, p2.
Row 15 K1, yfrn, p5, k6, yo, k1, yo, k6, p5, yon, k1. (29 sts)
Row 16 P2, k5, p15, k5, p2.
Row 17 K1, yfrn, p6, skpo, k11, k2tog, p6, yon, k1. (29 sts)
Row 18 P2, k6, p13, k6, p2.
Row 19 K1, yfrn, p7, skpo, k9, k2tog, p7, yon, k1. (29 sts)
Row 20 P2, k7, p11, k7, p2.
Row 21 K1, yfrn, p8, skpo, k7, k2tog, p8, yon, k1. (29 sts)
Row 22 P2, k8, p9, k8, p2.
Row 23 K1, yfrn, p9, skpo, k5, k2tog, p9, yon, k1. (29 sts)
Row 24 P2, k9, p7, k9, p2.
Row 25 K1, yfrn, p10, skpo, k3, k2tog, p10, yon, k1. (29 sts)
Row 26 P2, k10, p5, k10, p2.
Row 27 K1, yfrn, p11, skpo, k1, k2tog, p11, yon, k1. (29 sts)
Row 28 P2, k11, p3, k11, p2.
Row 29 K1, yfrn, p12, sl 1, k2tog, psso, p12, yon, k1. (29 sts)
Row 30 Purl.
Row 31 Inc in first st, k27, inc in last st. (31sts)
Rows 32–33 Purl.
Row 34 [K2tog, yfd) to last 3 sts, k3tog. (29 sts)
Row 35 Purl.
Row 36 P2tog, purl to last 2 sts, p2tog. (27 sts)
Row 37 Knit.
Row 38 As Row 36. (25 sts)
Row 39 Purl.
Rep Rows 34–39 three times more, then Rows 34–37 once. (3 sts)
P3tog.
Bind (cast) off.

TO COMPLETE
Make four motifs and join seams together with "petals" together at center to form one large square. For the single size, make 35 squares and join together in seven lines of five squares. For the double size, make 42 squares and join with seams together in seven lines of six squares.

EDGING
Cast on 4 sts.
Row 1 Yo, k2, yo, k2tog. (5 sts)
Row 2 Knit.
Row 3 Yo, k3, yo, k2tog. (6 sts)
Row 4 Knit.
Row 5 Yo, k4, yo, k2tog. (7 sts)
Row 6 Knit.
Row 7 Yo, k5, yo, k2tog. (8 sts)
Row 8 Knit.
Row 9 Yo, k6, yo, k2tog. (9 sts)
Row 10 Knit.
Row 11 Bind (cast) off 5 sts, k1, yo, k2tog. (4 sts)
Row 12 Knit.
These 12 rows form pattern, rep these rows until required length is obtained to fit throw.
Bind (cast) off.
Sew edging to throw; if necessary make a pleat at each corner.

TASSELS
Cut 10in. (26cm) lengths of cotton yarn. Take four strands, fold in half then slot loop through one hole in edging. Thread tassel ends through loop to make a knot. Trim ends level. Repeat for each tassel spaced evenly all round throw.

baby cot blanket

A cot blanket is a great start to life, particularly when it is lovingly made from a soft, luxurious yarn. This project is perfect for both beginners and more advanced knitters. The edging is very simple and the squares take no time at all.

size

Approx. 34 x 30in. (85 x 75cm)

materials

Light worsted (DK) yarn, such as Rooster Almerino DK
2 x 1¾oz (50g) balls—approx. 248yd (225m)—of light pink (A)
4 x 1¾oz (50g) balls—approx. 496yd (450m)—of cream (B)
2 x 1¾oz (50g) balls—approx. 248yd (225m)—each of light blue (C), light brown (D)
Needle size: US 5 (3.75mm)
Yarn sewing needle

gauge (tension)

21 sts and 28 rows over 4in. (10cm) square using stockinette (stocking) stitch. Change needle size if necessary to achieve the required gauge (tension).

SQUARES (MAKE 20 IN EACH COLOR)
Cast on 18 sts.
Work in st st for 26 rows.
Bind (cast) off.

TO COMPLETE
Sew in ends.
Embroider French knots on each side of cream-color squares using an equal mix of A, C, and D.
Sew squares together into ten rows of eight squares each using mattress stitch.
Sew rows together using mattress stitch, ensuring that a bound (cast) off edge of each square is positioned at top and bottom of the blanket.

EDGING (MAKE APPROX. 60 TRIANGLES)
Cast on 7 sts.
Row 1 K2, yo, k2tog, yo, k3. (8 sts)
Row 2 Knit.
Row 3 K2, yo, k2tog, yo, k4. (9 sts)
Row 4 Knit.
Row 5 K2, yo, k2tog, yo, k5. (10 sts)
Row 6 Knit.
Row 7 K2, yo, k2tog, yo, k6. (11 sts)
Row 8 Knit.
Row 9 K2, yo, k2tog, yo, k7. (12 sts)
Row 10 Knit.
Row 11 K2, yo, k2tog, yo, k8. (13 sts)
Row 12 Knit.
Row 13 K2, yo, k2tog, yo, k9. (14 sts)
Row 14 Knit.
Row 15 K2, yo, k2tog, yo k10. (15 sts)
Row 16 Bind (cast) off 8 sts, knit to end. (7 sts)

Rep Rows 1–16 until there are enough triangles to fit around each edge of the blanket.
Bind (cast) off.

TO COMPLETE
Sew edging to the blanket using slipstitch.

tip

For a perfect fit, sew the edging of the blanket around the blanket using slipstitch as you are working the edging.

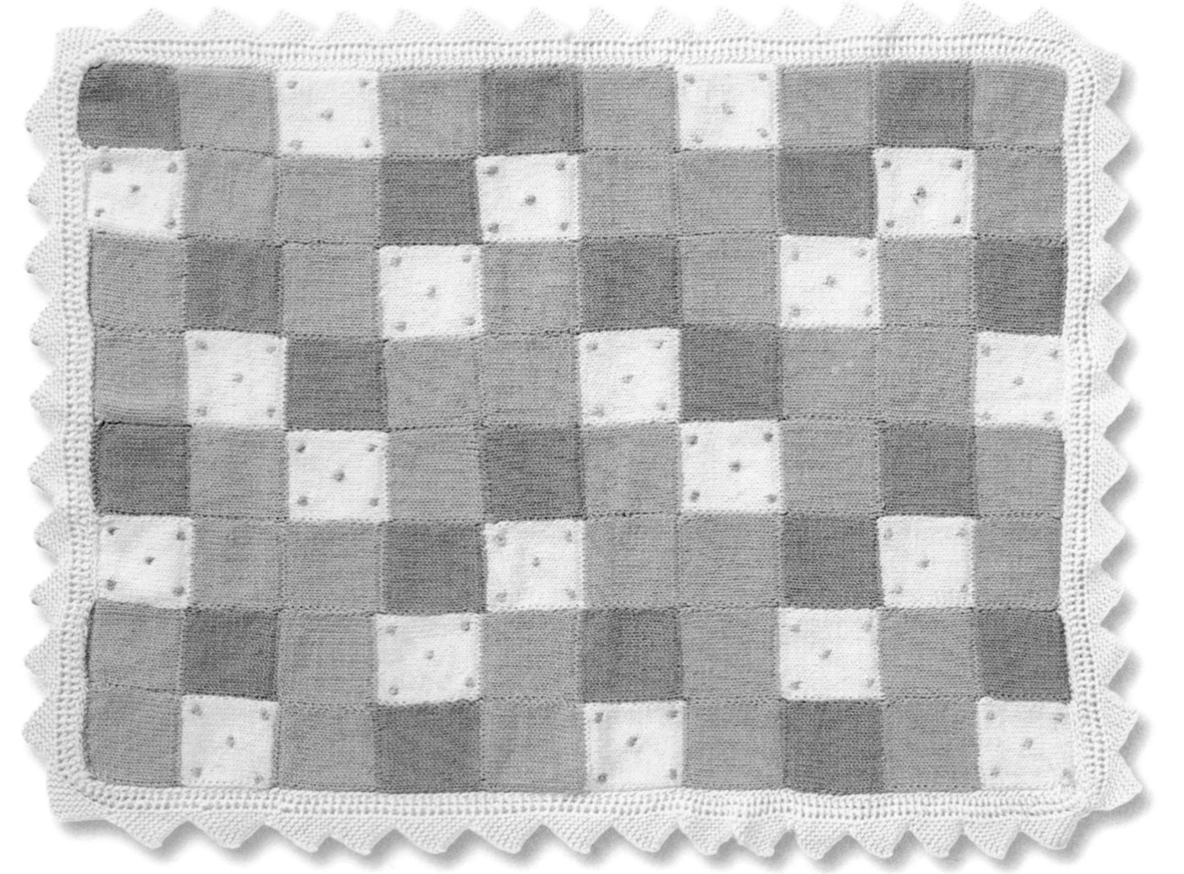

toddler blanket

This is a really special blanket; the yarn is a combination of alpaca and super soft merino wool and the motifs a pretty mixture of pictures and textures. The images are inspired by things babies love: bright colors, a heart, a boat, a flower, and a ladybird.

size

Blanket: approx. 47 x 45in. (117 x 112cm)
Each square: approx. 12 x 12in. (30 x 30cm)

materials

Alpaca and merino wool mix worsted (Aran) yarn, such as Rooster Almerino Aran
13 x 1¾oz (50g) balls—approx. 1339yd (1222m)—of light brown (A)
2 x 1¾oz (50g) balls—approx. 206yd (188m)—of red (B)
1 x 1¾oz (50g) ball—approx. 103yd (94m) —each of pink (C), yellow (D), purple-red (E), cream (F), blue-green (G), green (H), light pink (I), pale blue (J)
Needle size: US 8 (5mm)
Yarn sewing needle

gauge (tension)

16 sts and 24 rows over 4in. (10cm) square using stockinette (stocking) stitch. Change needle size if necessary to achieve the required gauge (tension).

SQUARES

Cast on 62 sts using A.
Foll chart (see pages 98–99) for each square, using st st throughout, and intarsia for color motifs. Foll charts to purl where indicated on knit row on textured motifs.
Bind (cast) off.

EDGING (MAKE 4)

Cast on 7 sts using A.
Row 1 K2, yo, k2tog, yo, k to end. (8 sts)
Row 2 Knit.
Rows 3–14 Rep Rows 1 and 2 six times. (14 sts)
Row 15 Rep Row 1. (15 sts)
Row 16 Bind (cast) off 8 sts, k to end. (7 sts)
These 16 rows make one triangle. Rep these rows 14 times more to make a strip of 15 triangles.
Bind (cast) off.

TO COMPLETE

Sew squares together to make blanket, following the photograph. Sew one strip of edging to each edge of blanket.

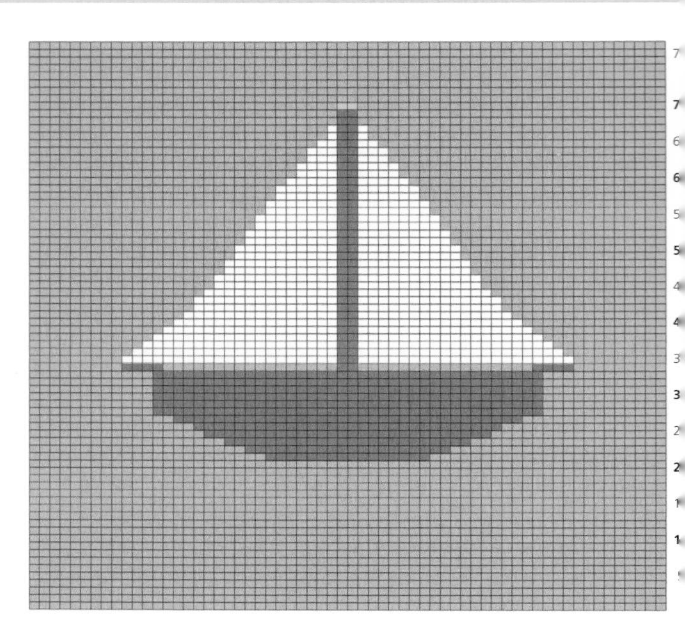

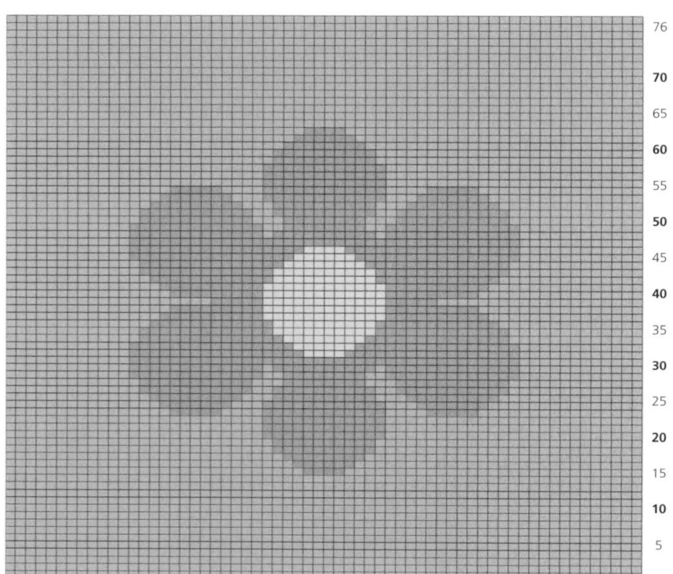

TODDLER BLANKET CHARTS

See page 97 for instructions.

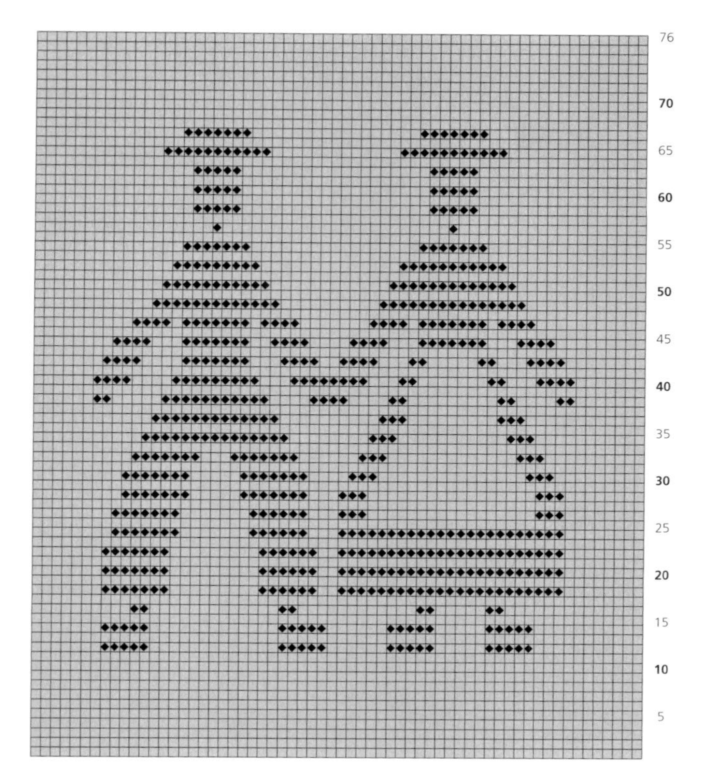

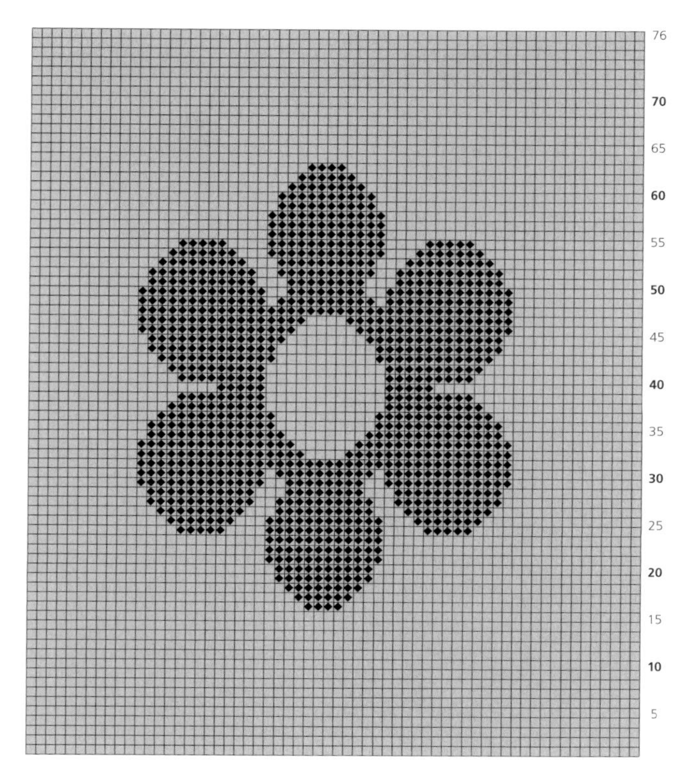

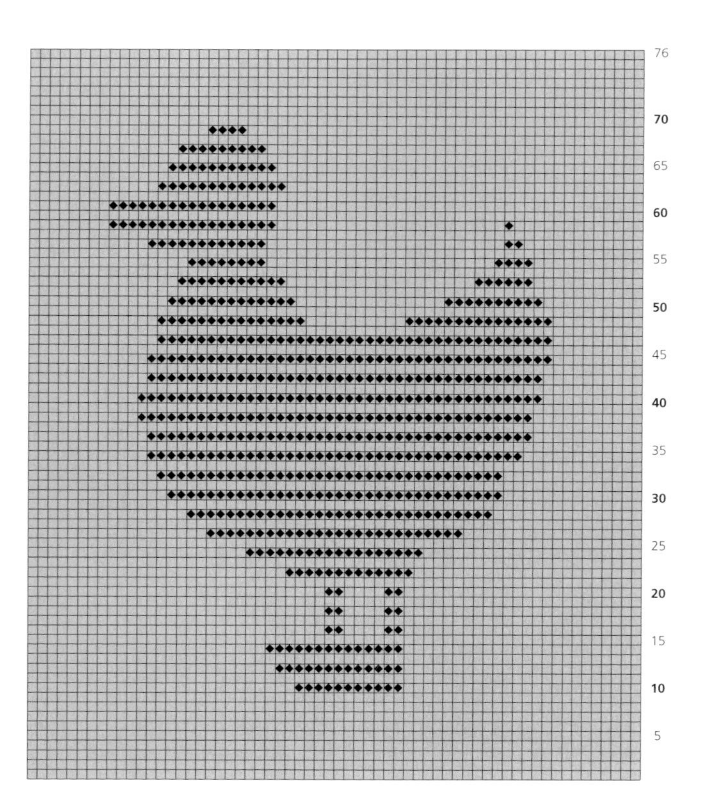

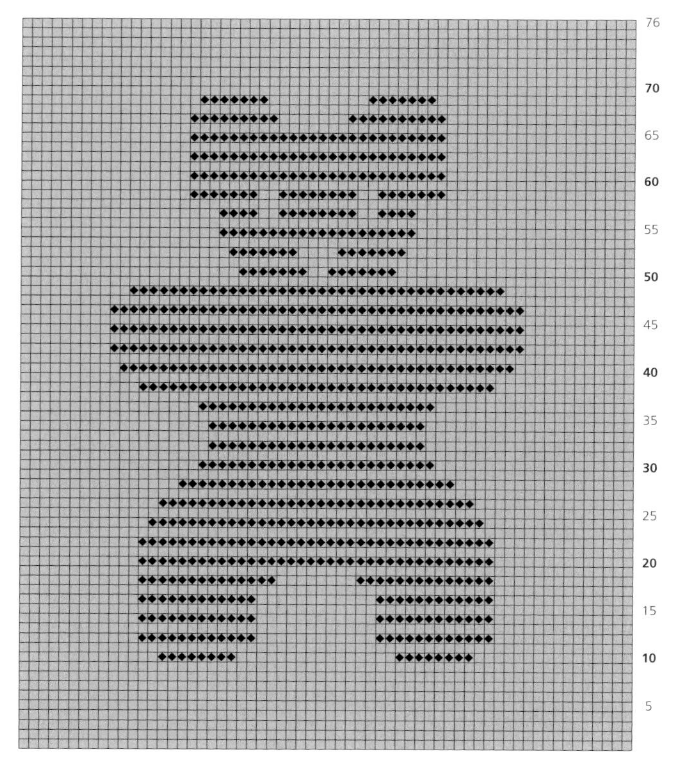

◆ = Purl on RS, knit on WS
☐ = knit on RS, purl on WS

embroidered throw

It's a real pleasure to be able to combine simple embroidery onto knitting. This embroidered throw uses traditional embroidered motifs to create an heirloom blanket that will make a treasured gift or personal treat in your own home.

size

Approx. 54 x 38in. (135 x 95cm)

materials

BACKGROUND SQUARES

Merino light worsted (DK) yarn, such as Debbie Bliss Rialto DK

18 x 1¾oz (50g) balls—approx. 2070yd (1890m)—in off-white

Needle size: US 6 (4mm)

Circular needle: 24in. (60cm) US 6 (4mm) (optional)

EMBROIDERY

Daisy bunches: Small amounts of yarn in silver, pale pink, yellow, green, mid blue

Hen: Small amount of yarn in dark plum

Goose: Small amounts of yarn in silver, yellow, black, yellow

Tree: Small amounts of yarn in dark plum, green, black

Yarn sewing needle

gauge (tension)

22 sts and 30 rows over 4in. (10cm) square using stockinette (stocking) stitch. Change needle size if necessary to achieve the required gauge (tension).

BACKGROUND SQUARES (MAKE 12)

Using US 6 (4mm) needles cast on 66 sts.

Beginning with a knit row, work 90 rows in st st.

Bind (cast) off.

TO COMPLETE

Sew squares together using backstitch in three rows of four then join rows to make one large square.

TOP AND BOTTOM EDGING

Using the circular needle, pick up and knit 193 sts evenly across the top of the throw.

Row 1 Sl 1, [k1, p1] to end.

Row 2 Sl 1, M1, [k1, p1] to last st, M1, k1. (195 sts)

Row 3 Sl 1, [p1, k1] to end.

Row 4 Sl 1, M1, [p1, k1] to last st, M1. (197 sts)

Rep Rows 1–4 six more times. (221 sts)

Bind (cast) off in seed (moss) stitch.

Rep edging at bottom of throw.

SIDE EDGINGS (MAKE 2)

Using the circular needle, cast on 2 sts.

Inc section. Row 1 K1, p1.

Row 2 Sl 1, M1, p1. (3 sts)

Row 3 K1, p1, k1.

Row 4 Sl 1, M1, p1, k1. (4 sts)

Row 5 Sl 1, p1, k1, p1.

Row 6 Sl 1, M1, k1, p1, k1. (5 sts)

Row 7 Sl 1, p1, k1, p1, k1.

Row 8 Sl 1, M1, p1, k1, p1, k1. (6 sts)

Row 9 Sl 1, p1, k1, p1, k1, p1.

Row 10 Sl 1, M1, [k1, p1] to end. (7 sts)

Row 11 Sl 1, [p1, k1] to end.

Row 12 Sl 1, M1, [p1, k1] to end. (8 sts)

Row 13 Sl 1, [p1, k1] to end.

Rep Rows 10–13 four more times and then Rows 10–11 once. (17 sts)

Straight section. Next row Sl 1, [p1, k1] to end.

Next row Sl 1, [p1, k1] to end.

These last two rows form seed (moss) stitch section. Rep these 2 rows for a further 358 rows or until the seed (moss) stitch section of side edging, when slightly stretched, fits along the side of the throw to the bound (cast) off edge of the 4th square.

Dec section. Next row Sl 1, k2tog, [p1, k1] to end.

Next row Sl 1, [p1, k1] to end.

Next row Sl 1, k2tog, [k1, p1] to end.

Next row Sl 1, [p1, k1] to end.

Rep these last four rows until 2 sts rem on needle.

Next row K2tog.

Bind (cast) off.

TO COMPLETE
Attach side edgings to throw using mattress stitch. Join corners of side edgings with corners of top and bottom edgings with mattress stitch.

EMBROIDERY
Split the wool and use only one strand as you would embroidery floss.

Thread a tapestry needle and follow the templates to embroider the designs on the squares.

tips
When sewing up your squares, make sure that the three squares that appear on the top and bottom part of the throw have the bound (cast) off edging on the outer edge of the throw. It will then be easier to pick up sts on these edges when working the seed (moss) stitch top and bottom edging of the throw.

When you are making the French knots, support the knot at the back as it is forming to prevent it from slipping through to the back of your work.

floral bunting

Bunting is the best way of cheering up a room or giving a festive air to a tea party or celebration. This pretty floral bunting has a vintage and charming feel that will brighten the soul. The flowers take very little yarn and are an ideal way of using up all those left over scraps.

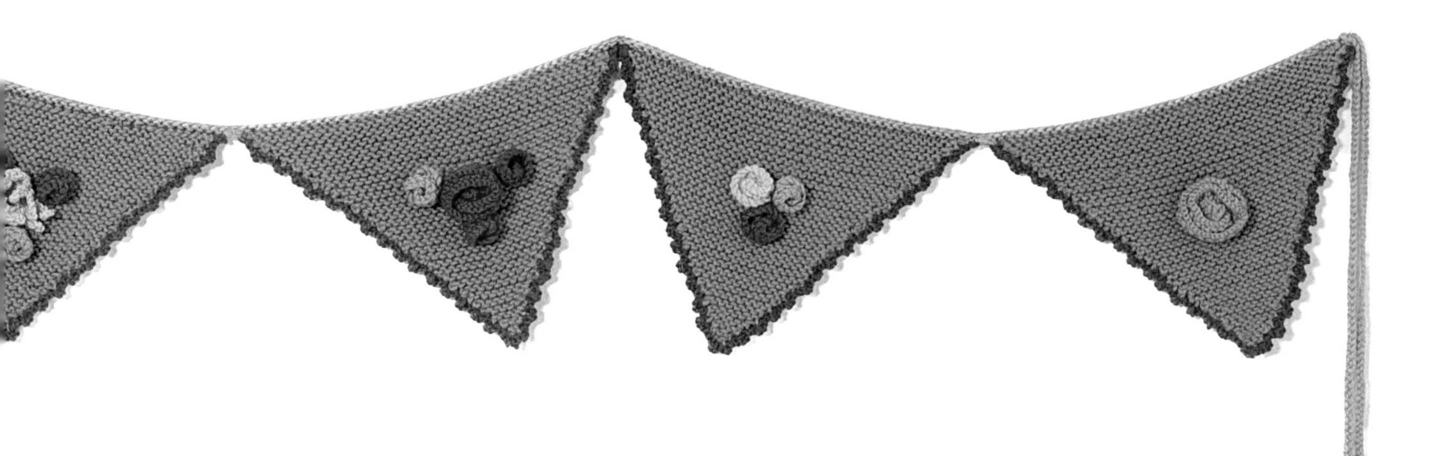

size

Bunting: 72in. (180cm) long, excluding ties
Each flag: 7½ x 9in. (19 x 22.5cm)

materials

FLAGS
Cashmere and merino wool mix worsted (Aran) yarn, such as Debbie Bliss Cashmerino Aran
4 x 1¾oz (50g) balls—approx. 384yd (360m)—of green (A)
Needle size: US 8 (5mm)

EDGING, FLOWERS, AND TIES
Pure wool light worsted (DK) yarn, such as Rowan Pure Wool DK
1 x 1¾oz (50g) ball—approx. 137yd (125m)—in each of purple-red (B), purple (C) dark red (D), pink (E), deep pink (F), yellow (G)
Needle size: US 6 (4mm) in 14–16in. (35–40cm) length
Yarn sewing needle

gauge (tension)

18 sts and 24 rows over 4in. (10cm) square using stockinette (stocking) stitch. Change needle size if necessary to achieve the required gauge (tension).

FLAGS (MAKE 8)
Cast on 41 sts using US 8 (5mm) needles and A.
Rows 1–2 Knit.
Row 3 K2tog, k to last 2 sts, k2tog. (39 sts)
Rep Rows 1–3 until 3 sts remain.
Next row K3tog.
Bind (cast) off.

SIDE EDGINGS
Using US 6 (4mm) needles and B, C, or E, with RS facing and starting from top left hand edge, pick up and knit 32 sts evenly along one side of flag.
Next row K1, cast on 1st, *bind (cast) off 3 sts, slip next st off rh needle onto lh needle, cast on 1 st; rep from * until there is 1 st left on rh needle.
Bind (cast) off.
Repeat on other side of flag.
At end of last picot, join picots from both sides at the tip by slipping rh needle into the first picot stitch from first side, knit the stitch, turn, k2tog.

TOP EDGING AND JOINING FLAGS
Using US 6 (4mm) needles and E, with RS facing, pick up and knit into each st across top of each flag in turn, also knitting into top of last picot st of edging on each side. When all flags are on rh needle, turn and knit one row.
Bind (cast) off.

LARGE ROSES (MAKE 3)
Using US 6 (4mm) needles and D, E, F, or G, cast on 10 sts.
Row 1 (right side) Knit.
Rows 2, 4, 6 Purl.
Row 3 K into front and back of every st. (20 sts)
Row 5 K into front and back of every st. (40 sts)
Row 7 K into front and back of every st. (80 sts)
Row 8 Purl.
Bind (cast) off.

SMALL ROSES (MAKE 21)
Using US 6 (4mm) needles and B, C, D, E, F, or G, cast on 21 sts.
Rows 1–3 Knit.
Pass all sts one at a time over first st, until only first st remains on needle.
Bind (cast) off.

PICOT FLOWERS (MAKE 3)
Using US 6 (4mm) needles and B, C, D, E, F, or G, cast on 5 sts.
Row 1 K into front and back of each st. (10 sts)
Rows 2, 4 Purl.
Row 3 As Row 1. (20 sts)
Row 5 Bind (cast) off 1 st, * slip next st off rh needle onto lh needle, cast on 3 sts, bind (cast) off 5 sts; rep from * until 1 st is left on rh needle.
Bind (cast) off.

TO COMPLETE
On large and small roses, twist rose into a spiral and sew at back to hold in place. On picot flowers, sew up seam to join petals. Using a contrasting color yarn, thread the yarn sewing needle and sew 3 or 5 French knots into the center of flower. Place and pin the roses on each flag. Sew in place. Sew in all ends neatly at the back.

TIES (MAKE TWO)
Measure and cut six strands of E each 59in. (150cm) long. Knot three strands at one end and then braid. Knot the other end and trim strands to neaten. Rep with other three strands. Thread a tie into the top edge on each side of bunting.

christmas tree garland

This is a bright and cheery Christmas project to hang over your fireplace during the festive season. You could also make individual Christmas trees to use as decorations on the tree itself.

size

Garland: 38in. (95cm) long, excluding ties
Each tree: 5½ x 2½in. (14 x 6.5cm)

materials

Alpaca and merino mix light worsted (DK) yarn, such as Rooster Almerino DK
2 x 1¾oz (50g) balls—approx. 248yd (225m)—of green (A)
1 x 1¾oz (50g) ball—approx. 124yd (112.5m)—of red (B)
Needle size: US 6 (4mm)
Yarn sewing needle

gauge (tension)

21 sts and 28 rows over 4in. (10cm) square using stockinette (stocking) stitch. Change needle size if necessary to achieve the required gauge (tension).

special abbreviation

kfb—knit into front and back of next st

CHRISTMAS TREE (MAKE 8)

Cast on 10 sts using A.
Work in seed (moss) stitch for 7 rows.
Row 8 Cast on 5 sts, k to end. (15 sts)
Row 9 Cast on 5 sts, k to end. (20 sts)
Rows 10–11 Knit.
Row 12 K1, k2tog, k to last 3 sts, k2tog, k1. (18 sts)
Row 13 Knit.
Rep Rows 12–13 four times more. (10 sts)
Row 22 Cast on 4 sts, k to end. (14 sts)
Row 23 Cast on 4 sts, k to end. (18 sts)
Rows 24–25 Knit.
Row 26 *K1, k2tog, k to last 3 sts, k2tog, k1. (16 sts)
Row 27 Knit.
Rep Rows 26–27 four times more. (8 sts)
Row 36 Cast on 4 sts, k to end. (12 sts)
Row 37 Cast on 4 sts, k to end. (16 sts)
Rows 38–39 Knit.
Row 40 K1, k2tog, k to last 3 sts, k2tog, k1. (14 sts)
Row 41 Knit.
Rep Rows 40–41 four times more. (6 sts)
Row 49 [K3tog] twice. (2 sts)
Row 50 K2tog.
Bind (cast) off.

BOBBLES (MAKE 48)

Cast on 3 sts using B.
Row 1 Knit.
Row 2 Kfb, k1, kfb. (5 sts)
Row 3 Knit.
Row 4 K2tog tbl, k to last 2 sts, k2tog. (3 sts)
Row 5 Knit.
Bind (cast) off.

TO COMPLETE

Sew running st around the edge of each bobble in turn and pull up the thread to form a bobble. Secure ends of yarn and sew a bobble in place on end of each tree branch.

GARLAND

Cast on 162 sts using B.
Knit one row.
Bind (cast) off.

Sew top of each Christmas tree to garland spaced evenly along length. Cut six lengths of yarn B each approx. 12in. (30cm) in length. Braid three lengths together and attach at one end to use as ties, then rep at the other end.

springtime teapot cover flowers

This is a great way to use up odd lengths of spare yarn. I made the teapot cover from an old recycled woolen blanket; first I dyed it in the washing machine and then decorated it with simple knitted flowers and a collection of old buttons.

size

To fit a standard size teapot

materials

Alpaca and merino wool mix light worsted (DK) yarn, such as Rooster Almerino DK
⅜oz (10g)—approx. 28yd (25m)—each of yellow, purple
Pure wool light worsted (DK) yarn, such as Rowan Pure Wool DK
⅜oz (10g)—approx. 28yd (25m)—each of pink, dark red, ocher, blue-red, purple-red
14 assorted buttons
Needle size: US 6 (4mm)
Yarn sewing needle
Sewing needle and thread

gauge (tension)

Gauge (tension) is not important on this project.

FLOWERS (MAKE 2 IN EACH COLOR)
Cast on 8 sts.
Row 1 Sl 1, k7.
Row 2 Sl 1, k5, turn. (2 sts remain on lh needle)
Row 3 Sl 1, k3, turn. (2 sts remain on needle)
Row 4 Sl 1, k3, turn. (2 sts remain on needle)
Row 5 Sl 1, k5 turn.
Row 6 Sl 1, k6 (leaving 1st on left needle), turn
Row 7 Sl 1, bind (cast) off until 1 st remains.
Cast on 7 sts (8 sts).
Rep Rows 1–7 four more times, casting on 7 sts at end each time, then rep once more.
Bind (cast) off last st, leaving a long tail of yarn.

TO COMPLETE
Thread tail of wool on flower into the yarn sewing needle and sew flower together. Stitch round inside of flower hole, reducing size of hole. Sew in ends. Repeat on all flowers.

Place a button in center of a flower and stitch to cover using sewing thread. Repeat to sew seven flowers on each side. Make a few stitches beneath corners of each flower to attach them to cover and stop them curling upward.

angel shawl

Charming and romantic, this lacy shawl weighs hardly anything at all. The pattern is easy to work but really makes the most of the supersoft alpaca yarn.

size

Approx. 70 x 24in. (175 x 60cm)

materials

Alpaca, silk, and cashmere mix laceweight (2ply) yarn, such as Bluefaced Angel Lace
2 x 3½oz (100g) hanks—approx. 2625yd (2400m)—of white
Needle size: US 5 (3.75mm) and US 2–3 (3mm)
Yarn sewing needle

gauge (tension)

Gauge (tension) is not important on this project.

SHAWL
Cast on 161 sts using US 5 (3.75mm) needles.
Row 1 (wrong side) Purl.
Row 2 K1, *yo, k3, sl 1, k2tog, psso, k3, yo, k1; rep from * to end.
Rep Rows 1–2 three times more.
Row 9 Purl.
Row 10 K2tog, *k3, yo, k1, yo, k3, sl 1, k2tog, psso; rep from * to last 9 sts, k3, yo, k1, yo, k3, skpo.
Rep Rows 9–10 three times more.
Rows 1–16 form pattern, rep these 16 rows until work measures approximately 175cm (70in), ending on either a Row 8 or Row 16.

EDGING (MAKE 4)
Cast on 10 sts using US 2–3 (3mm) needles.
Row 1 (right side) Sl 1, k2, yo, k2tog, *[yo] twice, k2tog; rep from * once more, k1.
Row 2 K3, [p1, k2] twice, yo, k2tog, k1.
Row 3 Sl 1, k2, yo, k2tog, k2, *[yf] twice, k2tog; rep from * once more, k1.
Row 4 K3, p1, k2, p1, k4, yo, k2tog, k1.
Row 5 Sl 1, K2, yo, k2tog, k4, *[yf] twice, k2tog; rep from * once more, k1.
Row 6 K3, p1, k2, p1, k6, yo, k2tog, k1.
Row 7 Sl 1, k2, yo, k2tog, k11.
Row 8 Bind (cast) off 6 sts, k6 (not incl st left on needle after binding/casting off), yo, k2tog, k1.
These 8 rows form pattern. Work as set until edging is length of side.
Bind (cast) off.

TO COMPLETE
Sew edging pieces onto sides of main piece. Stitch edging together at corners.

seashell scarf

A beautiful lace scarf made with little scallop-shaped stitches. This pattern knits up beautifully in Rooster Almerino, which is an alpaca/merino mix and perfectly soft next to the skin.

size
Approx. 70in. (175cm) long

materials
Alpaca and merino mix light worsted (DK) yarn, such as Rooster Almerino DK
4 x 1¾oz (50g) balls—approx. 496yd (450m)—of green-blue
Needle size: US 8 (5mm) and US 3 (3.25mm)

gauge (tension)
21 sts and 28 rows over 4in. (10cm) square using stockinette (stocking) stitch. Change needle size if necessary to achieve the required gauge (tension).

special abbreviation
Cluster 5—pass next 5 sts onto rh needle dropping extra loops, pass these 5 sts back onto lh needle, [k1, p1, k1, p1, k1] into all 5 sts tog wrapping yarn twice around needle for each st

SCARF
Cast on 37 sts using US 8 (5mm) needles.
Row 1 Knit.
Row 2 P1, *p5 wrapping yarn twice around needle for each st, p1; rep from * to end.
Row 3 K1, [Cluster 5, k1] to end.
Row 4 P1, *k5 dropping extra loops, p1; rep from *to end.
Row 5 Knit.
Row 6 P4, p5 wrapping yarn twice around needle for each st, *p1, p5 wrapping yarn twice around needle for each st; rep from * to last 4 sts, p4.
Row 7 K4, Cluster 5, *k1, Cluster 5; rep from *to last 4 sts, k4.
Row 8 P4, k5 dropping extra loops, *p1, k5 dropping extra loops; rep from * to last 4 sts, p4.
Rows 1–8 form pattern, rep these 8 rows until work measures 74in. (185cm) ending with a Row 8.
Bind (cast) off.

SCALLOPED ENDS (BOTH ALIKE)
Using US 3 (3.25mm) needles, pick up and knit 37 sts along cast on edge.
Row 1 Knit.
Row 2 K3, *M1, k1, M1, sl 1, sl 1, k2tog, psso, k3; rep from * to end.
Row 3 Knit.
Bind (cast) off.
Rep on bound (cast) off edge.

patchwork scarf

This scarf was inspired by a crocheted shawl my mother made for me, using this gorgeous yarn. The color palette available is perfect and these patchwork squares show off all the different shades beautifully.

size

Approx. 74 x 11½in. (188 x 29cm)

materials

Mohair and silk mix laceweight (2ply) yarn, such as Rowan Kid Silk Haze

EDGING
2 x ⅞oz (25g balls—approx. 460yd (420m) —of violet (A)

COLORWAY ONE
1 x ⅞oz (25g ball—approx. 230yd (210m) —each of green (B), gray-brown (C), pink (D)

COLORWAY TWO
1 x ⅞oz (25g ball—approx. 230yd (210m) —each of bright pink (E), blue-green (F), pale green (G)

COLORWAY THREE
1 x ⅞oz (25g ball—approx. 230yd (210m) —of cream (H), red-orange (I), dark gray (J)

Needle size: US 4 (3.5mm)

gauge (tension)

19 sts and 34 rows over 4in. (10cm) using stockinette (stocking) stitch. Change needle size if necessary to achieve the required gauge (tension).

SCARF
Cast on 60 sts using A.
Rows 1–4 Knit.
Colorway One. Next row K3 in A, change to B, k18, change to C, k18, change to D, k18, k3 in A.
Next row K3 in A, p18 in D, p18 in C, p18 in B, k3 in A.
Rep last two rows another 12 times (26 rows each square)
Change color sequence as follows:
Colorway Two. Next row K3 in A, change to E, k18, change to F, k18, change to G, k18, k3 in A.
Next row K3 in A, p18 in G, p18 in F, p18 in E, k3 in A.
Rep last two rows another 12 times (26 rows each square)
Change color sequence as follows:
Colorway Three. Next row K3 in A, change to H, k18, change to I, k18, change to J, k18, k3 in A.
Next row K3 in A, p18 in J, p18 in I, p18 in H, k3 in A.
Rep last two rows another 12 times. (26 rows each square)
Rep the three color sequences, alt the colors in the 9-block sequence by following the chart. Cont until scarf measures 74in. (188cm), or 25 squares.
Knit 4 rows in A.
Bind (cast) off loosely, using larger needle if necessary.

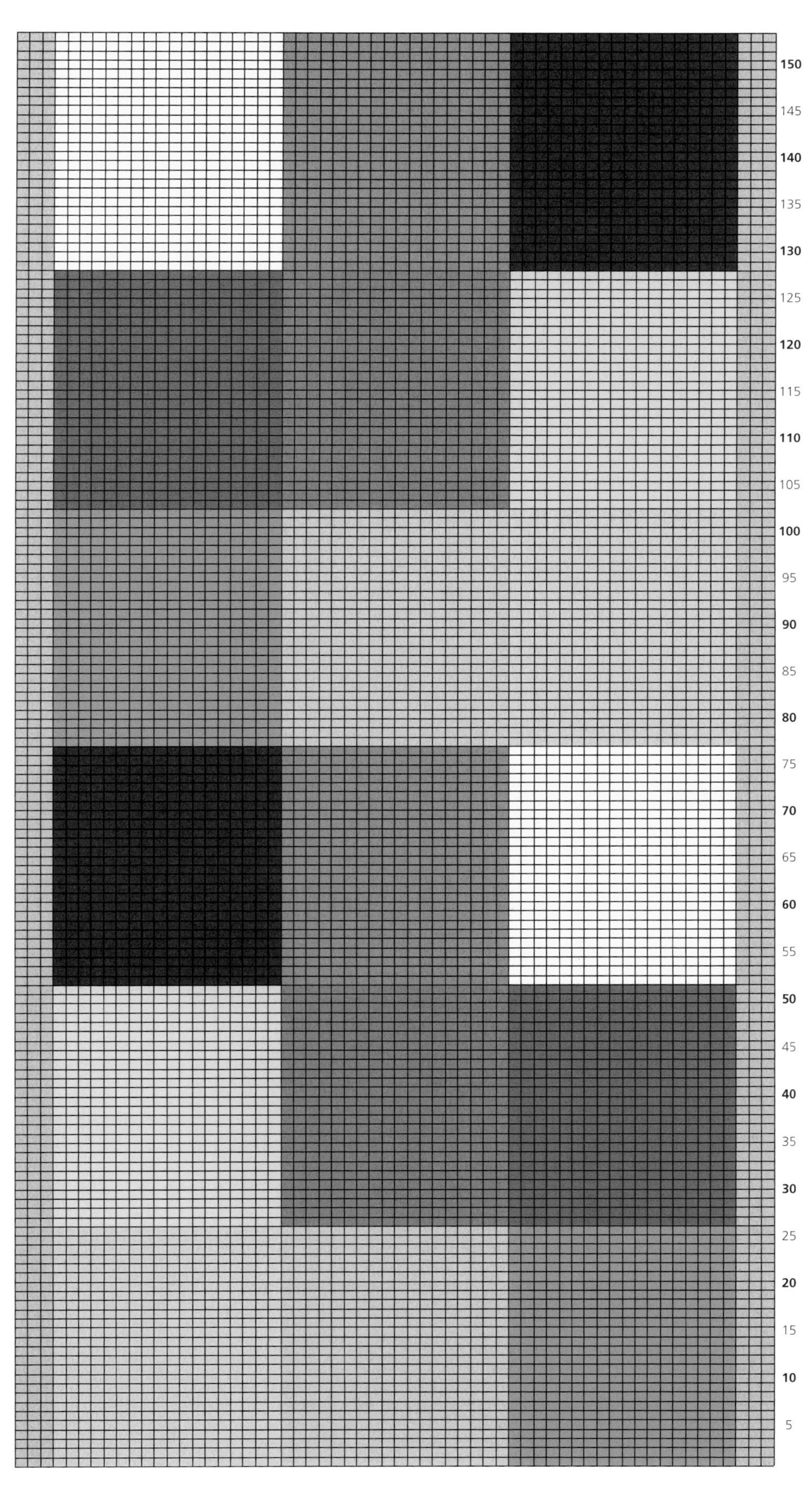

tip

Use the intarsia method when changing colors for the patchwork squares.

fringed shawl

This is based on a very popular crochet shawl I had some years ago, which was made in the same silky-soft Kid Silk Haze kid mohair. This is definitely going to be a big hit—don't be put off by the mohair, it's very comfortable to wear and looks spectacular.

size

Approx. 70 x 24in. (175 x 60cm)

materials

Mohair and silk mix laceweight (2ply) yarn, such as Rowan Kid Silk Haze
3 x $\frac{7}{8}$oz (25g ball—approx. 690yd (630m)—of pink (A)
2 x $\frac{7}{8}$oz (25g ball—approx. 460yd (420m)—of green (B)
Needle size: US 6 (4mm)

gauge (tension)

19 sts and 34 rows over 4in. (10cm) using stockinette (stocking) stitch. Change needle size if necessary to achieve the required gauge (tension).

SHAWL

Cast on 145 sts using A.

Row 1 Knit.

Row 2 (right side) K4, *sl 2, pass first sl st over 2nd and off needle, sl 1, pass 2nd sl st over 3rd and off needle, slip 3rd sl st back onto lh needle, [yo] twice (to make 2 sts), k 3rd sl st in usual way; rep from * to last 3 sts, k3.

Row 3 K5, *p1, k2; rep from * to last 2 sts, k2.

Rows 2–3 form pattern, rep these rows until work measures 70in. (175cm).

Bind (cast) off.

TASSELS

Cut 8in. (20cm) lengths of B for the tassels. Take 4 strands and fold in half. Insert loop through edge of shawl and thread tassel ends through loop, pulling tight to secure in place.

Attach tassels to edges of shawl at approx. 1$\frac{1}{4}$in. (3cm) intervals.

mirror pouch

A very delicate lacy cover for your makeup mirror or compact, made in a luxurious and supersoft mohair silk mix. It could also be used to keep a special piece of jewelry safe.

size

3 x 3in. (7.5 x 7.5cm)
To fit 2in. (5cm) compact mirror

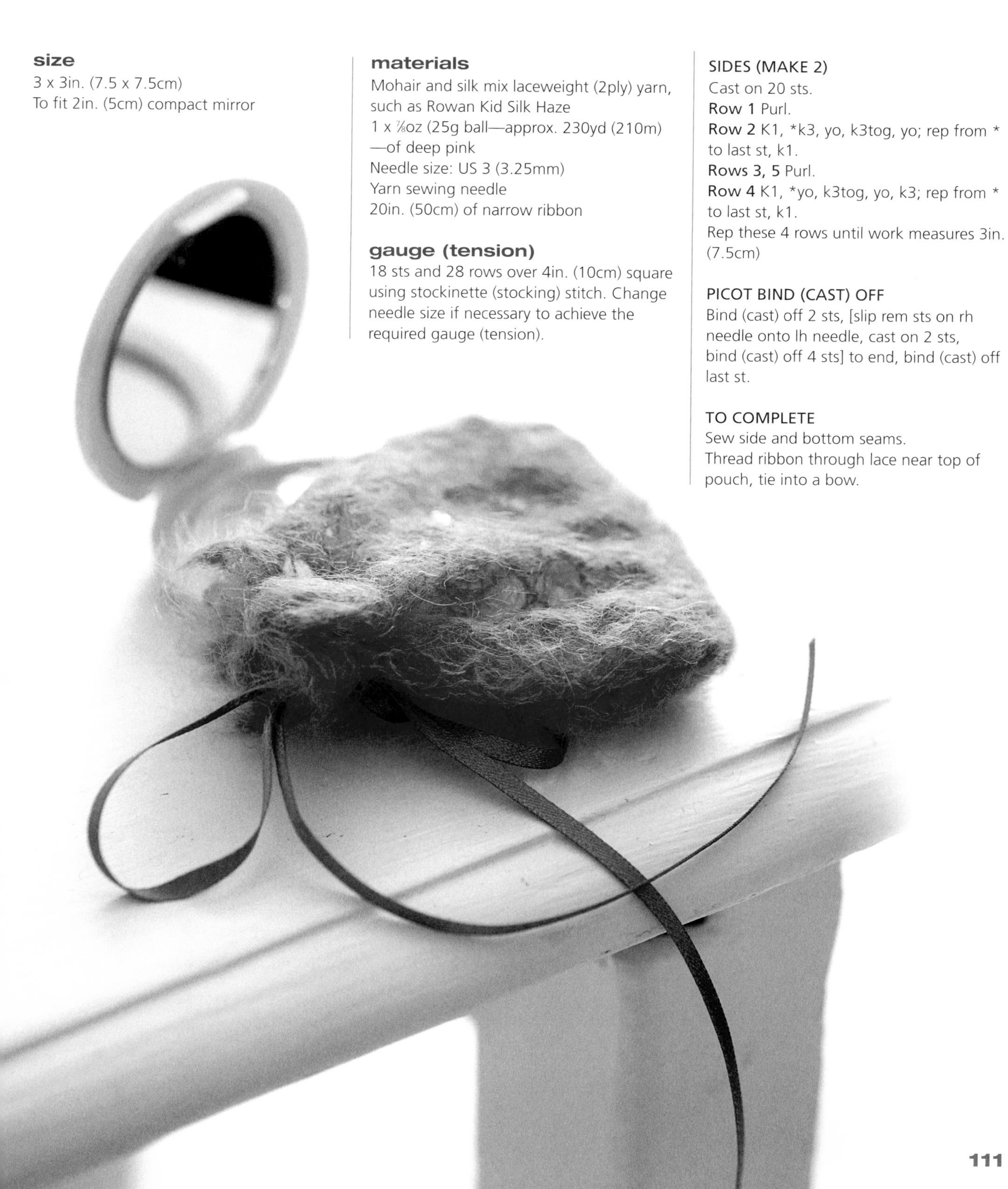

materials

Mohair and silk mix laceweight (2ply) yarn, such as Rowan Kid Silk Haze
1 x ⅞oz (25g ball—approx. 230yd (210m)—of deep pink
Needle size: US 3 (3.25mm)
Yarn sewing needle
20in. (50cm) of narrow ribbon

gauge (tension)

18 sts and 28 rows over 4in. (10cm) square using stockinette (stocking) stitch. Change needle size if necessary to achieve the required gauge (tension).

SIDES (MAKE 2)

Cast on 20 sts.
Row 1 Purl.
Row 2 K1, *k3, yo, k3tog, yo; rep from * to last st, k1.
Rows 3, 5 Purl.
Row 4 K1, *yo, k3tog, yo, k3; rep from * to last st, k1.
Rep these 4 rows until work measures 3in. (7.5cm)

PICOT BIND (CAST) OFF

Bind (cast) off 2 sts, [slip rem sts on rh needle onto lh needle, cast on 2 sts, bind (cast) off 4 sts] to end, bind (cast) off last st.

TO COMPLETE

Sew side and bottom seams.
Thread ribbon through lace near top of pouch, tie into a bow.

homemade home picture

Get an old picture frame and knit yourself an artwork! This is a great housewarming present—you could copy the colors of the new house itself and add personal touches to make it a really unique gift.

size

Approx. 8 x 7½in. (20 x 19cm)

materials

Light worsted (DK) yarn, such as Rooster Almerino DK
1 x 1¾oz (50g) balls—approx. 124yd (112.5m)—each of pale blue (sky), green (grass/butterfly), pale pink (house), cream (windows/seagull), light gray (upper windows), blue-green (door), dark gray (roof/tree trunk/seagull eye), beige (roof eaves), yellow (seagull beak/butterfly), bright pink (butterfly), dark green (tree)
Needle size: US 6 (4mm)

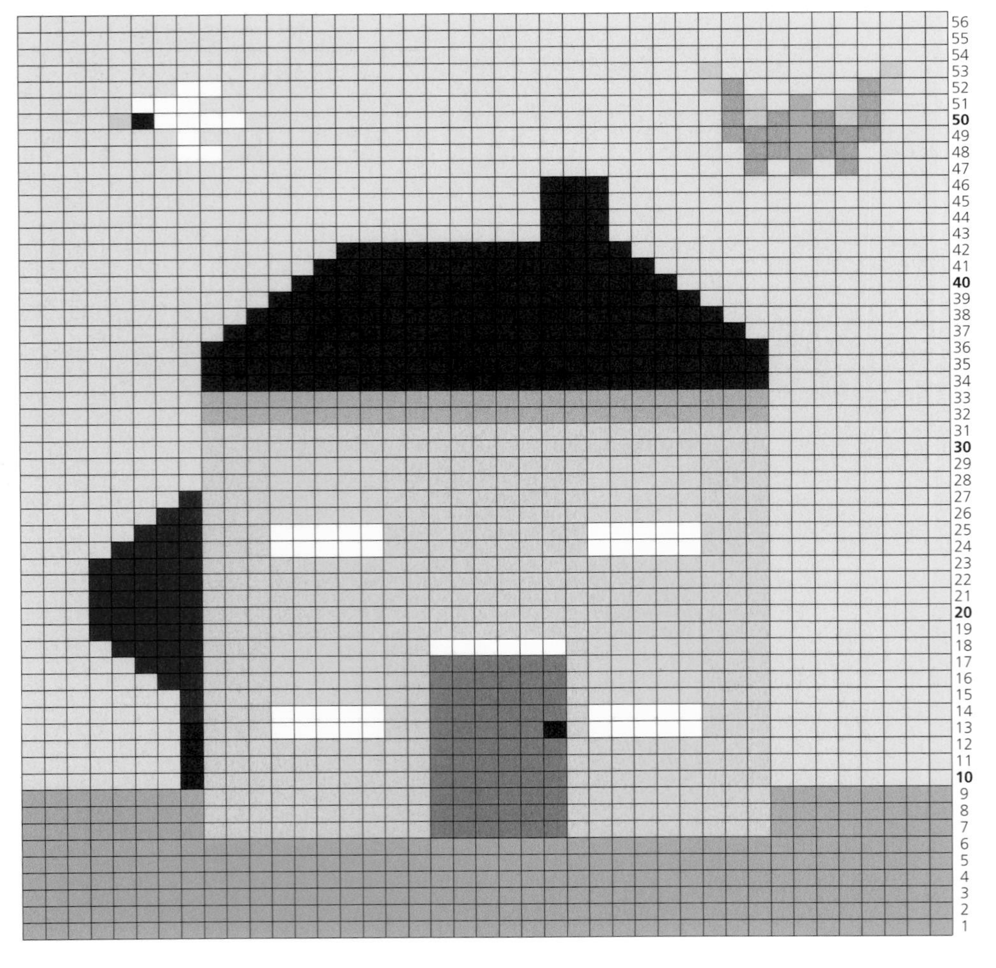

gauge (tension)

21 sts and 28 rows over 4in. (10cm) using stockinette (stocking) stitch. Change needle size if necessary to achieve the required gauge (tension).

PICTURE

Cast on 41 sts and work 56 rows in st st following the chart.
Bind (cast) off.

TO COMPLETE

Block and press the knitted picture and place it into a frame.

tip

If you press the picture onto Bondaweb, it makes it more manageable and easier to fix in place into a picture frame.

pompom draft excluder

Any excuse for a draft excluder and some pompoms—even if you don't have a draft! This is a lovely present for the child in your life.

size

Approx 32in. (80cm) long and 9½in. (24cm) in diameter

materials

DRAFT EXCLUDER
Cotton light worsted (DK) yarn, such as Debbie Bliss Cotton DK
2 x 1¾oz (50g) balls—approx. 184yd (168m)—each of white (A), navy (B), red (C), green (D)
Needle size: US 6 (4mm)
Yarn sewing needle
Toy stuffing

POMPOMS
Alpaca and merino wool mix worsted (Aran) yarn, such as Rooster Almerino Aran
3 x 1¾oz (50g) balls—approx. 309yd (282m)—of red (E)
Piece of cardboard

gauge (tension)

20 sts and 28 rows over 4in. (10cm) square using stockinette (stocking) stitch. Change needle size if necessary to achieve the required gauge (tension).

DRAFT EXCLUDER
Cast on 48 sts in A.
Work 4 rows in st st.
*Change to B.
Work 4 rows in st st.
Change to C.
Work 4 rows in st st.
Change to D.
Work 4 rows in st st.
Change to A.
Work 4 rows in st st.
Rep this sequence from * until work measures approx. 32in. (80cm), ending with the last row of a four-row rep (approx. 224 rows).
Bind (cast) off.

TO COMPLETE
With RS tog, sew seam along length. Gather one end together with a running stitch and pull tightly. Secure ends tightly.
Turn right side out and stuff. Secure other end with a gather as before.
Make two large pompoms as described in Method 1 on page 172 and sew securely to each end of draft exluder.

seed stitch mug cozy

These charming knitted cup covers will help to insulate your tea or coffee and keep it nice and hot in the cup. Seed (moss) stitch creates a wonderfully textured surface that is comforting to hold.

size

To fit an average mug approx. 4in. (10cm) high and 10in. (26cm) in diameter

materials

Alpaca and merino wool mix worsted (Aran) yarn, such as Rooster Almerino Aran
1 x 1¾oz (50g) ball—approx. 103yd (94m)—of green
Needle size: US 8 (5mm)
Yarn sewing needle
2 x snaps (press studs)
Needle and thread
2 x decorative buttons

gauge (tension)

19 sts and 23 rows over 4in. (10cm) using stockinette (stocking) stitch. Change needle size if necessary to achieve the required gauge (tension).

CURVED BOTTOM MUG
Cast on 37 sts.
Row 1 Knit.
Row 2 K3, inc in next st, [k5, inc in next st] 5 times. (43 sts)
Row 3 K1, *p1, k1; rep from * to end.
Rows 4–16 Work in seed (moss) st (k1, p1).
Row 17 Cast on 5 sts, starting with a purl st, seed (moss) st to end. (48 sts)
Row 18 Seed (moss) st to end.
Row 19 K1, p1, yon, k2tog, seed (moss) st to end.
Rows 20–21 Seed (moss) st.
Row 22 Knit.
Bind (cast) off.

STRAIGHT BOTTOM MUG
Cast on 43 sts.
Row 1 Knit.
Row 2 K1, *p1, k1; rep from * to end.
Work as Rows 3–22 from curved bottom mug.
Bind (cast) off.

TO COMPLETE
Sew side seam up to base of handle. Stitch two parts of a snap (press stud) onto reverse of button tab and matching area on RS of cover. Sew on button to correspond with position of snap (press stud). Place cup inside cover and fasten.

ripple mug cozy

This is a great textured-stitch mug cover that is created using a very simple knit and purl design. Why not make one for all your mugs?

size

To fit an average mug approx. 4in. (10cm) high and 10in. (26cm) in diameter

materials

Alpaca and merino wool mix worsted (Aran) yarn, such as Rooster Almerino Aran
1 x 1¾oz (50g) ball—approx. 103yd (94m)—of pink
Needle size: US 8 (5mm)
Yarn sewing needle
2 x snaps (press studs)
Needle and thread
2 x decorative buttons

gauge (tension)

19 sts and 23 rows over 4in. (10cm) using stockinette (stocking) stitch. Change needle size if necessary to achieve the required gauge (tension).

CURVED BOTTOM MUG
Cast on 37 sts.
Rows 1–2 Knit.
Row 3 K3, inc in next st, [k5, inc in next st] 5 times, k3. (43 sts)
Row 4 Knit.
Row 5 Purl.
Row 6 K1, *p2, k1; rep from * to end.
Row 7 Purl.
Rep Rows 4–7 once.
Row 12 Cast on 5 sts, k to end.
Row 13 Purl.
Row 14 P2, yfrn, p2tog, p1, k1, [p2, k1] to end.
Row 15 Purl.
Rows 16–17 Knit.
Bind (cast) off.

STRAIGHT BOTTOM MUG
Cast on 43 sts.
Rows 1–3 Knit.
Work as Rows 4–17 from curved bottom mug.
Bind (cast) off.

TO COMPLETE
Sew side seam up to base of handle. Stitch two parts of a snap (press stud) onto reverse of button tab and matching area on RS of cover. Sew on button to correspond with position of snap (press stud). Place cup inside cover and fasten.

chicken out pillow cover

This pillow (cushion) cover is made in four separate pieces for the front, which are sewn together, and there is one large piece at the back.

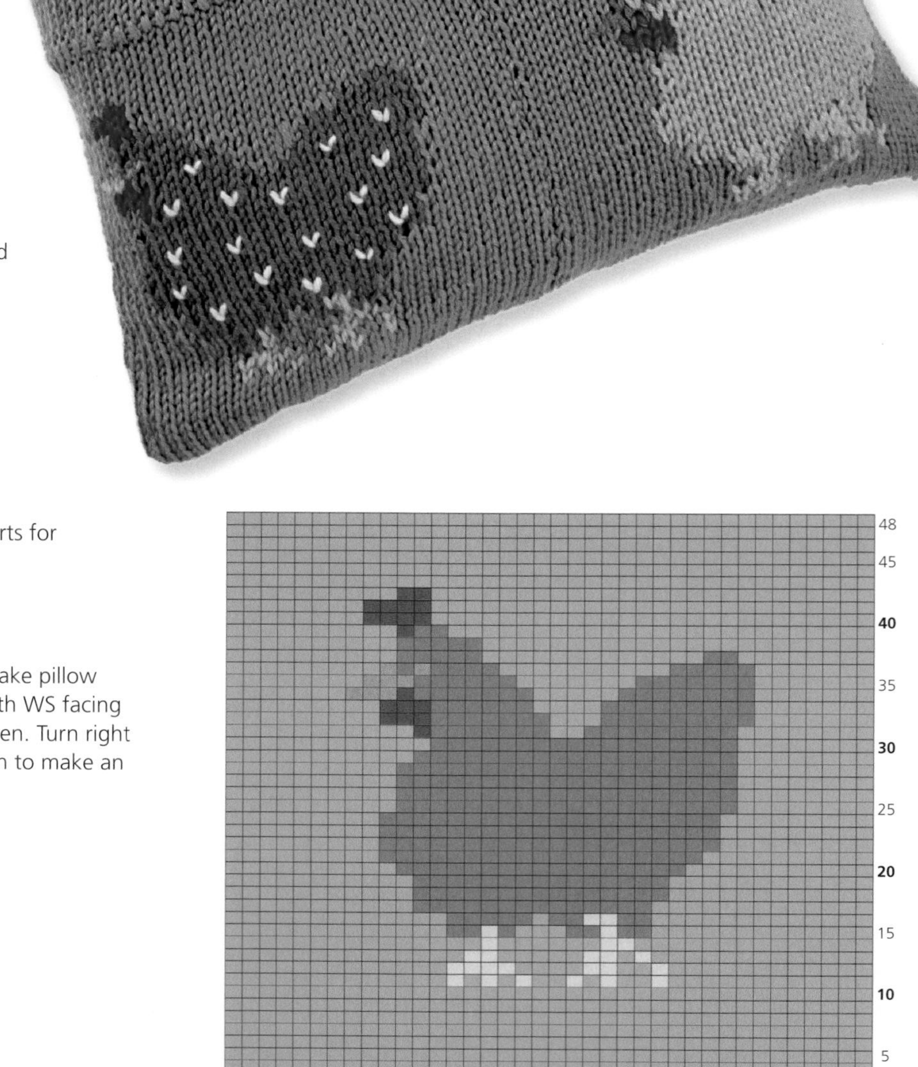

size

To fit a 16in. (40cm) pillow form

materials

Alpaca and merino wool mix worsted (Aran) yarn, such as Rooster Almerino Aran
4 x 1¾oz (50g) ball—approx. 412yd (376m)—of green (A)
1 x 1¾oz (50g) ball—approx. 103yd (94m)—each of cream (B), green-blue (C), beige (D), yellow (E)
Small amount of red (F)
Needle size: US 8 (5mm)
Yarn sewing needle
16in. (40cm) pillow form

gauge (tension)

16 sts x 24 rows over 4in. (10cm) square using stockinette (stocking) stitch. Change needle size if necessary to achieve the required gauge (tension).

BACK

Cast on 76 sts using A.
Knit 96 rows in st st.
Bind (cast) off.

FRONT (MAKE 4)

Cast on 38 sts using A.
Knit 48 rows in st st, following one of the charts for each hen.
Bind (cast) off.

TO COMPLETE

Join the four hen motif squares together to make pillow (cushion) cover front. To join back to front, with WS facing sew up bottom and side seams leaving top open. Turn right side out, insert pillow form. Use mattress stitch to make an invisible seam at the top.

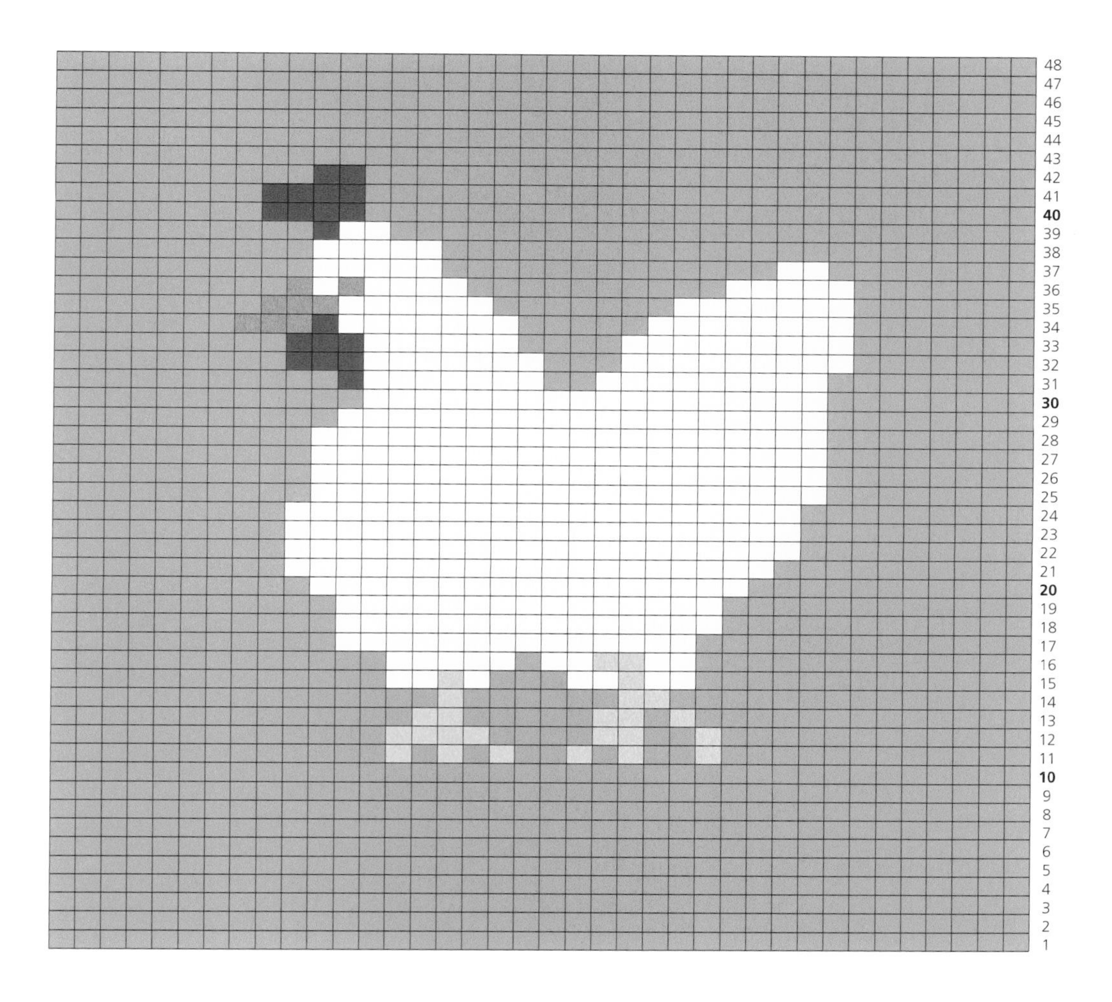
48
47
46
45
44
43
42
41
40
39
38
37
36
35
34
33
32
31
30
29
28
27
26
25
24
23
22
21
20
19
18
17
16
15
14
13
12
11
10
9
8
7
6
5
4
3
2
1

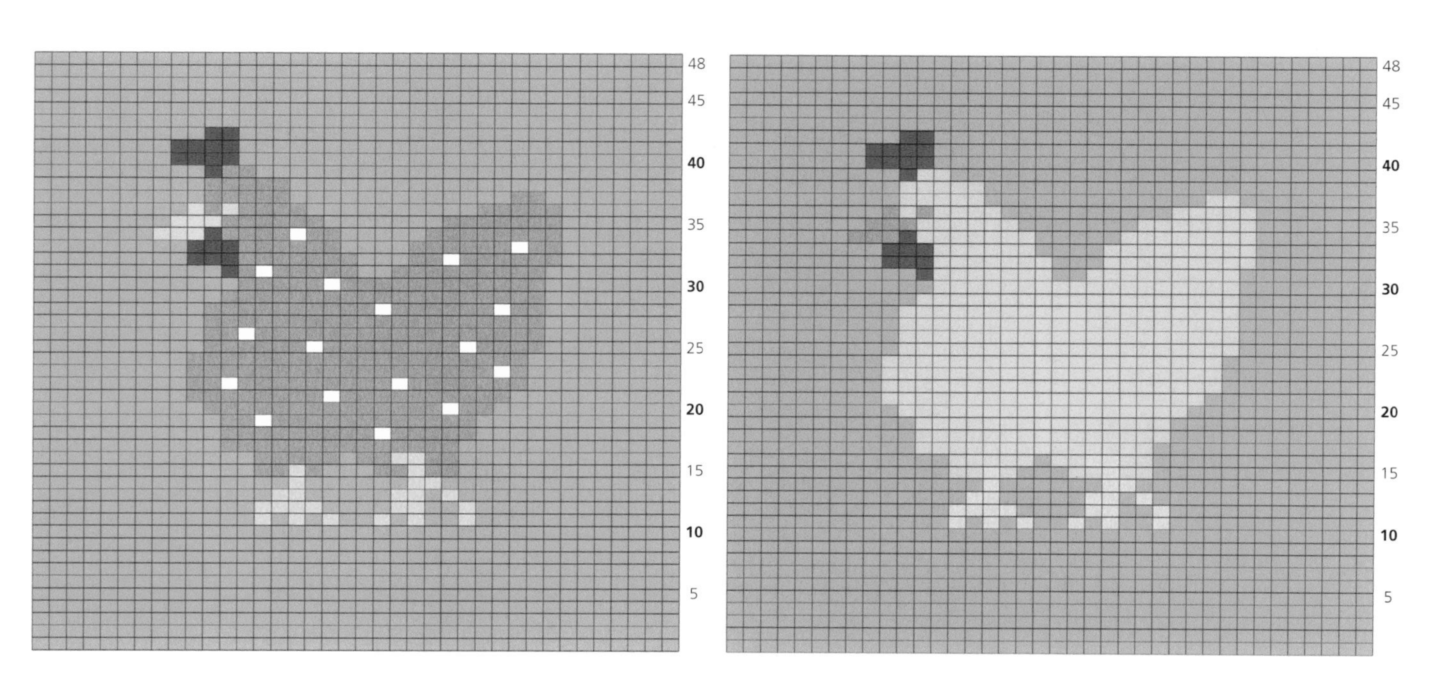
48
45
40
35
30
25
20
15
10
5
48
45
40
35
30
25
20
15
10
5

fair isle pillow cover

This is a traditional Fair Isle pattern, mixing large and small-scale designs to create a colorful pretty pillow (cushion) to decorate your home. The front of the cover is in a Fair Isle pattern, and the back is plain. It is knitted starting at the back, in just one piece.

size

To fit a 16in. (40cm) pillow form (cushion pad)

materials

Alpaca and merino wool mix worsted (Aran) yarn, such as Rooster Almerino Aran
4 x 1¾oz (50g) balls—approx. 412yd (376m)—of cream (A)
1 x 1¾oz (50g) ball—approx. 103yd (94m)—each of pink (B), green (C), blue-green (D)
Needle size: US 8 (5mm)
Yarn sewing needle
5 x medium size buttons
16in. (40cm) pillow form

gauge (tension)

19 sts and 23 rows over 4in. (10cm) stockinette (stocking) stitch square. Change needle size if necessary to achieve the required gauge (tension).

COVER

Cast on 76 sts using A.

Buttonhole band. Rows 1–4 Work in seed (moss) st (k1, p1).

Row 5 Seed (moss) st for 5 sts, bind (cast) off 2 sts, *seed (moss) st for 13 sts, bind (cast) off 2 sts; rep from * to last 5 sts, seed (moss) st to end.

Row 6 Seed (moss) st for 5 sts, cast on 2 sts *seed (moss) st for 14 sts, cast on 2 sts; rep from * to last 5 sts, seed (moss) st to end.

Rows 7–10 Work in seed (moss) st.

Bottom flap. Change to st st (1 row knit, 1 row purl) and work 12 more rows.

Front. With RS facing and starting with a knit row, begin foll chart working from right to left (knit row), left to right (purl row).

Each knit row K6 in A, foll chart, k5 in A.

Each purl row P5 in A, foll chart, p6 in A.

Cont in this way for 77 rows of chart.

Top flap. Working in st st and using A only, cont until work measures 33in. (83cm) from beg of seed (moss) st buttonhole band.

Button band. Work 10 rows seed (moss) st for back button band.

Bind (cast) off.

TO COMPLETE

With WS facing, place a pin marker 3in. (7.5cm) down from the top edge on each side. Fold bottom edge up to pin markers. Sew side seams together leaving top flap free. Turn right side out, fold top flap over bottom flap and mark button positions to match buttonholes. Sew on buttons and insert pillow form (cushion pad).

seed stitch pillow cover

This is a very simple, yet very classy pillow (cushion) cover. It's knitted in an alpaca and merino mixture of fibers, which make it supersoft, and the seed (moss) stitch pattern gives it a very attractive texture. The cover is all made in one piece.

size

To fit a 16in. (40cm) pillow form

materials

Alpaca and merino wool mix worsted (Aran) yarn, such as Rooster Almerino Aran
6 x 1¾oz (50g) balls—approx. 618yd (564m)—of cream
Needle size: US 8 (5mm)
Yarn sewing needle
5 x medium size buttons
16in. (40cm) pillow form

gauge (tension)

21 sts and 35 rows in seed (moss) stitch over 4in. (10cm) square. Change needle size if necessary to achieve the required gauge (tension).

COVER

Cast on 84 sts.
Work in seed (moss) st (k1, p1), until work measures 33in. (83cm). (290 rows)

BUTTONHOLE BAND

Work in seed (moss) st for 3 rows.
Next row (buttonhole) Seed (moss) st for 4 sts, *bind (cast) off 1 st, seed (moss) st for 18 sts; rep from * three more times, bind (cast) off 1 st, seed (moss) st for 4 sts. (5 buttonholes made)
Next row Seed (moss) st for 4 sts, *cast on 1 st, seed (moss) st for 18 sts; rep from * three more times, cast off 1 st, seed (moss) st for 4 sts.
Work in seed (moss) st for 3 more rows.
Bind (cast) off.

TO COMPLETE

With WS facing, place a pin marker 3in. (7.5cm) down from top edge on each side. Fold bottom edge up to pin markers. Sew side seams together leaving top flap free. Turn right side out, fold top flap over bottom flap and mark button positions to match buttonholes. Sew on buttons and insert pillow form.

flower pillow cover

This colorful pillow (cushion) cover is knitted in just one piece, with a flower front, plain back, and seed (moss) stitch button bands.

size
To fit a 16in. (40cm) pillow form

materials
Alpaca and merino wool mix worsted (Aran) yarn, such as Rooster Almerino Aran
4 x 1¾oz (50g) balls—approx. 412yd (376m)—of yellow (A)
1 x 1¾oz (50g) ball—approx. 103yd (94m)—each of pink (B), cream (C)
Needle size: US 8 (5mm)
Yarn sewing needle
5 x medium sized buttons
16in. (40cm) pillow form

gauge (tension)
19 sts and 23 rows over 4in. (10cm) square using stockinette (stocking) stitch. Change needle size if necessary to achieve the required gauge (tension).

COVER
Cast on 76 sts, using A.
Buttonhole band. Rows 1–4 Work in seed (moss) st (k1, p1).
Row 5 Seed (moss) st for 5 sts, bind (cast) off 2 sts, *seed (moss) st for 13 sts, bind (cast) off 2 sts; rep from * 3 times, seed (moss) st to end.
Row 6 Seed (moss) st for 5 sts, cast on 2 sts *seed (moss) st for 14 sts, cast on 2 sts; rep from * 3 times, seed (moss) st to end.
Rows 7–10 Work in seed (moss) st.
Change to st st, starting with a knit row, and work 26 rows.
Next row K19, foll chart to last 19 sts, k19.
Next row P19, foll chart to last 19 sts, p19.
Cont in this way for 47 rows of chart.
Cont in st st using A only until work measures 33in. (83cm) from beginning of seed (moss) st buttonhole band.
Button band. Work 10 rows in seed (moss) st.
Bind (cast) off.

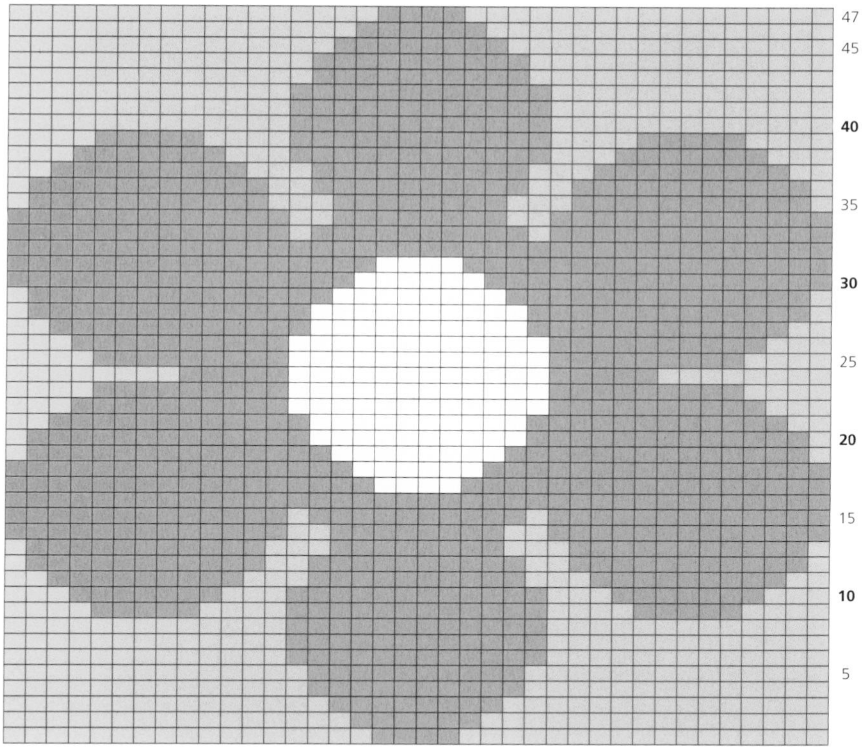

47
45
40
35
30
25
20
15
10
5

TO COMPLETE
With WS facing, place a pin marker 3in. (7.5cm) down from the top edge on each side. Fold bottom edge up to pin markers. Sew side seams together leaving top flap free. Turn right side out, fold top flap over bottom flap, and mark button positions to match buttonholes. Sew on buttons and insert pillow form.

baby bibs

These make interesting and original gifts for when a baby is born. The light worsted (DK) cotton used makes the bib easier to wash and it is worked on small needles to make a tightly-knit fabric so that any dribbles are quick to clean up!

size

Approx. 7¾ x 6½in. (18 x 16.5cm)

materials

Pure cotton light worsted (DK) yarn, such as Rowan Handknit DK

BIB 1
1 x 1¾oz (50g) ball—approx. 93yd (85m)—each of cream (A), pink (B), red (C)

BIB 2
1 x 1¾oz (50g) ball—approx. 93yd (85m)—each of blue (A), blue-green (B), cream (C)

Needle size: US 4 (3.5mm) and US 2 (2.75mm) circular
Stitch holder

gauge (tension)

26 sts and 36 rows over 4in. (10cm) square using stockinette (stocking) stitch. Change needle size if necessary to achieve the required gauge (tension).

BIB
Cast on 31 sts using US 4 (3.5mm) needles and A.
Change to B.
Rows 1, 3, 5, 7, 9 (wrong side) Purl.
Row 2 K1, M1, k29, M1, k1. (33 sts)
Row 4 K1, M1, k31, M1, k1. (35 sts)
Row 6 K1, M1, k33, M1, k1. (37 sts)
Row 8 K1, M1, k35, M1, k1. (39 sts)
Row 10 K1, M1, k37, M1, k1. (41 sts)
Row 11 Purl to end.
Row 12 Begin foll chart for next 18 rows.
Cont in st st and B only and work for 10 rows more.

SHAPE NECKLINE
Row 1 (right side) K12, bind (cast) off 17 sts, k12.
Place first set of 12 sts on stitch holder, cont working on rem 12 sts.
Rows 2, 4, 6, 8, 10, 12 Purl.
Row 3 Bind (cast) off 2 sts, k10. (10 sts)
Row 5 Bind (cast) off 1 st, knit to end. (9 sts)
Row 7 Bind (cast) off 1 st, with 1 st already on rh needle from bind (cast) off, k5 more, k2tog. (7 sts)
Row 9 Bind (cast) off 1 st, with 1 st already on rh needle from bind (cast) off, k3 more, k2tog. (5 sts)

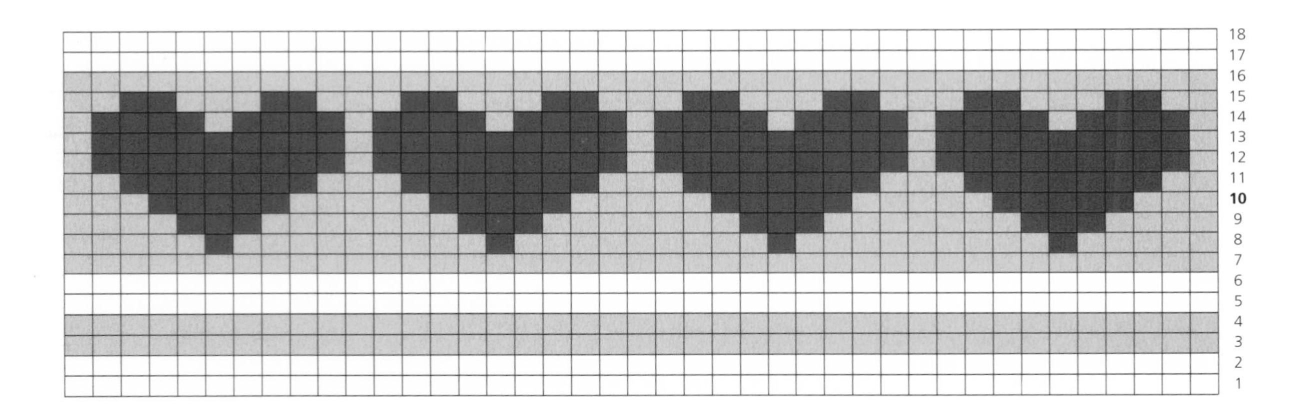

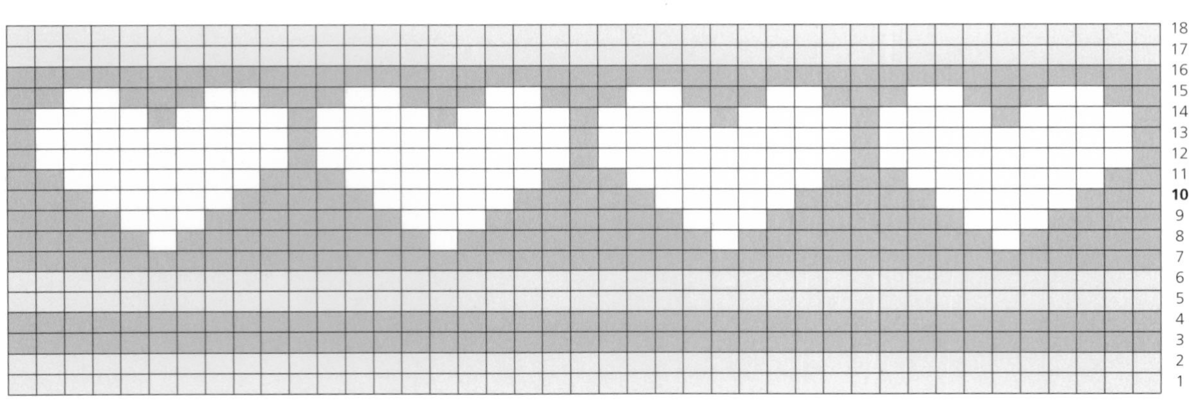

Row 11 Bind (cast) off 1 st, with 1 st already on rh needle from bind (cast) off, k1 more, k2tog. (3 sts)
Row 13 Sl 1, k2tog, psso. Cut yarn, pull tail through last st and bind (cast) off.
Rejoin yarn to 12 sts on holder and work other side, reversing shaping.
Bind (cast) off.

NECK EDGING
With RS facing pick up 43 sts along neckline edge of bib using A and US 2 (2.75mm) circular needles.
Knit 3 rows.
Bind (cast) off.

TIES AND OUTER EDGING
Using US 2 (2.75mm) circular needle and B cast on 50 sts.
With RS facing pick up 49 sts evenly along left edge, 36 sts evenly along bottom, and another 49 sts up right edge of bib, then cast on another 50 sts, turn. (234 sts).
Knit 3 rows, turning at the end of each row as normal.
Bind (cast) off.

heart lavender pillow

A tiny treat to put inside either your drawers or your wardrobe to keep your clothes smelling fresh and sweet, or on your bed to give you a soothing night's sleep. Add a tassel at each corner for a little extra glamour.

size
To fit lavender-filled fabric inner bag 6in. (15cm) square

materials
Pure wool light worsted (DK) yarn, such as Rowan Pure Wool DK

CUSHION 1
1 x 1¾oz (50g) ball—approx. 137yd (125m)—each of cream (A), deep pink (B)

CUSHION 2
1 x 1¾oz (50g) ball—approx. 137yd (125m)—each of deep red (A), pink (B)

CUSHION 3
1 x 1¾oz (50g) ball—approx. 137yd (125m)—each of navy (A), dark pink (B)

CUSHION 4
1 x 1¾oz (50g) ball—approx. 137yd (125m)—each of green (A), dark pink (B)

Needle size: US 6 (4mm)
Yarn sewing needle

gauge (tension)
22 sts and 30 rows over 4in. (10cm) square using stockinette (stocking) stitch. Change needle size if necessary to achieve the required gauge (tension).

FRONT
Cast on 34 sts using A.
Working in st st throughout, foll chart for 44 rows.
Bind (cast) off.

BACK
Cast on 34 sts using A.
Work 44 rows in st st.
Bind (cast) off.

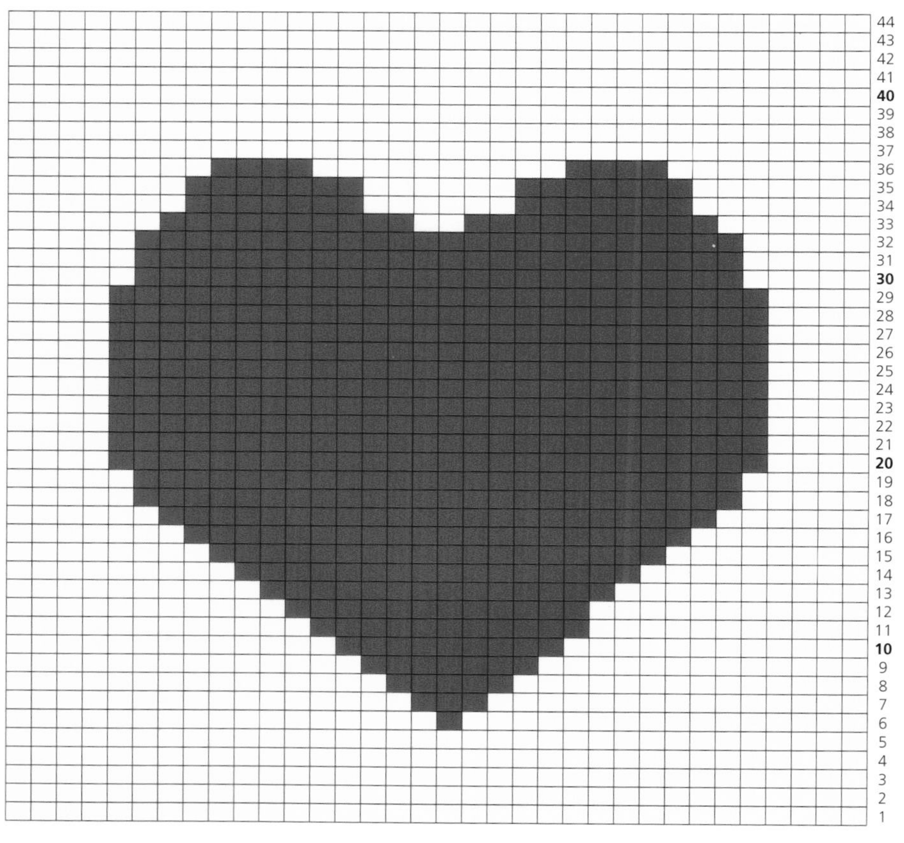

TO COMPLETE
Sew up three sides of pillow, leaving top open. Insert lavender-filled inner bag, and then sew up top of cover using mattress stitch.

beaded purse

This is such a pretty little purse, just the right size for your coins and cards! The beads add an extra touch of texture and sparkle, as well as more color, to the design.

size

Approx. 6in. (15cm) wide x 4in. (10cm) deep

materials

Pure cotton light worsted (DK) yarn, such as Rowan Handknit DK
1 x 1¾oz (50g) ball—approx. 93yd (85m)—of green
Needle size: US 6 (4mm)
50 x beads in purple
6in. (15cm) zipper
Fabric for lining 8 x 11½in. (20 x 30cm)

gauge (tension)

20 sts and 28 rows over 4in. (10cm) square using stockinette (stocking) stitch. Change needle size if necessary to achieve the required gauge (tension).

special abbreviation

Pb—place bead

PURSE
Cast on 33 sts.
Row 1 (right side) K4, *p1, k7; rep from * to last 5 sts, p1, k4.
Row 2 P3, *k1, p1, k1, p5; rep from * to last 6 sts, k1, p1, k1, p3
Row 3 K2, *p1, k3; rep from * to last 3 sts, p1, k2.
Row 4 P1, * k1, p5, k1, p1; rep from * to end.
Row 5 *P1, k3, Pb, k3, rep from * to last st, p1.
Row 6 As Row 4.
Row 7 As Row 3.
Row 8 As Row 2.
Row 9 K4, *p1, k3, Pb, k3; rep from * to last 5 sts, p1, k4.
Rep Rows 2–9 until work measures 8in. (20cm).
Bind (cast) off.

TO COMPLETE
Block finished piece and steam. Measure knitted piece and cut the lining to fit, allowing an extra ⅝in. (1.5cm) all around for the seams. Fold lining in half RS together and stitch zipper to top edges. Sew up two sides using sewing machine or hand stitching. Press out seams of lining.

Sew up side seams of knitted piece, and with RS of piece facing insert lining to fit, positioning zipper in center at top. Using yarn, sew top seam over each end of zipper.
Using thread in same color as yarn, sew knitted piece to zipper, taking care to position stitches in zipper behind top of lining.

tip

Beads must be threaded onto the yarn before you begin knitting. To knit in a bead, knit up to the stitch before you want the bead, bring the yarn and bead to the front of the work, slip the next stitch purlwise, bring the yarn to the back of the work, leaving the bead at the front, then knit the next stitch. The bead should fall in the center of each diamond.

cable hot water bottle cover

Don't burn your toes on your hot water bottle; just knit this cover in a lovely supersoft yarn and keep your feet warm and comfortable.

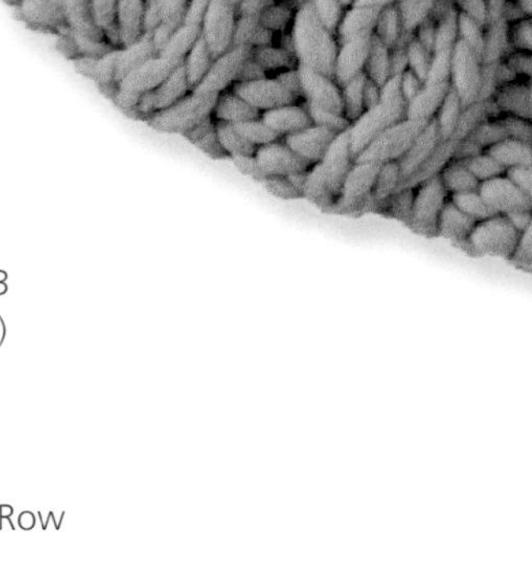

size

Approx 8¾ x 13in. (22 x 32cm)
To fit hot water bottle approx. 8¾in. (22cm) wide x 10½in. (26cm) deep

materials

Wool and cashmere chunky weight yarn, such as Debbie Bliss Como
1 x 1¾oz (50g) ball—approx. 46yd (42m)—of pale olive green
Needle size: US 11 (8mm)
Cable needle
Yarn sewing needle

gauge (tension)

10 sts and 16 rows over 4in. (10cm) square using stockinette (stocking) stitch. Change needle size if necessary to achieve the required gauge (tension).

special abbreviation

C4B (cable 4 back)—slip next 2 sts onto a cable needle and hold at back of work, knit next 2 sts from lh needle, then knit sts from cable needle

COVER (MAKE 2)

Cast on 24 sts
Row 1 P3, [k3, p2] 3 times, k3, p3.
Row 2 K3, [p3, k2] 3 times, p3, k3.
Row 3 P3, [k3, p2] 3 times, k3, p3.
Inc row K3, [p1, M1 purlwise, p2, k2] 3 times, p1, M1 purlwise, p2, k3. (28 sts)
Row 5 P3, [C4B, p2] 3 times, C4B, p3.
Row 6 K3, [p4, k2] 3 times, p4, k3.
Row 7 P3, [k4, p2] 3 times, k4, p3.
Rows 8–10 Rep Rows 6–7 once, then Row 6 again.
Rep Rows 5–10 five times more, then Rows 5–7 once.
Dec row K3, [p1, p2tog, p1, k2] 3 times, p1, p2tog, p1, k3. (24 sts)
Eyelet row K2, [yo, k2tog, k2] 5 times more, k2.
Next row P, dec 2 sts evenly across row.
Next row K2, [p2, k2] to end.
Next row P2, [k2, p2] to end.
Rep last 2 rows once more.
Work 4 rows 2 x 2 rib, inc one st on the end of the last row. (50 rows)

PICOT BIND (CAST) OFF

Bind (cast) off 2 sts, [sl rem st on rh needle back onto lh needle, cast on 2 sts, bind (cast) off 4 sts] to end.

TO COMPLETE

Press pieces according to yarn band instructions. Sew side seams.

MAKE TIE

Cut three lengths of yarn each 32in. (80cm), knot strands tog at one end and braid, then knot other end to secure. Thread braid through eyelets, starting and ending at the two center eyelets. Insert hot water bottle and tie braid into a bow.

fair isle hot water bottle cover

This is a simple Fair Isle pattern in a nice cozy thick yarn, with a pretty picot cast off.

size

Approx 8¾ x 13in. (22 x 33cm)
To fit hot water bottle approx. 8¾in. (22cm) wide x 10½in. (26cm) deep

materials

Wool and cashmere chunky weight yarn, such as Debbie Bliss Como
3 x 1¾oz (50g) balls—approx. 138yd (126m)—of light gray (A)
1 x 1¾oz (50g) ball—approx. 46yd (42m)—each of lilac (B), plum (C), lime green (D)
Needle size: US 11 (8mm)
Yarn sewing needle

gauge (tension)

10 sts and 15 rows over 4in. (10cm) using stockinette (stocking) stitch. Change needle size if necessary to achieve the required gauge (tension).

COVER (MAKE 2)

Cast on 28 sts using A.
Working in st st, and starting with a K row, follow the chart for Rows 1–27, then rep Rows 9–21 once more.
Cont in A only.
Eyelet row K3, *bind (cast) off 1 st, k2; rep from * to last 3 sts, k3.
Next row P3, *cast on 1 st, p2; rep from * to last 3 sts, p3.
Work 4 rows 2 x 2 rib, inc 1 st on end of last row. (46 rows)

PICOT BIND (CAST) OFF

Change to B.
Bind (cast) off 2 sts, [sl rem st on rh needle back onto lh needle, cast on 2 sts, bind (cast) off 4 sts] rep to last st, bind (cast) off last st.

TO COMPLETE

Press pieces according to yarn band instructions.
Sew side seams.

TIE

Cut one length of 32in. (80cm) in each of A, B, and C. Knot strands tog at one end and braid, then knot other end to secure.
Thread braid through eyelets, starting and ending at the two center eyelets.
Insert hot water bottle in cover and tie braid into a bow.

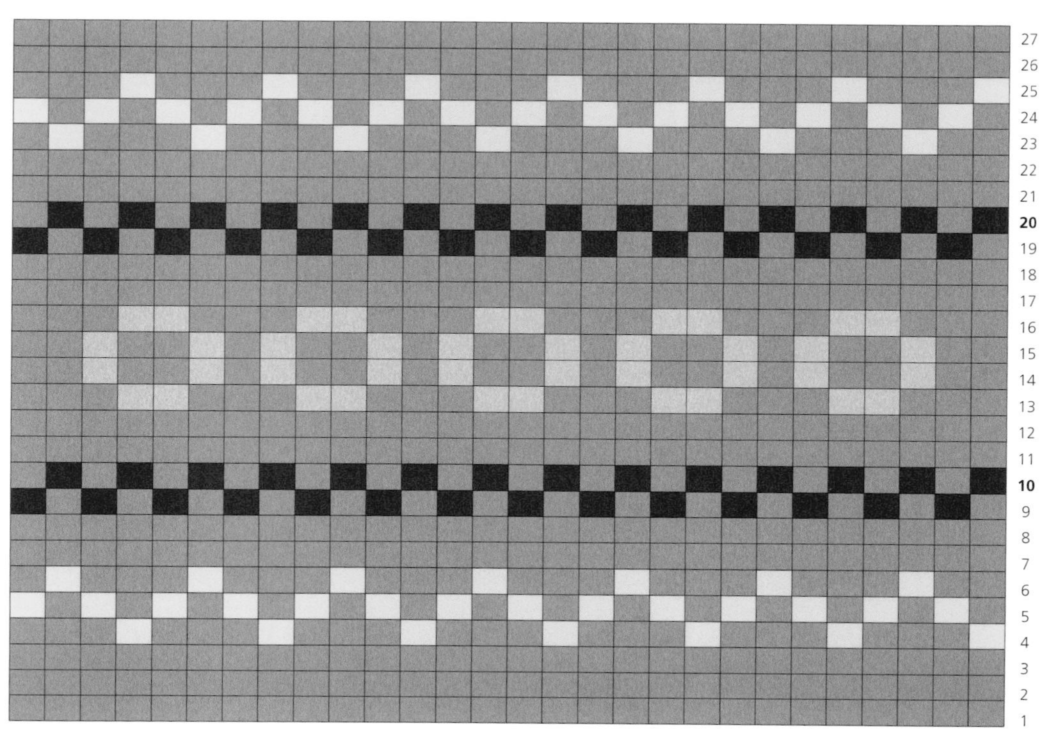

veggie shopping bag

This bag is just a great shopping carrier. If you line the bag and the handles with a firm fabric, it will be strong enough to take all your vegetables home. The sides are worked in seed (moss) stitch for a wonderfully textured look.

size

Approx 12½ x 15in. (32 x 38cm)

materials

Alpaca and merino wool mix worsted (Aran) yarn, such as Rooster Almerino Aran
5 x 1¾oz (50g) balls—approx. 515yd (470m)—of gray-brown (A)
1 x 1¾oz (50g) ball—approx. 103yd (94m)—of green (B)
Pure wool light worsted (DK) yarn, such as Rowan Pure Wool DK
1 x 1¾oz (50g) ball—approx. 137yd (125m)—of orange (C)
Needle size: US 8 (5mm) and US 6 (4mm)
Stitch holder
Yarn sewing needle
Toy stuffing
Fabric for bag lining 16 x 36in. (40 x 90cm)
Fabric for straps 25 x 2in. (62.5 x 5cm)
Sewing needle and thread

gauge (tension)

20 sts x 32 rows over 4in. (10cm) square using stockinette (stocking) stitch. Change needle size if necessary to achieve the required gauge (tension).

special abbreviation

Kfb—knit into front and back of same st

BAG

Cast on 62 sts using US 8 (5mm) needles and A.
Row 1 *K1, pl; rep from * to end.
Row 2 *P1, k1; rep from * to end.
Rep Rows 1 and 2 until work measures 15in. (38cm).
Bind (cast) off.

STRAPS (MAKE TWO)

Cast on 8 sts using US 8 (5mm) needles and A.
Row 1 *K1, pl; rep from * to end.
Row 2 *P1, k1; rep from * to end.
Rep Rows 1 and 2 until work measures 24in. (60cm).
Bind (cast) off.

CARROTS (MAKE 1 LARGE, 2 SMALL)

Cast on 2 sts using US 6 (4mm) needles and C.
Row 1 [Kfb] twice. (4 sts)
Row 2 Purl.
Row 3 Kfb, k2, kfb. (6 sts)
Row 4 Purl.
Row 5 Kfb, k4, kfb. (8 sts)
Row 6 Purl.
Cont inc by 1 st at each end of every k row in this way to 18 sts (small carrot) or 24 sts (large carrot).
Cont straight, working in st st until work measures 4in. (10cm) for small carrot or 5½in. (14cm) for large one.
Do not bind (cast) off. Leave sts on holder and cut yarn leaving a long end.

CARROT TOPS (MAKE 4 FOR EACH CARROT)

*Cast on 18 sts using B and US 6 (4mm) needles, bind (cast) off 17 sts (leaving last st on needle); rep from * three times. (4 sts)
Cut yarn, leaving 6in. (15cm) end.
Thread yarn end into a needle, pass through rem 4 sts, pull tight and secure.

TO COMPLETE

With WS of bag pieces facing, join front and back by sewing up the side and bottom seams, leaving the top open.
To finish carrots, sew up sides and stuff each with toy stuffing. Sew four leaves onto pulled-up end of each carrot. Sew carrots onto front of bag.

LINING

Cut two pieces of lining fabric to same size as bag, leaving ⅝in. (1.5cm) allowance for seams on each of three sides and 1in. (2.5cm) at top. With RS together pin and machine stitch side and bottom seams. Trim bottom corners and press out seams. Turn top over by 1in. (2.5cm) and press. Insert lining into knitted bag and pin in place around top. Hand sew a few stitches at each end of bottom of bag to prevent the lining from riding up inside.

STRAPS

Measure straps and cut strap lining double the width of the knitted piece, adding ⅝in. (1.5cm) for hem at ends.
With wrong side facing, fold each side to center so that sides meet. Press. Fold each end under by ⅝in. (1.5cm) and press. The length and width should now measure as knitted strap.
Place the lining onto the knitted strap with folded sides down and facing the knitted strap. Pin and hand sew in place. Repeat for 2nd strap.

TO INSERT STRAPS

Place a pin marker 3in. (8cm) in from each outside seam of bag. At one side, push one end of strap down between lining and knitted piece at the pin marker by approx. 1½in. (3.5cm), pin in place. Repeat on same side with other end of same strap. Repeat for second strap on other side.
Hand sew lining to knitted piece around the top, incorporating straps as you sew and stitching the straps onto bag both on outside and inside of bag. Reinforce straps onto bag by hand or machine, by sewing a square of stitches securely around strap ends where they have been inserted between the bag and lining.

dishcloths

These are really fun gifts and make great little presents when you are dropping in to see someone for dinner or lunch—and may just mean that you can avoid washing the dishes afterward!

size

Approx. 10 x 10in. (25 x 25cm)

materials

Pure cotton light worsted (DK) yarn, such as Rowan Handknit DK

DISHCLOTH 1

1 x 1¾oz (50g) ball—approx. 93yd (85m)—each of pink (A), blue-green (B), green (C)

DISHCLOTH 2

1 x 1¾oz (50g) ball—approx. 93yd (85m)—each of rust (C), gray (D)

Needle size: US 10 (6mm)

gauge (tension)

19 sts x 28 rows over 4in. (10cm) square using stockinette (stocking) stitch. Change needle size if necessary to achieve the required gauge (tension).

DISHCLOTH 1

Cast on 45 sts using A.

Rows 1–8 Knit.

Change to B.

Rows 9–16 Knit.

Change to C.

Rows 17–24 Knit.

Rep Rows 1–24 until 72 rows have been completed.

Bind (cast) off.

DISHCLOTH 2

Cast on 45 sts using C.

Rows 1–8 Knit.

Change to D.

Rows 9–16 Knit.

Rep Rows 1–16 until 72 rows have been completed.

Bind (cast) off.

advent calendar pockets

A very cute idea for an advent calendar; the little pockets are just the right size to hold Christmas sweets, chocolates, or advent gifts. Make 24 pockets and tie them onto the Christmas tree or add string or ribbon and hang them somewhere in your home for a real seasonal treat.

size

Each pocket: 3 x 4in. (7.5 x 10cm)

materials

Merino light worsted (DK) yarn, such as Debbie Bliss Rialto DK
6 x 1¾oz (50g) balls—approx. 689yd (630m)—in red (A)
3 x 1¾oz (50g) balls—approx. 345yd (315m)—in white (B)
Needle size: US 6 (4mm)
13¼yd (12m) of ½in. (1cm) wide Christmas ribbon

gauge (tension)

22 sts and 30 rows over 4in. (10cm) square using stockinette (stocking) stitch. Change needle size if necessary to achieve the required gauge (tension).

POCKETS (MAKE 1 FOR EACH NUMBER)
Cast on 18 sts using A.
Rows 1–3 Knit.
Row 4 K8, bind (cast) off 2 sts, k to end. (8 sts on each side of buttonhole)
Row 5 K7, knit into front and back of next 2 sts, knit to end.
Rows 6–7 Knit.
Row 8 Purl.
Cont working in st st for a further 30 rows, then foll relevant chart (see pages 132–135) for next 14 rows to insert each day number.
Row 53 Knit.
Row 54 Purl.
Rows 55–56 Knit.
Row 57 K8, bind (cast) off 2 sts, k to end. (8 sts on each side of ribbon hole)
Row 58 K8, knit into front and back of next 2 sts, k8.
Rows 59–61 Knit.
Bind (cast) off.

TO COMPLETE
With RS tog, sew up side seams, leaving top open. Turn RS out. Cut ribbon into 24 equal strips and thread each strip through ribbon holes ready to tie.

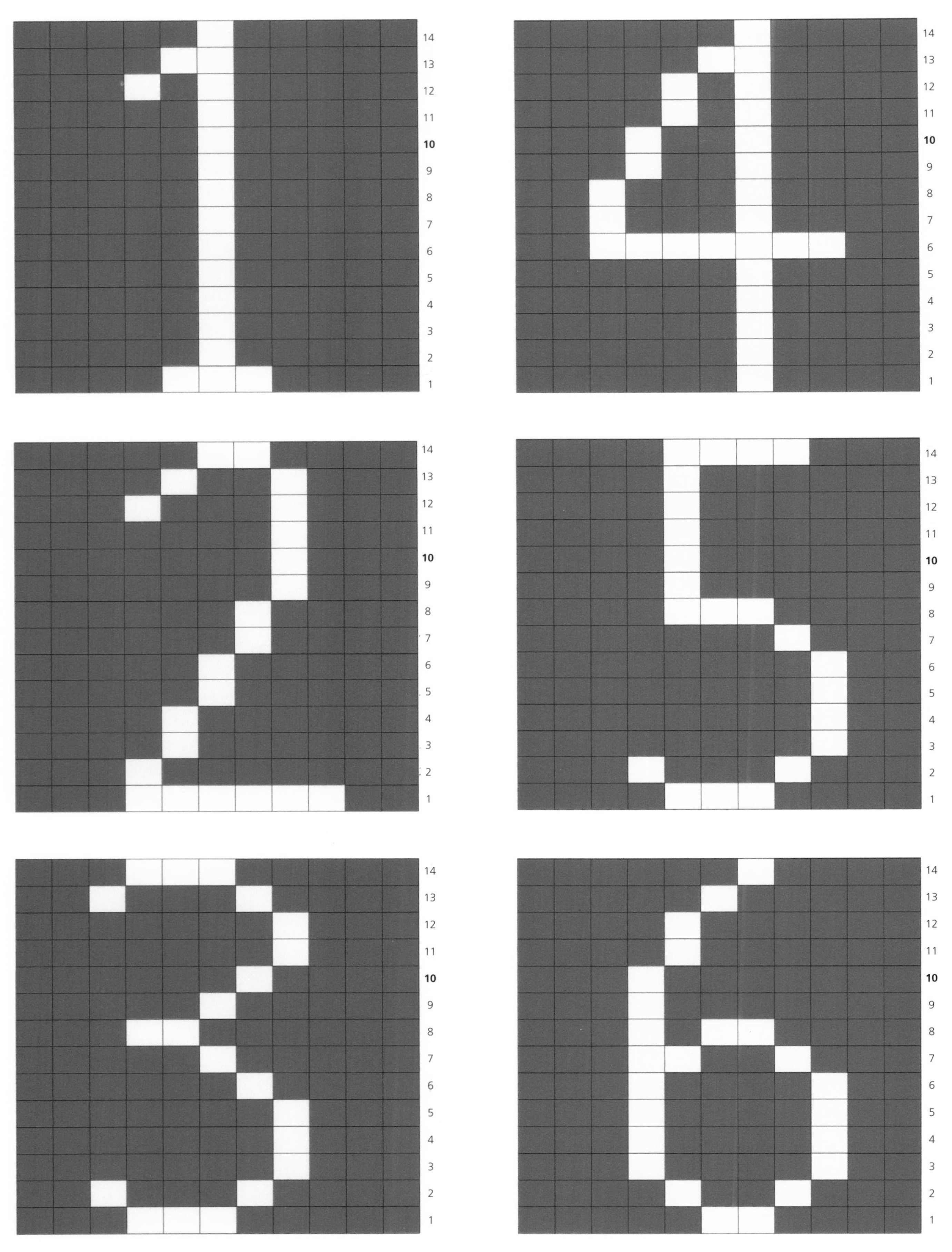
14
13
12
11
10
9
8
7
6
5
4
3
2
1

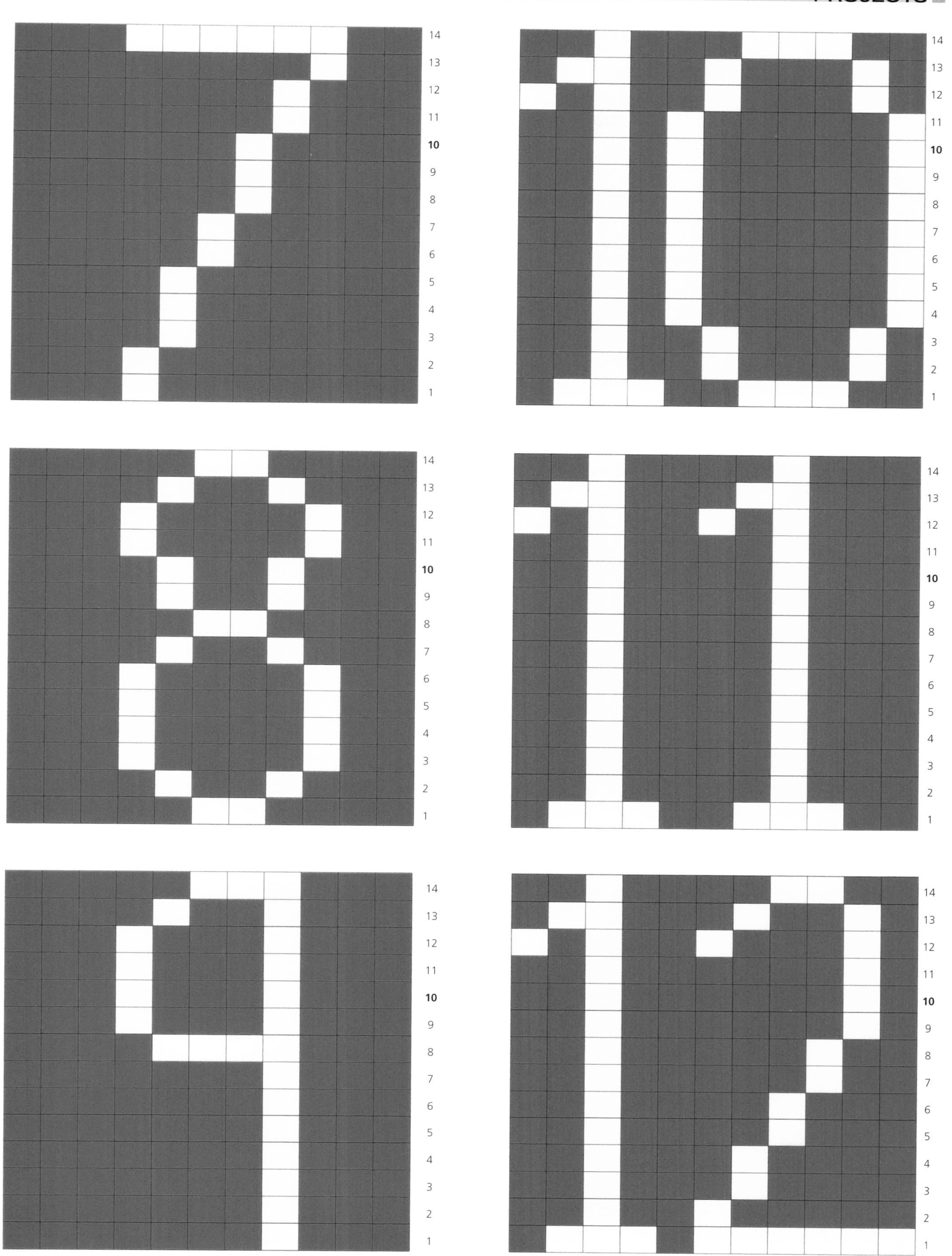
14
13
12
11
10
9
8
7
6
5
4
3
2
1

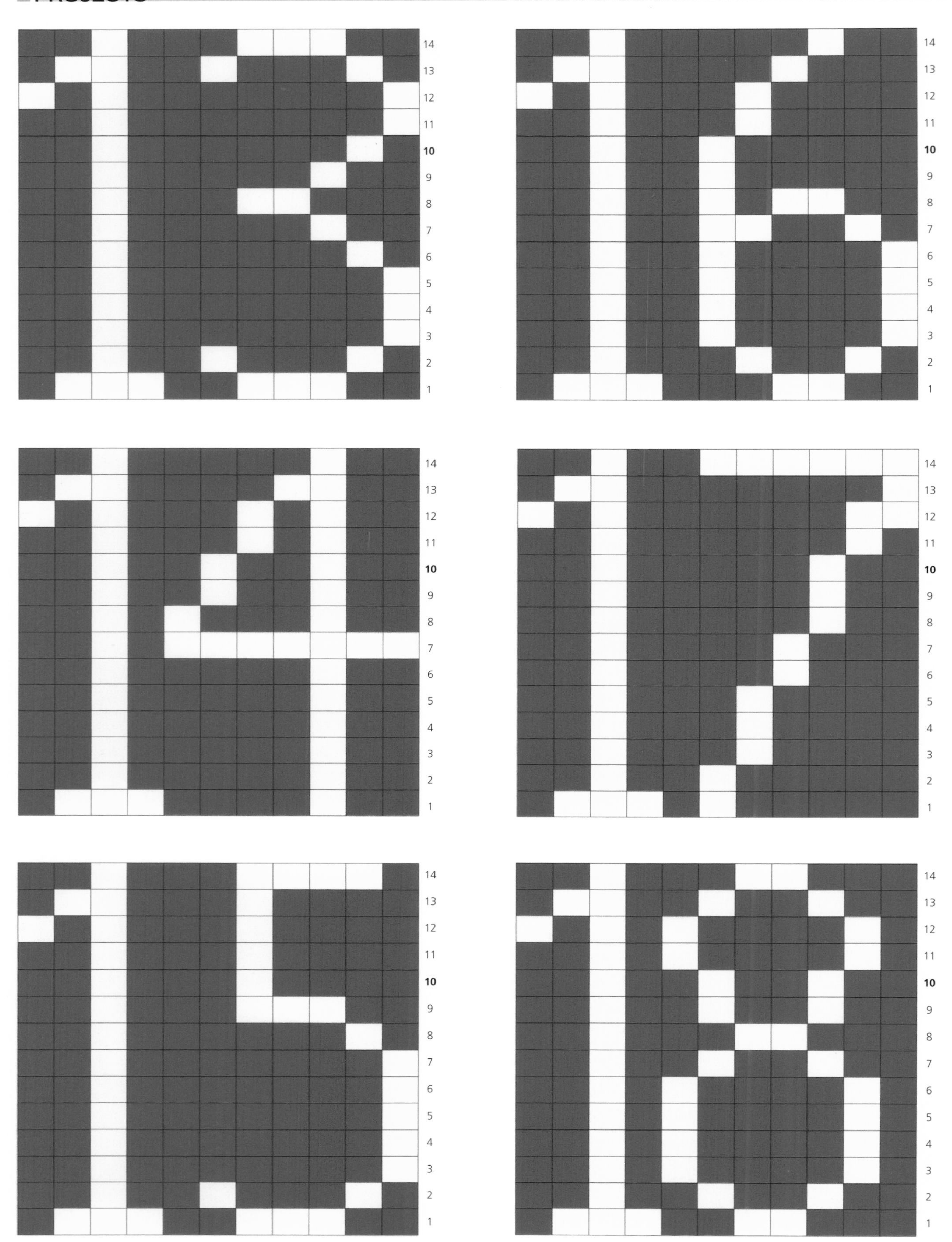
14
13
12
11
10
9
8
7
6
5
4
3
2
1

14
13
12
11
10
9
8
7
6
5
4
3
2
1

knitting needle roll

This is such a handy piece of equipment. There is a little felt patch for you to keep your sewing needles and a pocket for your scissors, cable needles, and row counters. This one has been worked in self-patterning yarn to achieve a subtle blend of colors—just like magic knitting.

size

Approx. 18 x 15in. (46 x 38cm)

materials

Wool, mohair, and silk mix self-patterning yarn, such as Noro Blossom
2 x 1¾oz (50g) balls—approx. 197yd (180m)—of bright multicolor
Needle size: US 7 (4.5mm)
Felt piece 4 x 3in. (10 x 7.5cm)
Fabric for linings and pocket 1yd (1m)
39in. (1m) of ⅝in. (1.5cm) wide ribbon

gauge (tension)

16 sts and 22 rows over 4in. (10cm) square using stockinette (stocking) stitch. Change needle size if necessary to achieve the required gauge (tension).

OUTER COVER

Cast on 64 sts.
Work in st st until work measures 20in. (50cm).
Bind (cast) off.

TO COMPLETE

Block and press. When working on the main knitted piece from now on, the longest side becomes the width of the needle roll hold and the shorter side becomes the depth.

LINING

Measure the knitted piece and cut main lining to size adding on ⅝in. (1.5cm) on all sides for seam allowances. Pin, press, and sew a ⅝in. (1.5cm) seam on all sides.

For inner lining, cut a piece of fabric the same width as main lining but make the depth 3in. (7.5cm) shorter, adding on ⅝in. (1.5cm) on all sides for seam allowances. Sew seam of top edge with a zigzag stitch. Pin, press, and sew a ⅝in. (1.5cm) seam on all sides.

For accessory pocket, cut a piece of fabric 4 x 5in. (10 x 13cm) adding on ⅝in. (1.5cm) on all sides for seam allowances. Fold the top seam, press, pin and sew using a zigzag stitch. Fold side and bottom seams, press and pin. Pin in place onto center rh side of inner lining. Sew using a zigzag stitch.

Cut a piece of felt approx. 4 x 3in. (10 x 7.5cm). Without folding a seam, zigzag the top edge. Pin felt in place on lh side of lining. Zigzag stitch the side and bottom edges onto inner lining.

Pin inner lining to main lining, matching bottom edges, leaving 3in. (7.5cm) gap at top. Sew inner lining to main lining using straight stitch, leaving top open. For knitting needle pockets, starting at the top edge of the inner lining, sew vertically down to the bottom in vertical lines approx. 1in. (2.5cm) apart for one pair of needles or 2in. (5cm) apart for two pairs of needles—start each line of stitching afresh, do not stitch across at the ends. Pin the whole lining piece onto the wrong side of the knitted piece.

Cut ribbon in half. Insert one end between the lining and main piece half way down on lh side (with lining facing), pushing in by approx. 1in. (2.5cm). Hand sew lining onto knitted piece, incorporating the end of the ribbon.

Starting from opposite end to ribbon end, roll up needle case. Pin and sew other ribbon end onto knitted piece to correspond with first ribbon end. Insert needles and accessories into holder and tie with ribbons.

tip

As with many of the projects in this book, the roll is worked in one piece and fits 14in. (35cm) length knitting needles. If you want it to fit larger size needles, just cast on more stitches.

bee mobile

These are cute little flying bees. They make a great hanging mobile for babies, but adults will love them too.

size

Each bee approx. 4½in. (11.5cm) in length

materials

Alpaca and merino mix light worsted (DK) yarn, such as Rooster Almerino DK
1 x 1¾oz (50g) ball—approx. 124yd (112.5m)—of yellow (A)
1 x 1¾oz (50g) ball—approx. 124yd (112.5m)—of cream (B)
Merino light worsted (DK) yarn, such as Debbie Bliss Rialto DK
1 x 1¾oz (50g) ball—approx. 115yd (105m)—in black (C)
Scrap of red yarn or embroidery floss (D)
Needle size: US 3 (3.25mm)
Yarn sewing needle
Toy stuffing
1¾yd (1.5m) of ½in. (1cm) wide ribbon

gauge (tension)

21 sts x 28 rows over 4in. (10cm) square. Change needle size if necessary to achieve the required gauge (tension).

special abbreviation

Kfb—knit into front and back of same st

BEE (MAKE 3)
Cast on 8 sts using C.
Rows 1, 3 Purl.
Row 2 [Kfb] to end. (16 sts)
Row 4 [Kfb in 1 st, k1] to end. (24 sts)
Change to A.
Rows 5, 7 Purl.
Row 6 [Kfb in 1 st, k2] to end. (32 sts)
Row 8 Knit.
Change to C.
Work 4 rows st st.
Change to A
Work 4 rows st st.
Change to C.
Rows 17, 19 Purl.
Row 18 [K2, k2tog] to end. (24 sts)
Row 20 Knit.
Change to A.
Rows 21, 23 Purl.
Row 22 [K1, k2tog] to end. (16 sts)
Row 24 Knit.
Change to B.
Row 25 Purl.
Row 26 [K1, Kfb in next st] to end. (24 sts)
Work 9 rows st st.
Row 36 [K1, k2tog] to end. (16 sts)
Row 37 Purl.
Row 38 K2tog to end.
Thread yarn through rem sts and fasten off.

WINGS (MAKE 2 FOR EACH BEE)
Cast on 6 sts using B.
[Kfb] to end. (12 sts)
Work 15 rows garter st (knit all rows).
Break off yarn, leaving a long end. Thread yarn through rem sts. Pull tightly and fasten off.

TO COMPLETE
Gather cast on edge, and sew seam, leaving head until last. Stuff body firmly. Stuff head and sew up. Using B, sew running stitch around neck to tighten and secure. Sew wings on top of body. Embroider eyes using C and mouth using D.
For antennae, using C make a looped French knot on each side of head by wrapping yarn round needle three times and leaving a loop before going back into work to fasten off.
Cut three lengths of ribbon, each approx. 20in. (50cm) long. Sew between wings to create a hanging mobile.

beaded corsage

Feminine and delicate—this pretty flower is so luscious, it almost looks good enough to eat!

size

Flower: 4in. (10cm) diameter
With leaves extending to 7in. (17.5cm)

materials

Mohair and silk mix laceweight (2ply) yarn, such as Rowan Kid Silk Haze
1 x ⅞oz (25g ball—approx. 230yd (210m)—each of deep pink (A), pale violet (B), green (C)
Stitch holder
30 x glass seed beads in lilac
Safety pin or brooch pin (to secure at back)
Needle size: US 3 (3.25mm)

gauge (tension)

19 sts x 34 rows over 4in. (10cm) square using stockinette (stocking) stitch. Change needle size if necessary to achieve the required gauge (tension).

special abbreviation

Kfb—knit into front and back of same st

OUTER FLOWER (MAKE 3)

Cast on 10 sts using A.
Row 1 K1, *Kfb in next st; rep from * to end. (19 sts)
Rows 2, 4, 6 Purl.
Row 3 *Kfb in next st; rep from * to last st, k1. (37 sts)
Row 5 As Row 1. (73 sts)
Row 7 *K1, Kfb in next st; rep from * to last st, k1. (109 sts)
Row 8 With WS facing, bind (cast) off 3 sts, *sl st on rh needle to lh needle, cast on 2 sts, bind (cast) off 5 sts; rep from * to end.
Bind (cast) off.

INNER FLOWERS (MAKE 3)

Cast on 105 sts using B.
Row 1 K1, *k2, pass first st over 2nd st; rep from * to end. (53 sts)
Row 2 P1, [P2tog] to end. (27 sts)
Row 3 Knit.
Row 4 As Row 2. (14 sts)
Row 5 K2tog to end. (7 sts)
Place rem sts on st holder. Break off yarn leaving end of approx. 8in. (20cm).

LEAVES (MAKE 3)

Using yarn double throughout cast on 3 sts.
Row 1 Purl.
Row 2 K1, M1, k1, M1, k1. (5 sts)
Rows 3, 5 Purl.
Row 4 K2, M1, k1, M1, k2. (7 sts)
Row 6 K3, M1, k1, M1, k3. (9 sts)
Rows 7–9 Work in st st.
Row 10 K4, M1, k1, M1, k4. (11 sts)
Rows 11–13 Work in st st.
Row 14 K5, M1, k1, M1, k5. (13 sts)
Rows 15–21 Work in st st.
Row 22 K1, skpo, k7, k2tog, k1. (11 sts)
Row 23 and every foll alt row Purl.
Row 24 K1, skpo, k5, k2tog, k1. (9 sts)
Row 26 K1, skpo, k3, k2tog, k1. (7 sts)
Row 28 K1, skpo, k1, k2tog, k1. (5 sts)
Row 30 Skpo, k1, k2tog. (3 sts)
Row 32 Sl 1, k2tog, psso.
Bind (cast) off.

TO COMPLETE

Gather cast on sts on outer flower and fasten off tightly. Sew up short seam edges. On inner flower, draw yarn end through sts and fasten off. Sew up short seam edges. Rep on all rem flowers. Place each inner flower into an outer flower and attach from back. Thread beads, bunch up, and attach to flower centers. Bunch all three flowers together and attach at back. Spread out the leaves and attach together. Lay flowers on top of leaves and stitch in place.

tip

The outer flowers are knitted from inner edge by increasing; the inner flowers are knitted from outer edge by decreasing.

nursery blocks

These nursery blocks are really gorgeous, brightly colored, soft and squidgy, and a lovely gift for any baby—and they also include lots of charming motifs that toddlers will love.

size

4in. (10cm) cube

materials

SHEEP

Light worsted (DK) yarn, such as Rooster Almerino DK

1 x 1¾oz (50g) balls—approx. 124yd (112.5m)—each of green (background), pale blue (eye)

Merino light worsted (DK) yarn, such as Debbie Bliss Rialto DK

1 x 1¾oz (50g) balls—approx. 115yd (105m)—each of black (head/legs), off white (body)

BOAT

Merino light worsted (DK) yarn, such as Debbie Bliss Rialto DK

1 x 1¾oz (50g) balls—approx. 115yd (105m)—of red (background)

Light worsted (DK) yarn, such as Rooster Almerino DK

1 x 1¾oz (50g) balls—approx. 124yd (112.5m)—each of blue-green (boat), cream (sail)

CHICK

Merino light worsted (DK) yarn, such as Debbie Bliss Rialto DK

1 x 1¾oz (50g) balls—approx. 115yd (105m)—of red (background), yellow (chick)

Light worsted (DK) yarn, such as Rooster Almerino DK

1 x 1¾oz (50g) balls—approx. 124yd (112.5m)—each of pale pink (legs), bright pink (beak/head feather)

STRIPES 1

Light worsted (DK) yarn, such as Rooster Almerino DK

1 x 1¾oz (50g) balls—approx. 124yd (112.5m)—each of white, yellow, green

Merino light worsted (DK) yarn, such as Debbie Bliss Rialto DK

1 x 1¾oz (50g) balls—approx. 115yd (105m)—each of red, blue

FISH

Light worsted (DK) yarn, such as Rooster Almerino DK

1 x 1¾oz (50g) balls—approx. 124yd (112.5m)—each of pale blue (background), green (fish), white (eye/bubbles)

Merino light worsted (DK) yarn, such as Debbie Bliss Rialto DK

1 x 1¾oz (50g) balls—approx. 115yd (105m)—of red (lips)

STRIPES 2

Light worsted (DK) yarn, such as Rooster Almerino DK

1 x 1¾oz (50g) balls—approx. 124yd (112.5m)—each of red, cream, pink

Needle size: US 6 (4mm)

4in. (10cm) foam cube

Yarn sewing needle

gauge (tension)

21 sts and 28 rows over 4in. (10cm) square using stockinette (stocking) stitch. Change needle size if necessary to achieve the required gauge (tension).

special instructions

Knit the body of the sheep in seed (moss) stitch.

BLOCK SIDES (MAKE 6)

Cast on 23 sts.

Knit 30 rows foll a different chart for each side.

Bind (cast) off.

TO COMPLETE

Block and steam squares. Place onto cube and pin in place. Once in position, sew up each seam using mattress stitch.

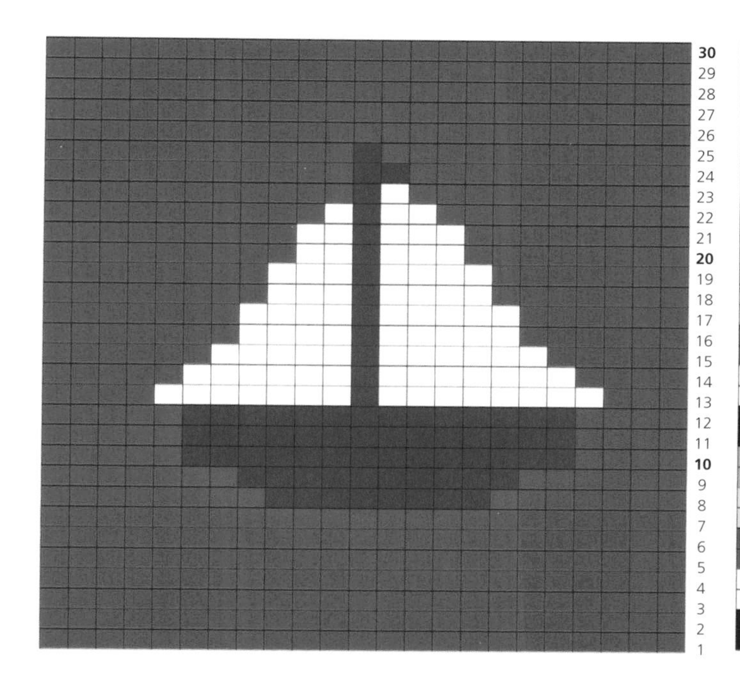
30
29
28
27
26
25
24
23
22
21
20
19
18
17
16
15
14
13
12
11
10
9
8
7
6
5
4
3
2
1

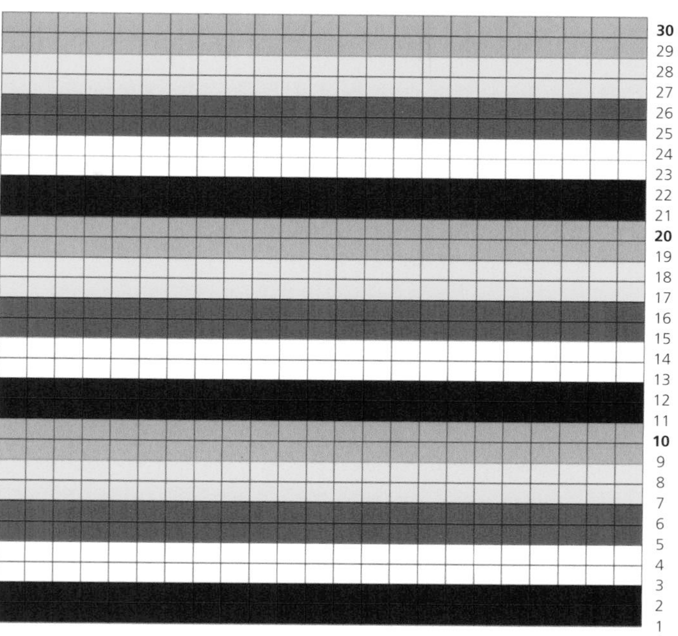
30
29
28
27
26
25
24
23
22
21
20
19
18
17
16
15
14
13
12
11
10
9
8
7
6
5
4
3
2
1

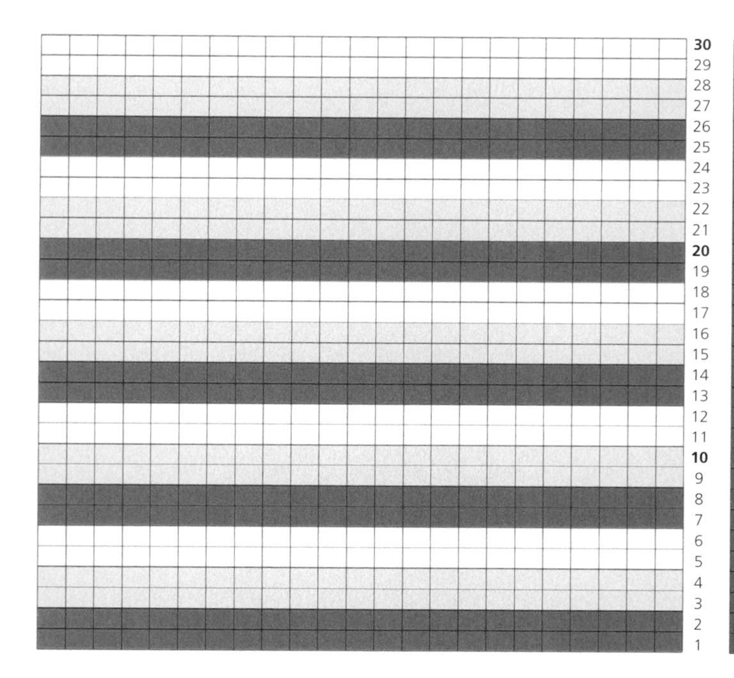
30
29
28
27
26
25
24
23
22
21
20
19
18
17
16
15
14
13
12
11
10
9
8
7
6
5
4
3
2
1

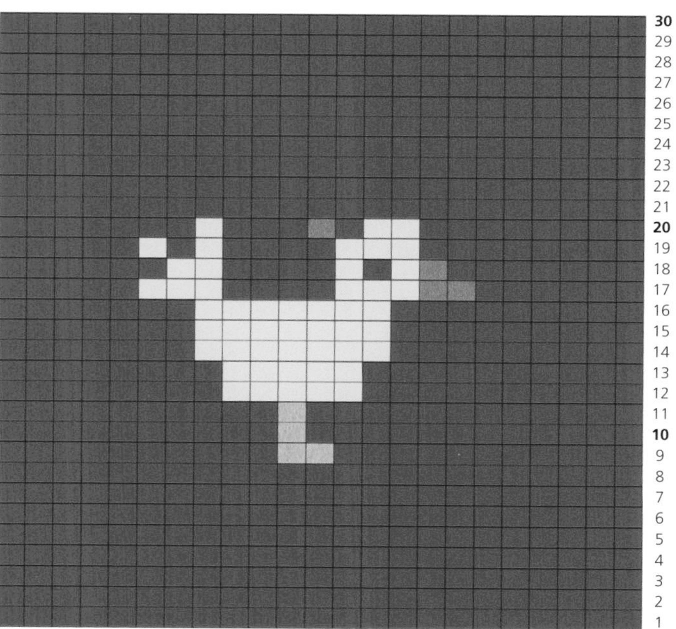
30
29
28
27
26
25
24
23
22
21
20
19
18
17
16
15
14
13
12
11
10
9
8
7
6
5
4
3
2
1

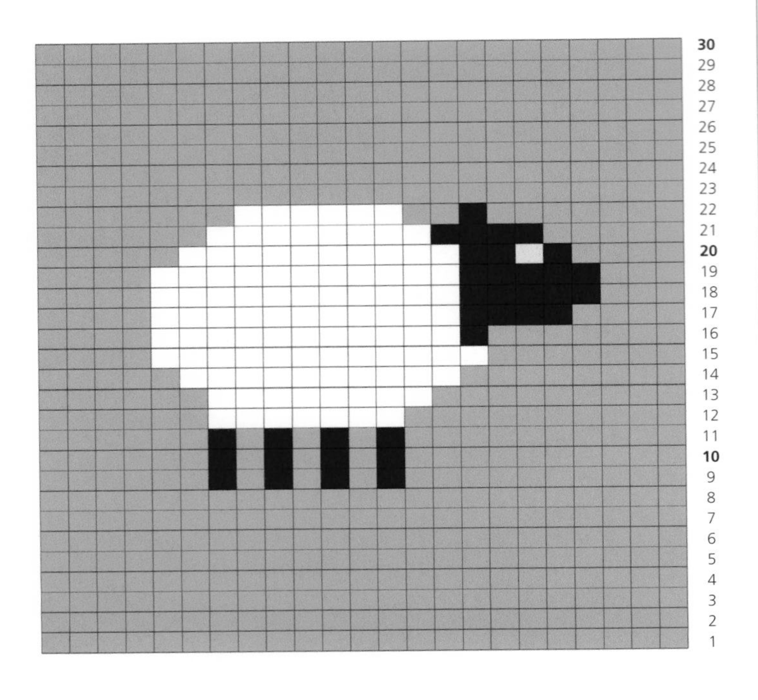

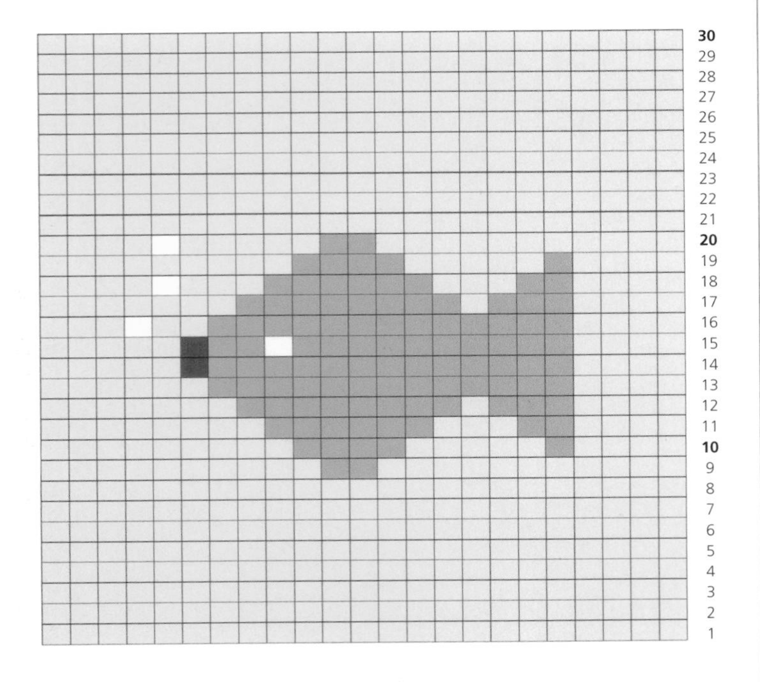

number blocks

These blocks feature numbers instead of motifs, so they are ideal to teach a slightly older child to count.

size

4in. (10cm) cube

materials

ONE
Light worsted (DK) yarn, such as Rooster Almerino DK
1 x 1¾oz (50g) balls—approx. 124yd (112.5m)—each of pale blue (background), red (number)

TWO
Light worsted (DK) yarn, such as Rooster Almerino DK
1 x 1¾oz (50g) balls—approx. 124yd (112.5m)—each of green (background), yellow (number)

THREE
Light worsted (DK) yarn, such as Rooster Almerino DK
1 x 1¾oz (50g) balls—approx. 124yd (112.5m)—each of green-blue (background), white (number)

FOUR
Light worsted (DK) yarn, such as Rooster Almerino DK
1 x 1¾oz (50g) balls—approx. 124yd (112.5m)—each of white (background), deep red (number)

FIVE
Light worsted (DK) yarn, such as Rooster Almerino DK
1 x 1¾oz (50g) balls—approx. 124yd (112.5m)—each of yellow (background), pale pink (number)

SIX
Light worsted (DK) yarn, such as Rooster Almerino DK
1 x 1¾oz (50g) balls—approx. 124yd (112.5m)—each of pale pink (background), blue-green (number)

Needle size: US 6 (4mm)
4in. (10cm) foam cube
Yarn sewing needle

gauge (tension)

21 sts and 28 rows over 4in. (10cm) square using stockinette (stocking) stitch. Change needle size if necessary to achieve the required gauge (tension).

BLOCK SIDES (MAKE 6)
Cast on 23 sts.
Knit 30 rows foll a different chart for each side.
Bind (cast) off.

TO COMPLETE
Block and steam squares. Place onto cube and pin in place. Once in position, sew up each seam using mattress stitch.

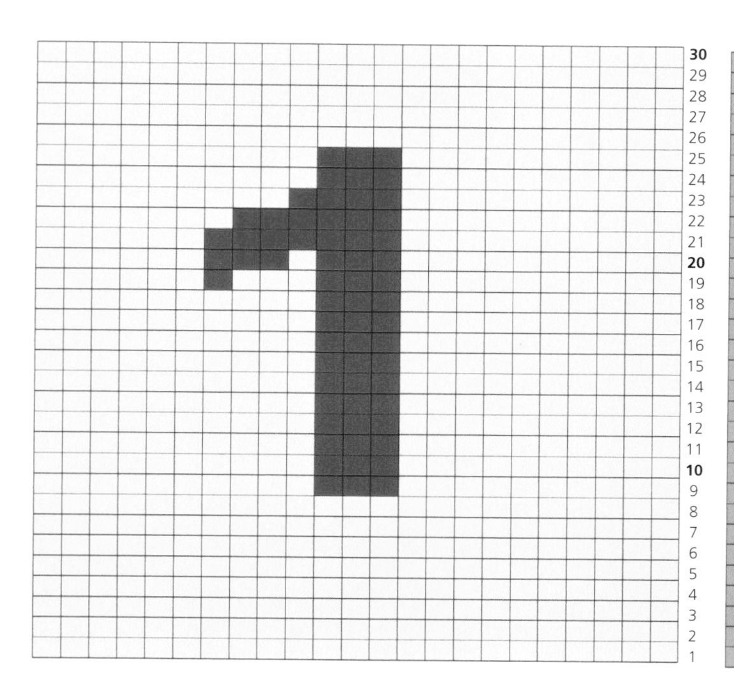

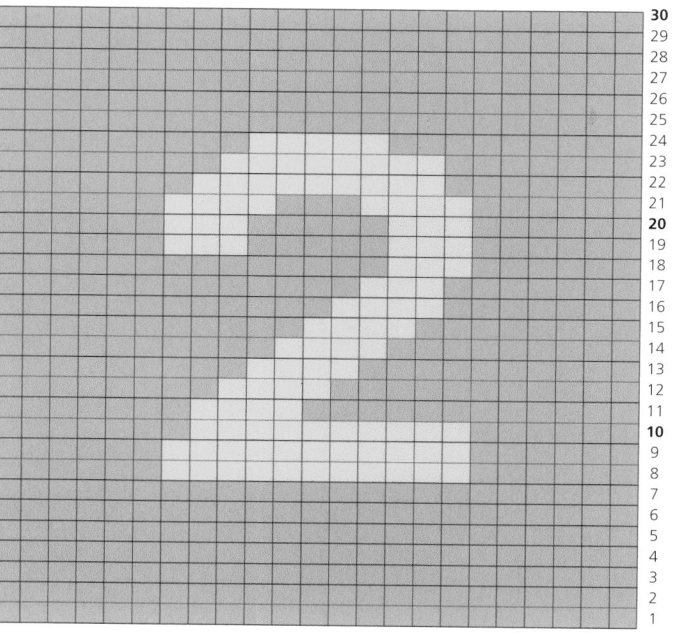

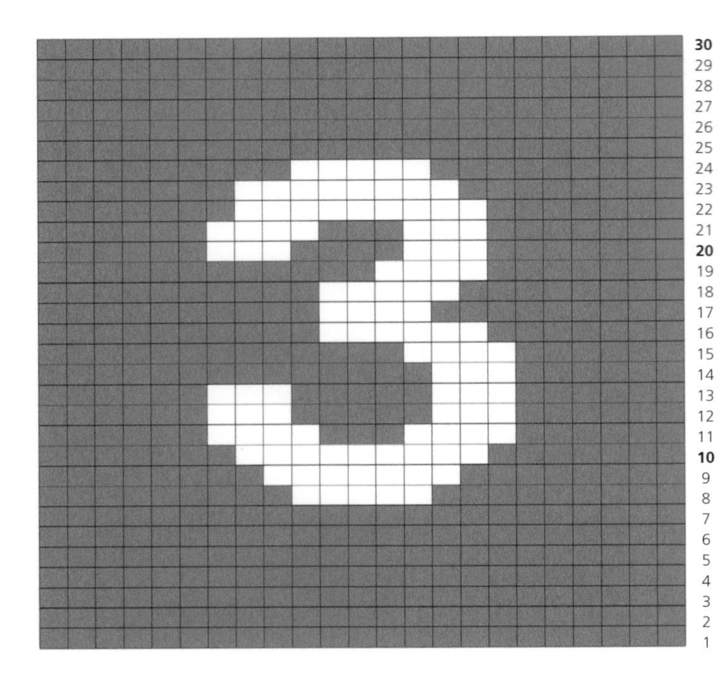

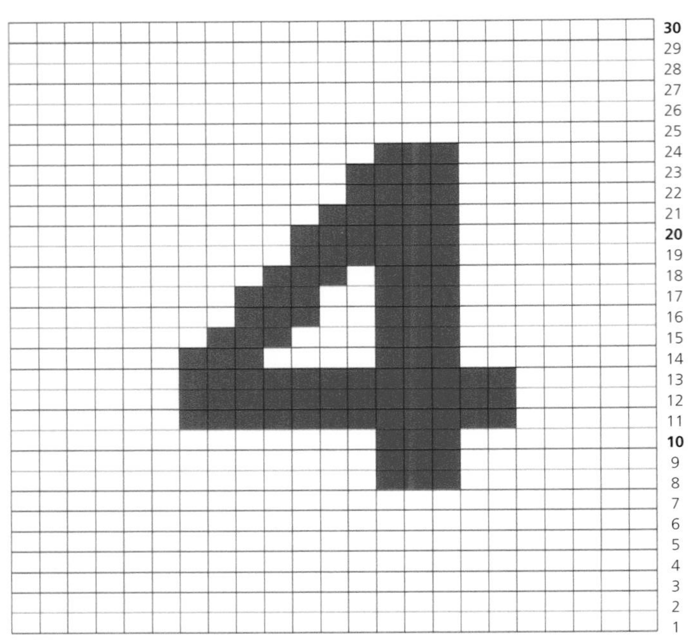

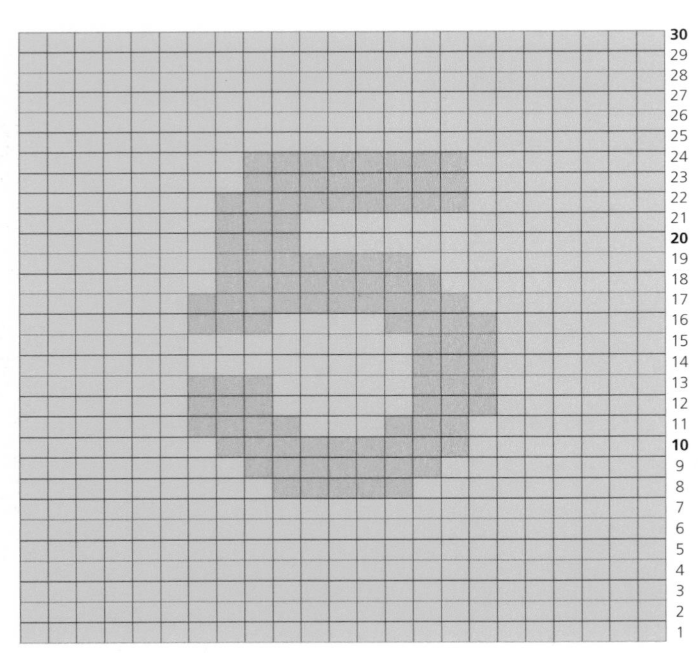

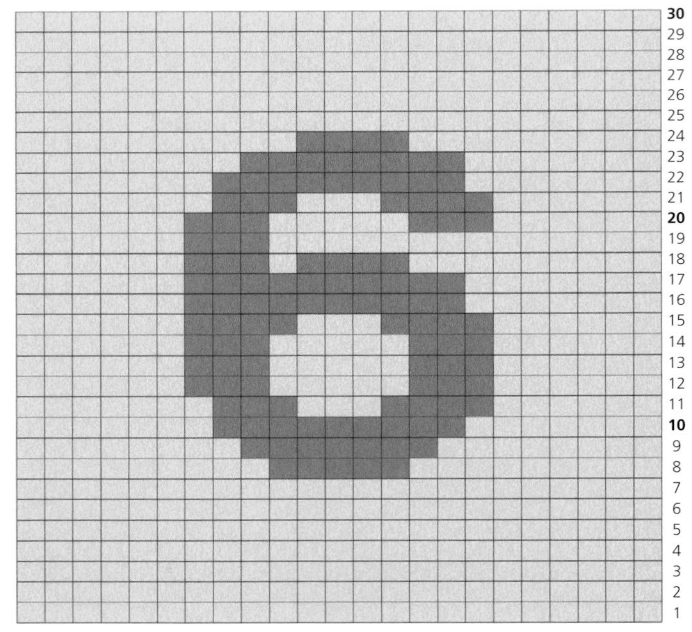

giant knitted bath mat

This bath mat was made using long strips of fabric sewn together and wound into one big ball. Giant needles can be bought or made from broom handles. The measurements below are just a guide—the mat may come out a different size depending on how big your needles are.

size

Approx. 22 x 32in. (56 x 81cm)

materials

5.5yd (5m) of cotton fabric 52in. (130cm) wide
Sewing needle and thread
Needle size: US 11 (7.5mm)

gauge (tension)

A specific gauge (tension) is not important on this project.

MAT

Cut fabric into 22 strips each 2in. (5cm) wide and 5.5yd (5m) long.
Sew each length of fabric together so that strips are one continuous length.
Wind strips into one big ball.
Cast on 20 sts.
Work in garter stitch (all rows knit) until mat measures 32in. (80cm) in length (approx. 48 rows).
Bind (cast) off loosely.
Weave in ends.

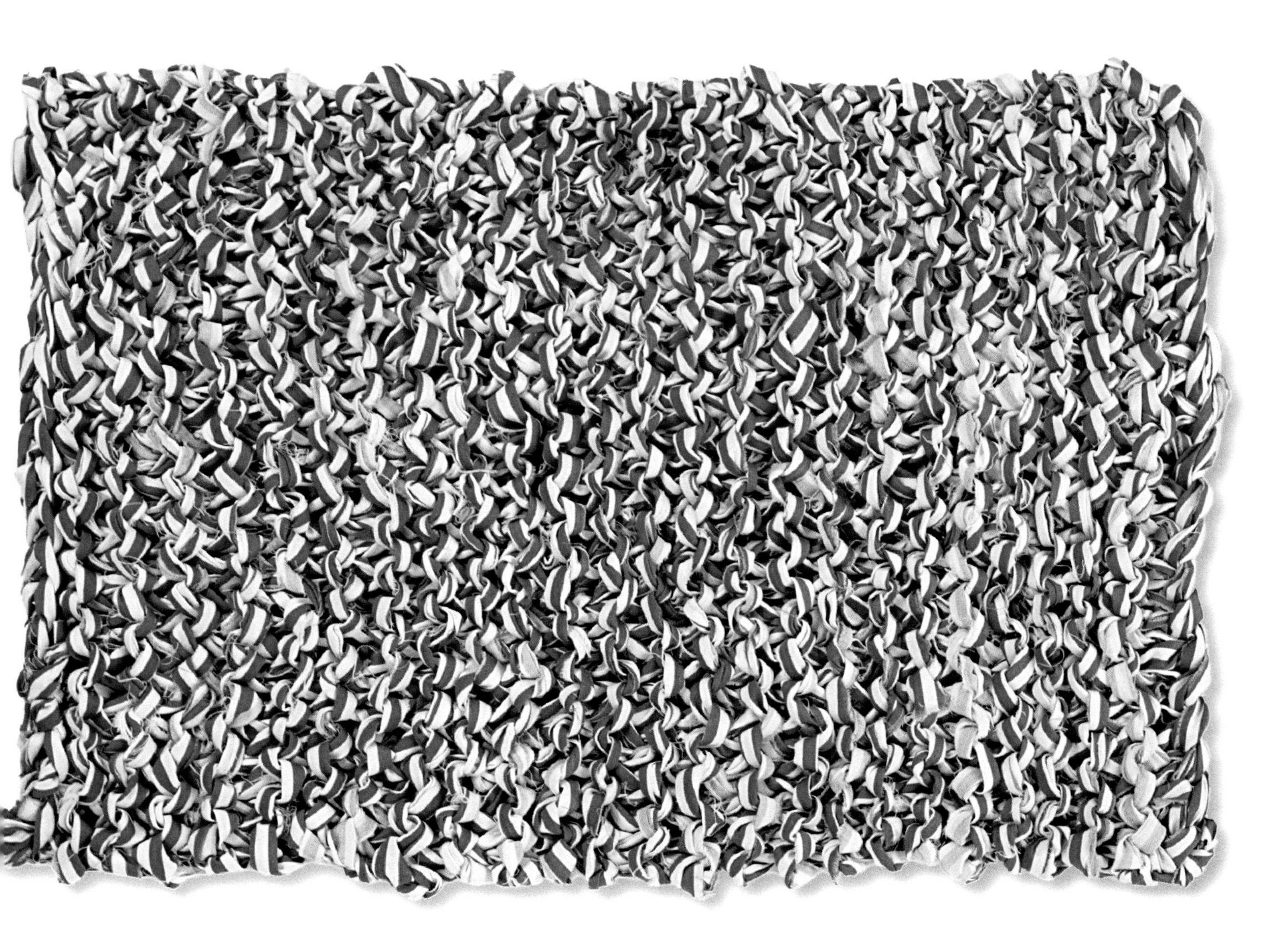

garter stitch pencil case

With self-patterning wool the colors always blend together beautifully and you get the effect of changing colors while using the same ball of wool. It's very effective on this simple pencil case.

size

8in. (20cm) wide x 4in. (10cm) deep

materials

Silk, mohair, and lamb's wool mix self-patterning yarn, such as Noro Silk Garden
1 x 1¾oz (50g) ball—approx. 109yd (100m)—of bright multicolor
Needle size: US 7 (4.5mm)
Fabric for lining 10 x 10in. (25 x 25cm)
Needle and thread
8in. (20cm) zipper
Buttons to decorate

gauge (tension)

21 sts and 28 rows over 4in. (10cm) square using stockinette (stocking) stitch. Change needle size if necessary to achieve the required gauge (tension).

CASE

Cast on 36 sts.
Work in garter stitch (all rows knit) until work measures 8in. (20cm)
Bind (cast) off.

TO COMPLETE

Block finished piece and steam. Measure knitted piece and cut the lining to fit, allowing an extra ⅝in. (1.5cm) all around for the seams. Fold the lining in half RS together and stitch zipper to top edges. Sew up two sides using the sewing machine or hand stitching. Press out seams of lining.
Sew up side seams of knitted piece, and with RS of piece facing insert lining to fit, positioning zipper in center at top. Using yarn, sew top seam over each end of zipper.
Using thread in same color as yarn, sew knitted piece to zipper, taking care to position stitches in zipper behind top of lining. Sew on buttons to decorate.

cupcake pincushion

This is a very simple little cupcake pattern that doesn't need to be knitted on four needles. It's just worked in one piece with the minimum of shaping.

size

3¼in. (8cm) at widest part x 3½in. (9cm) to top of cherry

materials

Alpaca and merino mix light worsted (DK) yarn, such as Rooster Almerino DK
1 x 1¾oz (50g) ball—approx. 124yd (112.5m)—each of white (A), pale pink (B), beige (C),
Alpaca and merino wool mix worsted (Aran) yarn, such as Rooster Almerino Aran
1 x 1¾oz (50g) ball—approx. 103yd (94m)—of red (D)
Needle size: US 3 (3.25mm) and US 5 (3.75mm)
Yarn sewing needle
Toy stuffing

gauge (tension)

21 sts and 28 rows over 4in. (10cm) square using stockinette (stocking) stitch. Change needle size if necessary to achieve the required gauge (tension).

PINCUSHION

Cast on 7 sts using US 3 (3.25mm) needles and A.
Row 1 Inc k wise into every st. (14 sts)
Row 2 and foll alt rows Purl.
Row 3 [K1, inc k wise into next st] to end. (21 sts)
Row 5 [K2, inc k wise into next st] to end. (28 sts)
Starting with a P row, work 3 rows st st.
Row 9 [K3, inc k wise into next st] to end. (35 sts)
Row 10 Purl.
Rows 11–12 Knit.
Change to US 5 (3.75mm) needles.
Shape sides. Row 1 [K1 into back of next st, p1] to last st, k1.
Row 2 K1, [k1, p1] to last 2 sts, k2.
Rep last 2 rows three times more.
Row 9 K1, p1, *[k1, p1, k1] into next st, p1, k1, p1; rep from * to last st, k1. (51 sts)
Starting with Row 2, rep Rows 2 and 1 three times, finishing with WS facing.
Row 16 Knit 1 row.
Change to C.
Rows 17–18 Starting with a k row, work in st st.
Change to B.
Rows 19–22 Work in st st.
Dec for top.
Row 23 [K2, k2tog] to last 3 sts, k3. (39 sts)
Rows 24–26 Starting with a p row, work in st st.
Row 27 [K1, k2tog] to end. (26 sts)
Row 28 Purl.
Row 29 K2tog to end. (13 sts)
Row 30 P2tog to last st, p1. (7 sts)
Break off yarn and thread through sts, draw up and fasten off.

CHERRY

Cast on 4 sts using US 3 (3.25mm) needles and D.
Row 1 Purl.
Row 2 Inc k wise into every st. (8 sts)
Rows 3–7 Starting with a p row, work in st st.
Row 8 k2tog to end. (4 sts).
Break off yarn and thread through sts.
Draw up and fasten off.

TO COMPLETE

With RS tog, sew side seams of cupcake leaving a gap for stuffing. Stuff cake and sew up gap. Stuff cherry and sew gap. Sew cherry on top of cake.

child's backpack

A very neat and appealing child's backpack. It has drawstring ties and a little pocket on the front to store all those tiny treasures.

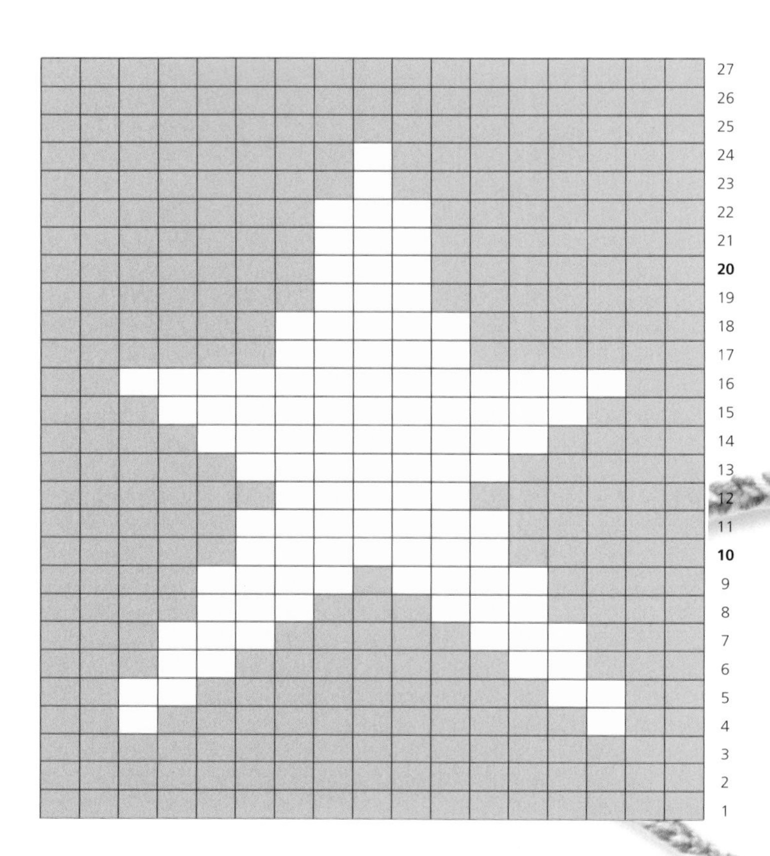

size

9in. (23cm) wide x 10½in. (27cm) deep

materials

Merino worsted (Aran) yarn, such as Debbie Bliss Rialto Aran
2 x 1¾oz (50g) balls—approx. 175yd (160m)—in pale blue (A)
1 x 1¾oz (50g) balls—approx. 87.5yd (80m)—in off-white (B)
Needle size: US 8 (5mm)
Yarn sewing needle

gauge (tension)

18 sts and 24 rows over 4in. (10cm) square using stockinette (stocking) stitch. Change needle size if necessary to achieve the required gauge (tension).

BACKPACK (ONE PIECE)

Cast on 42 sts using A.
Row 1 Knit.
Row 2 Knit.
Change to B.
Row 3 Knit.
Row 4 Knit.
Change to A
Eyelet row: **K1, *bind (cast) off 2 sts, k3; rep from * to last 2 sts, k2.
Next row K3, *cast on 2 sts, k4; rep from * to last st, k1.**
Change to B.
Work 2 rows knit.
Change to A.
Starting with a knit row, work in st st as set for 116 rows.
Change to B.
Work 2 rows knit.
Change to A.
Eyelet row: As previous eyelet row from ** to **.
Change to B.
Work 2 rows knit.
Bind (cast) off.

POCKET

Cast on 17 sts using A.
Foll chart for 27 rows working in st st.
Bind (cast) off.

TO COMPLETE

Sew side seams. Sew on pocket using blanket stitch and B.

TIES (MAKE 2)

Cut 6 strands of A and B each 85in. (212cm) in length, pair colors and knot at one end then braid three pairs together, knot at other end. Rep for 2nd tie with other three pairs.
Attach one end of tie to bottom corner of backpack (from inside), leave a loop and thread the other end through each eyelet, leaving a long tail on the other side. Rep on other side with second tie.

fingerless gloves

Using a beautiful supersoft wool gives these fingerless mittens a really luxurious feel. The pretty ruffled edgings are very elegant and the gloves are super easy as there is no shaping; they are knitted as a rectangular block with edgings added for a little glamour.

size

To fit an average hand

materials

Alpaca and silk mix worsted (Aran) yarn, such as Debbie Bliss Alpaca Silk Aran
2 x 1¾oz (50g) balls—approx. 142yd (130m)—of green (A)
1 x 1¾oz (50g) ball—approx. 71yd (65m)—of dark pink (B)
Needle size: US 8 (5mm)
Yarn sewing needle
4 x vintage buttons

gauge (tension)

18 sts and 24 rows over 4in. (10cm) square using stockinette (stocking) stitch. Change needle size if necessary to achieve the required gauge (tension).

special abbreviations

K1B—knit into back of st on right side rows
P1B—purl into back of st on wrong side rows

tip

It's best to pin the seam first, so that you can mark exactly where the thumbhole should fall before sewing up.

GLOVES

Cast on 30 sts using A.
Knit in st st until work measures approx. 8in. (20cm) or glove fits around hand with the sts running horizontally around hand.
Bind (cast) off.

PICOT EDGE (FINGER END)

With RS facing and using B, pick up and knit 24 sts along one side of knitted piece, (with sts running horizontally).
Next row Purl.
Next row K1, transfer st from rh needle back onto lh needle. *Cast on 2 sts, bind (cast) off 4 sts, transfer st from rh needle back onto lh needle; rep from * to end.

SCALLOPED SHELL EDGING (WRIST END)

Cast on 62 sts using B.
Row 1 K1, yo, *k5, slip the 2nd, 3rd, 4th and 5th sts just worked one by one over first st and off the needle, yo; rep from * to last st, k1.
Row 2 P1, *p1, yrn, P1B into next st, p1; rep from * to last st, p1.
Row 3 K2, K1B, *k3, K1B; rep from * to last st, k1.
Work 3 rows in garter st (all rows knit).
Bind (cast) off.

TO COMPLETE

With RS together sew shell edging onto edge opposite picot edge. Sew up seam on thumb side of each glove, leaving a hole for thumb to fit through. Turn RS out. Sew 2 buttons on cuff of each glove.

men's fingerless gloves

These are great knitted in a variety of different colors and are very popular with teenagers and adults alike. The mittens have a thumb and a ribbed cuff to help keep them in place on the wrist.

size

Small:large

materials

A pair of mittens uses 1 x 50g ball of wool.
For striped mitten:
Merino light worsted (DK) yarn, such as Debbie Bliss Rialto DK
¾ x 1¾oz (50g) balls—approx. 86yd (79m)—of black (A)
¼ x 1¾oz (50g) balls—approx. 29yd (27m)—of dark red (B)
Needle size: US 4 (3.5mm) and US 6 (4mm)

gauge (tension)

22 sts and 30 rows over 4in. (10cm) square using stockinette (stocking) stitch. Change needle size if necessary to achieve the required gauge (tension).

LEFT HAND

Cast on 34:36 sts using US 4 (3.5mm) needles and A.
Work 14 rows in single rib (k1, p1).
Change to US 6 (4mm) needles and work 6:8 rows in st st starting with a k row.
Shape thumb gusset. Row 1 K15:16, inc 1 st into each of next 2 sts, k17:18.
Row 2 and every alt row Purl.
Row 3 K15:16, inc 1 st, k2, inc 1 st, k17:18.
Rep Rows 2–3, three times more, working 2 sts more between inc on each rep. (44:46 sts)
Work 7 rows in st st.
Divide for thumb. Next row K27:28, turn, inc 1 st, p11, turn, inc 1 st, k12. (14 sts)
**Work on these 14 sts in st st for 3:5 rows.
Work the next 4:5 rows in single rib.
Bind (cast) off in rib.

JOIN FOR HAND

With RS of work facing and with rh needle, pick up and knit 1 st at base of thumb. Pick up and knit 1 st on other side of thumb (to join thumb). Knit to end.
Next row Purl across all sts. (34:36 sts)
Cont in st st for a further 7:9 rows.
Work a further 5:6 rows in single rib.
Bind (cast) off in rib.

RIGHT HAND

Work as left hand until thumb gusset is reached.
Shape thumb gusset. Row 1 K17:18, inc 1 st into each of next 2 sts, k17:18.
Row 2 and every alt row Purl.
Row 3 K17:18, inc 1 st, k2, inc 1 st, k15:16.
Rep Rows 2–3 three times more, working 2 sts more between inc on each rep. (44:46 sts)
Work in st st for 7 rows.
Divide for thumb. Next Row K29:30, turn, inc 1 st, p11, turn, inc 1 st, k12. (14 sts)
Work as left hand from ** to end.

TO COMPLETE

Sew up side and thumb seams. Sew in ends. Turn right side out.

child's pompom hat

This fun child's hat is knitted in a very easy stitch pattern. It is one size with no shaping so is a quick project that can be knitted in one or two evenings.

size

9in. (22.5cm) wide x 6in. (15cm) deep

materials

Alpaca and merino wool mix worsted (Aran) yarn, such as Rooster Almerino Aran 1 x 1¾oz (50g) ball—approx. 103yd (94m)—each of green (A), blue-green (B)
Needle size: US 8 (5mm)

gauge (tension)

22 sts x 17 rows over 4in. (10cm) square using US 8 (5mm) needles. Change needle size if necessary to achieve the required gauge (tension).

HAT
Cast on 45 sts using B.
Work 7 rows in st st.
Start pattern WS facing.
Row 1 In A, k1, purl to last st, k1.
Row 2 In B, k1, sl 1, *k1, sl 3; rep from * ending k1 sl 1, k1.
Row 3 In B, k1, *p3, sl 1; rep from * ending p3, k1.
Row 4 In A, k2, *sl 1, k3; rep from * ending sl 1, k2.
Row 5 In A, purl to last st, k1.
Row 6 In B, k1, *sl 3, k1; rep from * to end.
Row 7 In B, k1, pl, *sl 1, p3; rep from * ending sl 1, p1, k1.
Row 8 In A, k4, *sl 1, k3; rep from * ending k1.
These 8 rows form pattern, rep these rows until work measures approx. 12in. (30cm) ending with a Row 8.
Change to B and work 8 rows in st st starting with a purl row.
Bind (cast) off loosely.

TO COMPLETE
With RS tog, fold knitted piece in half and sew up the side seams using B. Turn right side out. Make two small pompoms as described in Method 2 on page 172 and sew securely to each top corner of hat.

tip

If you'd like to change the size, measure the head circumference and cast on stitches in multiples of 4 plus 1 to make the pattern work. There are approx. 5 (2) stitches per inch (cm). Then measure from the forehead, where the hat sits, across the back and knit to your personal measurements.

bobble purse

This is a cute, fun little makeup bag decorated with colorful bobbles. It's lined with fabric to stop the knitting from stretching when you add your stash of makeup. This is a handy pattern for using up scraps of wool on the bobbles.

size

Approx. 7½in. (19cm) wide x 5in. (13cm) deep

materials

Alpaca and merino wool mix worsted (Aran) yarn, such as Rooster Almerino Aran
1 x 1¾oz (50g) ball—approx. 103yd (94m)—of yellow (A)
Scraps—approx. 1¼yd (1m)—of various pinks, purples (B)
Needle size: US 8 (5mm)
Fabric for lining 10 x 12in. (25 x 30cm)
Sewing needle and thread
6in. (15cm) zipper

gauge (tension)

19 sts x 23 rows over 4in. (10cm) square using US 8 (5mm) needles. Change needle size if necessary to achieve the required gauge (tension).

PURSE

Cast on 40 sts in A.
Work in st st for 70 rows or until work measures approx. 10in. (25cm); foll chart to place bobbles, working these in B.
Bind (cast) off.

BOBBLE

Using contrast yarn, (k1, p1, k1, p1, k1) into next st, turn, p5, turn, k5, turn, p2tog, p1, p2tog, turn sl 1, k2tog, psso.
Break off yarn.

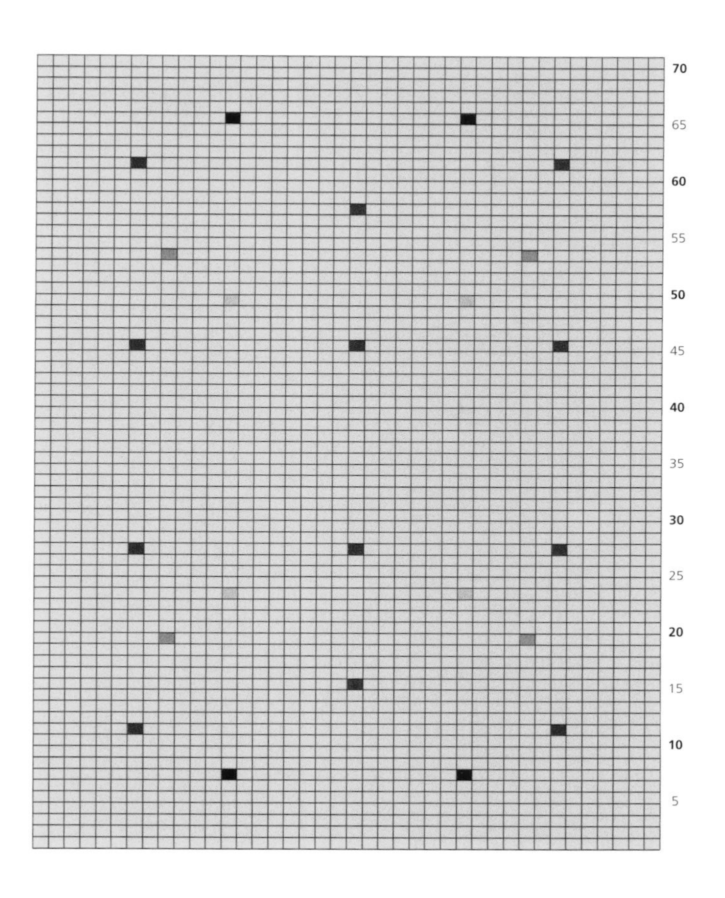

TO COMPLETE

Block finished piece and steam. Measure knitted piece and cut the lining to fit, allowing an extra ⅝in. (1.5cm) all around for the seams. Fold the lining in half RS together and stitch zipper to top edges. Sew up two sides using the sewing machine or hand stitching. Press out seams of lining.
Sew up side seams of knitted piece, and with RS of piece facing insert lining to fit, positioning zipper in center at top. Using yarn, sew top seam over each end of zipper.
Using thread in same color as yarn, sew knitted piece to zipper, taking care to position stitches in zipper behind top of lining.

needle case

For a very beautiful little gift make this needle case, which uses simple embossed diamond stitch and is lined with felt. It has been decorated on the inside with a patchwork panel, and an embroidered flower cut from the corner of a vintage handkerchief. Use whatever you have available to personalize—buttons, embroidery, patchwork—or just leave it plain.

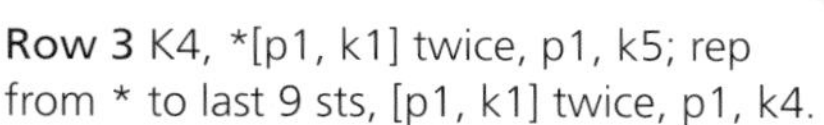

size

Approx 4¼ x 4in. (10.5 x 10cm)

materials

Cotton light worsted (DK) yarn, such as Rowan Cotton Glace
1 x 1¾oz (50g) ball—approx. 126yd (115m)—of dark pink
Needle size: US 3 (3.25mm)
Pale pink felt for lining 9 x 4in. (22.5 x 10cm)
White felt 7 x 3in. (17.5 x 7.5cm)
Sewing needle and thread
20in. (50cm) of ½in. (1cm) wide green gingham ribbon

gauge (tension)

23 sts x 32 rows over 4in. (10cm) square using US 8 (5mm) needles. Change needle size if necessary to achieve the required gauge (tension).

CASE

Cast on 43 sts.
Row 1 (right side) P1, k1, p1, *[k3, p1] twice, k1, p1; rep from * to end.
Row 2 P1, k1, *p3, k1, p1, k1, p3, k1; rep from * to last st, p1.
Row 3 K4, *[p1, k1] twice, p1, k5; rep from * to last 9 sts, [p1, k1] twice, p1, k4.
Row 4 P3, *[k1, p1] 3 times, k1, p3; rep from * to end.
Row 5 As Row 3.
Row 6 As Row 2.
Row 7 As Row 1.
Row 8 P1, k1, p1, *k1, p5, [k1, p1] twice; rep from * to end.
Row 9 [P1, k1] twice, *p1, k3, [p1, k1] 3 times; rep from * to last 9 sts, p1, k3, [p1, k1] twice, p1.
Row 10 As Row 8.
These 10 rows form pattern, rep these rows until work measures approx. 4in. (10cm).
Bind (cast) off.

TO COMPLETE

Sew in ends. Block and shape piece, press on wrong side.

LINING

Measure the knitted piece and cut a piece of pink felt approx. 8 x 3½in. (20 x 9cm) so it fits just on the inside and is slightly smaller than the knitted piece. Center felt on WS of knitted piece. Pin and hand sew around edges to hold in place.
Using pinking shears, cut a piece of white felt to approx. 7½ x 3in. (19 x 7.5cm). Center on top of pink felt and pin in place (do not sew). Fold needle case in half with knitted side facing upwards and felted pieces facing each other. Pin in place. Machine sew or backstitch by hand ⅝in. (1.5cm) in from folded line.
Cut the length of ribbon in half. Fold one end of ribbon inwards by approx. ¼in. (0.5cm). Stitch folded end of ribbon in center of inside edge of case. Rep on other side with other half of ribbon.
Decorate inside of needle case with a piece of patchwork, embroidery, or embroidered corner of a vintage handkerchief and sew in place.

heart ipod cover

A delightful little cover that will protect your iPod from scratches and scrapes, and is great as a gift for Valentine's Day.

size

2¼in. (5.5cm) wide x 3½in. (9cm) deep

materials

Pure alpaca light worsted (DK) yarn, such as Drops Classic Alpaca DK
1 x 1¾oz (50g) ball—approx. 98.5yd (90m)—cream (A)
Pure wool light worsted (DK) yarn, such as Rowan Pure Wool DK
1 x 1¾oz (50g) ball—approx. 137yd (125m)—deep pink (B)
Needle size: US 6 (4mm)
1 x small button

gauge (tension)

21 sts x 28 rows over 4in. (10cm) square. Change needle size if necessary to achieve the required gauge (tension).

COVER (MAKE 2)
Cast on 13 sts using A.
Rows 1–2 Knit.
Change to B.
Row 3 Knit.
Row 4 Purl.
Change to A.
Starting with a k row, work 6 rows st st.
Next row (right side) Foll chart, using B for motif, for next 14 rows.
Cont in A only work 6 rows st st.
Change to B.
Knit 2 rows.
Change to A.
Knit 2 rows.
Bind (cast) off.

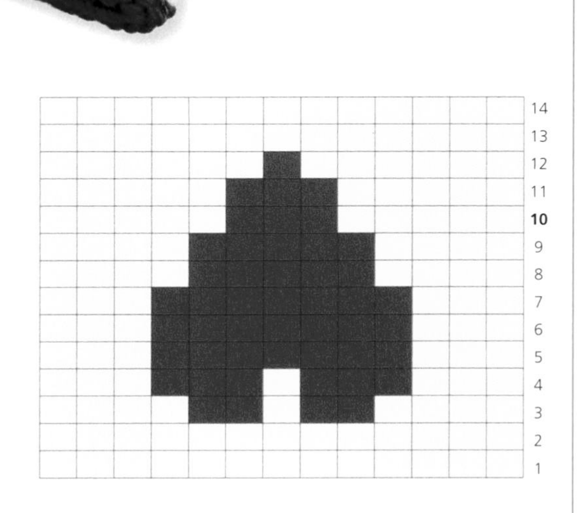

BUTTON TAB
On one piece pick up 5 sts at center top using A.
Knit 2 rows.
Next row K2, bind (cast) off 1 st, k2.
Next row K2, cast on 1 st, k2.
Knit 2 more rows.
Bind (cast) off.

TO COMPLETE
Sew side seams. Sew button to top center front to match buttonhole.

hound's-tooth ipod cover

This cover has a rather more masculine look.

size

2¼in. (5.5cm) wide x 3½in. (9cm) deep

materials

Alpaca light worsted (DK) yarn, such as UK Alpaca Superfine DK
1 x 1¾oz (50g) ball—approx. 144yd (132m)—of cream (A)
Alpaca light worsted (DK) yarn, such as Artesano Inca Mist
1 x 1¾oz (50g) ball—approx. 109yd (100m)—of dark blue (B)
Needle size: US 6 (4mm)
1 x small button

gauge (tension)

21 sts x 28 rows over 4in. (10cm). Change needle size if necessary to achieve the required gauge (tension).

COVER (MAKE 2)
Cast on 12 sts using A.
Rows 1–2 Knit.
Row 3 K1 in A, *k1 in B, k3 in A; rep from * to last 3 sts, k1 in B, k2 in A.
Row 4 *P3 in B, p1 in A; rep from * to end.
Row 5 *K3 in B, K1 in A; rep from * to end.
Row 6 P1 in A, *p1 in B, p3 in A; rep from * to last 3 sts, p1 in B, p2 in A.
Rows 3–6 form pattern, rep these rows until work measures approx. 3in. (7.5cm).
Knit 2 rows in A.

BUTTON TAB
On one piece pick up 5 sts at center top using A.
Knit 2 rows.
Next row K2, bind (cast) off 1 st, k2.
Next row K2, cast on 1 st, k2.
Knit 2 more rows.
Bind (cast) off.

TO COMPLETE
Sew side seams. Sew button to top center front to match buttonhole.

big wool handbag

This is a gorgeous bag; the super chunky Big Wool means that it knits up really quickly and the Fair Isle design on the front is a very simple one. Add a lining to make it stronger.

size

Approx. 10in. (25cm) deep x 9in. (23cm) wide

materials

Pure wool chunky yarn, such as Rowan Big Wool
2 x 3½oz (100g) balls—approx. 175yd (160m)—of charcoal (A)
1 x 3½oz (100g) balls—approx. 87.5yd (80m)—of deep pink (B), green (C)
Needle size: US 11 (8mm)
Fabric for lining 24 x 12in. (60 x 30cm)
Sewing needle and thread
1 x large button
1 x large snap (press stud)

gauge (tension)

8 sts and 11 rows over 4in. (10cm) square using stockinette (stocking) stitch. Change needle size if necessary to achieve the required gauge (tension).

SIDES (MAKE 2)

Cast on 31 sts using A.
Rows 1–13 Work in st st.
Row 14 Starting with a p row, foll chart for 9 rows.
Rows 23–35 Work in st st and A until work measures approx. 8¾in. (22cm) deep.
Rows 36–41 Work in garter stitch (all rows k).
Bind (cast) off in B, with right side facing.

HANDLES (MAKE 2)

Cast on 4 sts using A.
Work in garter stitch until handle measures 16in. (40cm)
Bind (cast) off.

TO COMPLETE

Sew side and bottom seam of bag. Sew on button.

LINING

Cut lining fabric to fit inside bag, adding ⅝in. (1.5cm) seam allowance on both sides and 1in. (2.5cm) at top edges. With RS tog, pin and machine sew side seams. Trim bottom corners and press out seams. Turn top over by 1in. (2.5cm) and press. Insert lining into knitted bag and pin in place around top edge. Catch corners of lining from inside to secure into bag.

Place pin marker 2½in. (6cm) from each outside seam of bag. At one side, push one end of strap approx. 1½in. (4cm) down between lining and knitted piece at the pin marker, pin in place. Repeat on same side with other end of same strap. Repeat for second strap on other side. Hand sew lining to knitted piece around the top, incorporating straps as you sew and stitching the straps onto the bag both on the outside and inside. Sew snap (press stud) to center of sides inside top.

lace panel leg warmers

These leg warmers have a certain "vintage" look, but the subtle color and lace panel makes them more elegant than eighties leg warmers—more "tame" than "Fame."

size

16in. (40cm) long x 13½in. (34cm) circumference

materials

Pure merino wool light worsted (DK) yarn, such as Rooster Rooster Baby
4 x 1¾oz (50g) balls—approx. 547yd (500m)—of pale green
Needle size: US 3 (3.25mm)

gauge (tension)

24 sts and 34 rows over 4in. (10cm) square using stockinette (stocking) stitch. Change needle size if necessary to achieve the required gauge (tension).

LEG WARMER (MAKE 2)
Cast on 82 sts.
Row 1 P2, [k2, p2] to end.
Row 2 K2, [p2, k2] to end.
Rep Rows 1–2 three times more, inc one st at center of Row 8. (83 sts)
Row 9 (right side) K36, p2, k2tog, [k1, yf] twice, k1, sl 1, k1, psso, p2, k36.
Row 10 and every alt row P36, k2, p7, k2, p36.
Row 11 K36, p2, k2tog, yf, k3, yf, sl 1, k1, psso, p2, k36.
Row 13 K36, p2, k1, yf, sl 1, k1, psso, k1, k2tog, yf, k1, p2, k36.
Row 15 K36, p2, k2, yf, sl 1, k2tog, psso, yf, k2, p2, k36.
Row 16 As Row 10.
Rows 9–16 form patt, rep these rows 13 times more, then Rows 9–15 once more.
Next row P36, k2, p3, p2 tog, p2, k2, p36. (82 sts)
Work 8 rows in 2x2 rib.
Bind (cast) off.

TO COMPLETE
Sew seam at back.

felted bag

This is a very simple way of felting—you simply knit and then throw the pieces in the washing machine to give a felted look. The bag is simply gorgeous; the pattern is easy and shows off the beautiful colors of the wool.

size

Each piece before felting 11½in. (29cm) wide x 8¾in. (22cm) deep
Handles before felting 2½ x 17½in. (6.5 x 44cm)
Finished bag approx.10in. (25cm) width x 7in. (17.5cm) deep
Finished handles approx. 2in. (5cm) wide x 16in. (40cm) long

materials

Pure wool self-patterning yarn, such as Noro Kureyon
1 x 1¾oz (50g) ball—approx. 109yd (100m)—of multicolor
Needle size: US 7 (4.5mm)
Fabric for lining 12 x 18in. (30 x 45cm)
Needle and thread
1 x large snap (press stud)

gauge (tension)

15 sts x 20 rows over 4in. (10cm) square using stockinette (stocking) stitch, before felting. Change needle size if necessary to achieve the required gauge (tension).

BAG SIDES (MAKE 2)

Using yarn doubled throughout, cast on 42 sts.
Work in st st until piece measures 11½in. (29cm).
Bind (cast) off.

HANDLES (MAKE 2)

Cast on 11 sts.
Work in st st until piece measures 17½in. (44cm).
Bind (cast) off on a knit row.

FLOWER

Cast on 60 sts.
Row 1 Knit.
Row 2 *K1, k2tog; rep from * to end. (40 sts)
Rows 3, 5 Purl.
Row 4 [K2tog] to end. (20 sts)
Row 6 [K2tog] to end. (10 sts)
Row 7 Purl.
Break off yarn, thread through rem sts, and fasten off.

FELTING

Sew in all ends before felting. Wash pieces twice on a hot machine wash, then leave to dry naturally. Press when fully dry.

TO COMPLETE

With wrong sides facing, sew up side seams. Sew flower onto front of bag.

LINING

Cut lining fabric to fit inside bag, adding ⅝in. (1.5cm) seam allowance on both sides and 1in. (2.5cm) at top edges. With RS tog, pin and machine sew side seams. Trim bottom corners and press out seams. Turn top over by 1in. (2.5cm) and press. Insert lining into knitted bag and pin in place around top edge. Catch corners of lining from inside to secure into bag.

Place pin marker 2in. (5cm) from each outside seam of bag. At one side, push one end of strap approx. 1½in. (4cm) down between lining and knitted piece at the pin marker, pin in place. Repeat on same side with other end of same strap. Repeat for second strap on other side. Hand sew lining to knitted piece around the top, incorporating straps as you sew and stitching the straps onto the bag both on the outside and inside. Sew snap (press stud) to center of sides inside top.

knitted bow

This bow makes a fun accessory to add to a bag or hat, or to decorate a gift. It is worked in single rib throughout, so is really easy to make.

size

Approx 6in. (15cm) to top of bow x 7¾in. (19.5cm) long to tips

materials

Light worsted (DK) yarn, such as Rooster Almerino DK
1 x 1¾oz (50g) ball—approx. 124yd (112.5m)—of bright pink
Needle size: US 6 (4mm)
Yarn sewing needle

gauge (tension)

21 sts x 28 rows over 4in. (10cm) square using US 8 (5mm) needles. Change needle size if necessary to achieve the required gauge (tension).

BOW LOOPS (MAKE 2)

Cast on 22 sts.
Work 5½in. (14cm) in single rib (k1, p1).
Bind (cast) off.

TAIL (MAKE 2)

Cast on 2 sts.
Row 1 Inc in first st, cont in single rib to end.
Row 2 Work in rib to end.
Rep Rows 1–2 until there are 22 sts.
Cont in rib until work measures 5½in. (14cm).
Bind (cast) off.

CENTER

Cast on 16 sts and work in single rib until work measures 3in. (7.5cm).
Bind (cast) off.

TO COMPLETE

Fold pieces for loops in half with bound (cast) off edge to cast on edge. Using a yarn sewing needle, gather and pleat loops at paired edges and sew securely to each other.
Pleat straight ends of the pointed tails and sew to base of loops near center. Wrap small center piece around and sew to form "knot" in center of bow.

cable neck warmer

This is a great little warmer to tuck under your coat. Made with a soft and luxurious mix of alpaca and silk, it will feel so comfortable against your skin.

size
9in. (22.5cm) deep x 21¼in. (54cm) circumference

materials
Alpaca and silk mix worsted (Aran) yarn, such as Debbie Bliss Alpaca Silk Aran
4 x 1¾oz (50g) balls—approx. 284yd (260m)—of gray
Needle size: US 8 (5mm)
Cable needle

gauge (tension)
18 sts x 24 rows over 4in. (10cm) square using US 8 (5mm) needles. Change needle size if necessary to achieve the required gauge (tension).

special abbreviation
C8B (cable 8 back)—sl next 4 sts onto cable needle and hold at back of work, k next 4 sts from lh needle, then k sts from cable needle

NECK WARMER
Cast on 158 sts.
Row 1 K2, [p2, k2] to end.
Row 2 P2, [k2, p2] to end.
Rep Rows 1–2 once more, then Row 1 again.
Row 6 Rib 6, [M1, rib 2, M1, rib 10] to last 8 sts, M1, rib 2, M1, rib 6. (184 sts)
Begin cable patt. Row 7 P4, [k8, p6] to last 12 sts, k8, p4.
Row 8 K4, [p8, k6] to last 12 sts, p8, k4.
Rows 9–10 As Rows 1–2.
Row 11 P4, [C8B, p6] to last 12 sts, C8B, p4.
Row 12 As Row 2.
Rows 13–16 Rep Rows 1–2 twice.
Rows 7–16 form cable pattern, rep these ten rows three times more, then Rows 7–15 once.
Next row K4, [p1, p2tog, p2, p2tog, p1, k6] to last 12 sts, p1, p2tog, p2, p2tog, p1, k4. (158 sts)
Rep Rows 1–2 three times.
Bind (cast) off in rib.

TO COMPLETE
Sew seam at back.

felted hearts

Years ago I bought some felted pieces wrapped in a bundle intending to do something with them, but they stayed sitting on the dresser for years. So many people saw them and wanted to buy them that it inspired me to design these striped heart bundles. They just look great hanging around the room, or tie them onto ribbon to make a pretty garland.

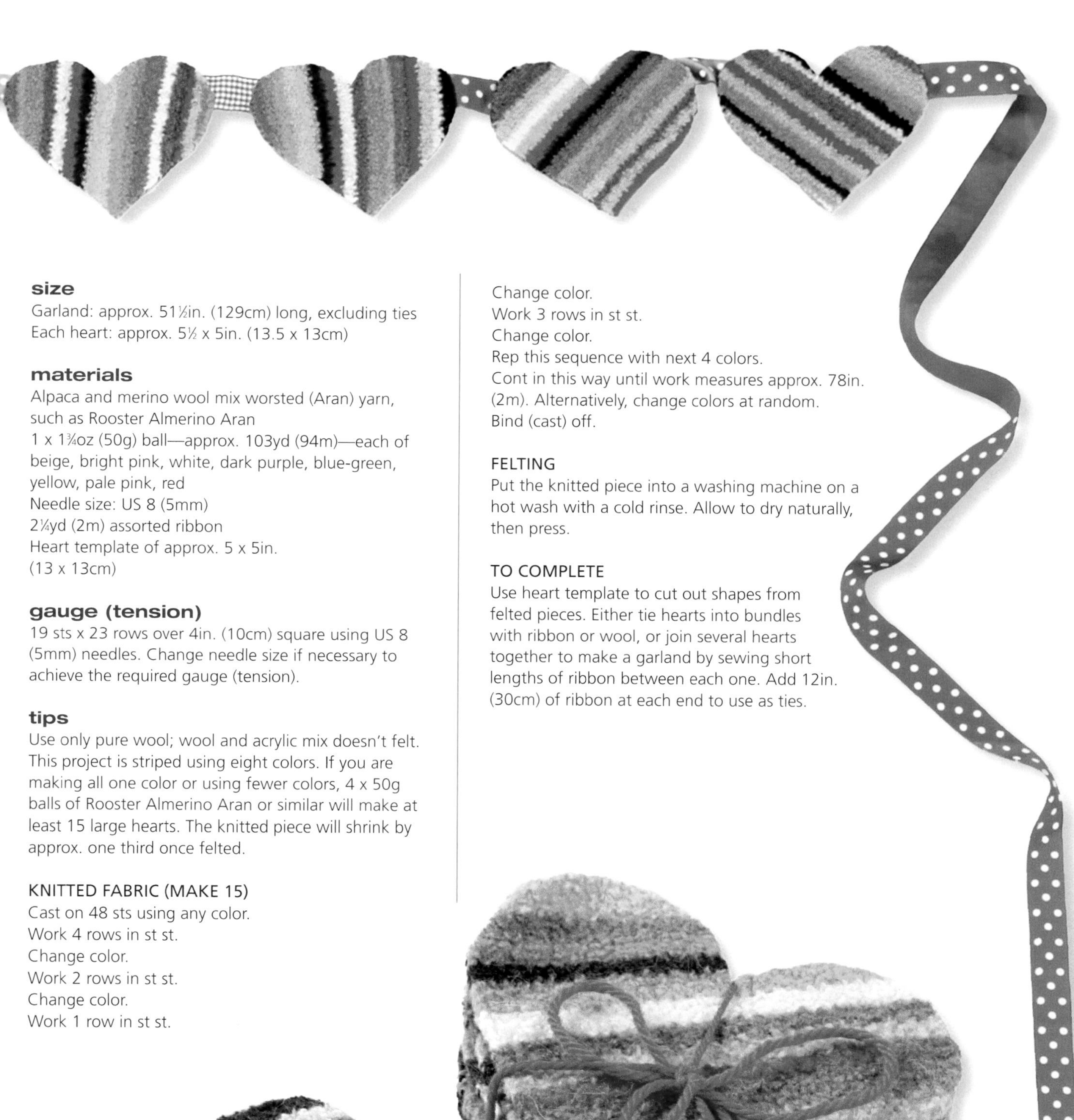

size

Garland: approx. 51½in. (129cm) long, excluding ties
Each heart: approx. 5½ x 5in. (13.5 x 13cm)

materials

Alpaca and merino wool mix worsted (Aran) yarn, such as Rooster Almerino Aran
1 x 1¾oz (50g) ball—approx. 103yd (94m)—each of beige, bright pink, white, dark purple, blue-green, yellow, pale pink, red
Needle size: US 8 (5mm)
2¼yd (2m) assorted ribbon
Heart template of approx. 5 x 5in. (13 x 13cm)

gauge (tension)

19 sts x 23 rows over 4in. (10cm) square using US 8 (5mm) needles. Change needle size if necessary to achieve the required gauge (tension).

tips

Use only pure wool; wool and acrylic mix doesn't felt. This project is striped using eight colors. If you are making all one color or using fewer colors, 4 x 50g balls of Rooster Almerino Aran or similar will make at least 15 large hearts. The knitted piece will shrink by approx. one third once felted.

KNITTED FABRIC (MAKE 15)

Cast on 48 sts using any color.
Work 4 rows in st st.
Change color.
Work 2 rows in st st.
Change color.
Work 1 row in st st.
Change color.
Work 3 rows in st st.
Change color.
Rep this sequence with next 4 colors.
Cont in this way until work measures approx. 78in. (2m). Alternatively, change colors at random.
Bind (cast) off.

FELTING

Put the knitted piece into a washing machine on a hot wash with a cold rinse. Allow to dry naturally, then press.

TO COMPLETE

Use heart template to cut out shapes from felted pieces. Either tie hearts into bundles with ribbon or wool, or join several hearts together to make a garland by sewing short lengths of ribbon between each one. Add 12in. (30cm) of ribbon at each end to use as ties.

part three

basic techniques

There are a lot of different techniques used in this book. If you're not familiar with them, use the guide in this section. There is always something new to learn in knitting and if you're not confident attempting a new technique on your own, try getting someone to show you how—there's nothing better than an experienced knitter to help you along the way.

the techniques

This first section describes basic knitting techniques, followed by some slightly more advanced techniques. It also demonstrates a few different methods for sewing up. The additional techniques section covers other skills, such as embroidery and making pompoms and tassels, which are needed for some of the projects in this book.

holding the yarn and needles

Although there is no particular right or wrong way to hold the yarn or needles, use the instructions below as a guide to help you obtain the correct gauge (tension) and knit comfortably. Over the years I've changed my style as knitting needles have changed. My grandmother taught me to knit with the needles under my armpits, which gave me a good control of the needles as a beginner. Most knitters will hold the yarn in the right hand with a needle in each hand. If you are left-handed try following the instructions reversing left and right, and use a mirror to reverse the diagrams.

holding the needles

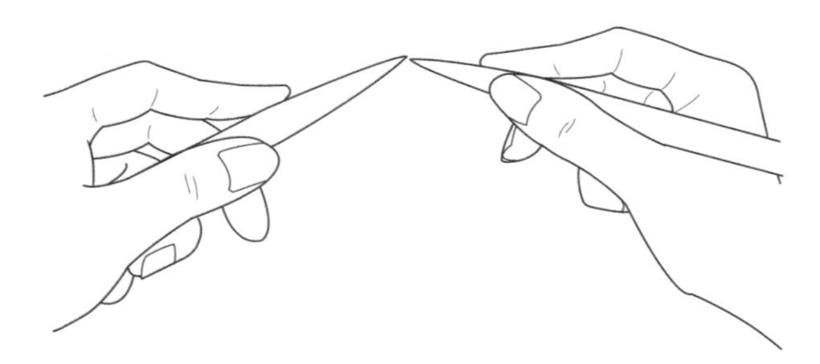

Pick up the left needle with your left hand supporting it with your finger lightly resting on the top. Pick up the right needle as you would a pen with the needle resting in the crook of your thumb. Hold it approx. 1in (2.5cm) from the tip of the needle. As you start knitting this hand will gently move up toward the tip of the needle and back down again.

holding the yarn

Hold both needles in the left hand while picking up the yarn in the right hand. Pick up the strand of yarn with the ball on your right. With the right hand, catch the strand of yarn with your little finger with your palm toward you, then turn your palm over lacing the yarn over the third, under the middle and over the first finger of the right hand.

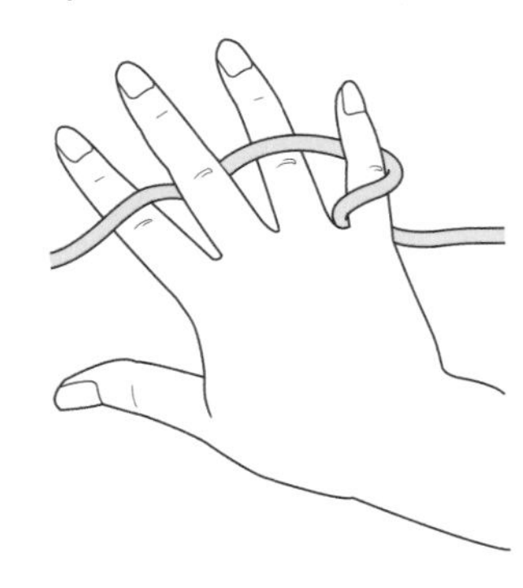

making a loop

Before you start knitting you'll need to make a loop, or first stitch. This is also called a slip knot.

1. Release at least 8in. (20cm) of yarn from the ball. Leave the tail of the yarn to the left and the ball on the right, wrap the yarn loosely around the first two fingers of your left hand, crossing the yarn over once. Place a needle under the back strand of the yarn and pull through to make a loop.

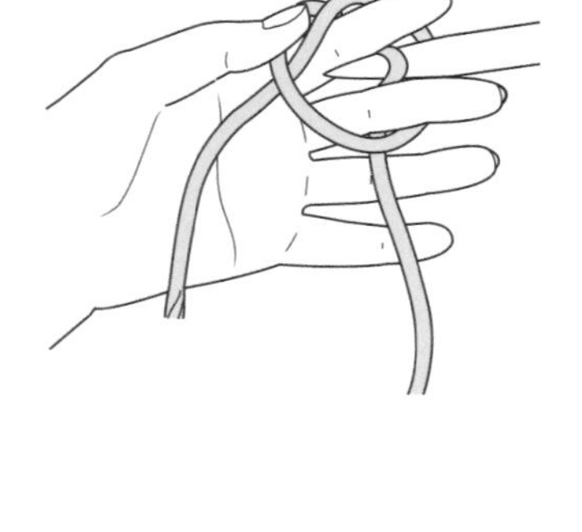

2. Gently slip your fingers away from the loop and lightly pull the end on the left to tighten the knot. It should be firm on the needle but not so tight that you can't fit the other needle through it.

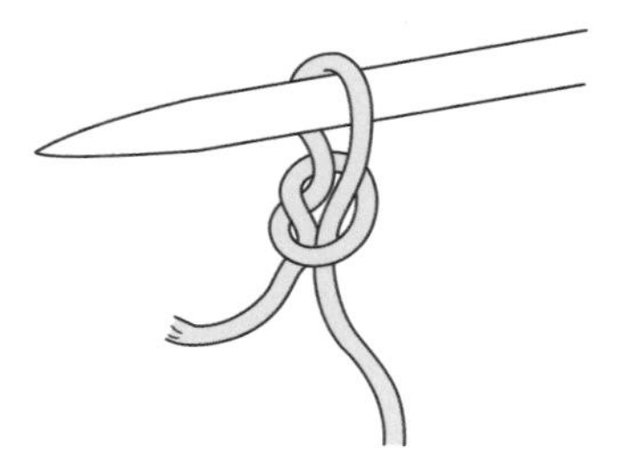

casting on

There are so many ways to cast on and as your experience grows you'll experiment with more, but when starting out try using one of these basic methods.

thumb method

Starting with a slip knot, leave a long tail of yarn approx 3 or 4 times the length of the proposed cast on edge, keeping the ball of yarn to your right and the long tail of yarn to your left. Hold the needle in your right hand.

1. Using the tail, make a loop with the yarn around your left thumb. Hold the yarn leading to the ball with your right hand. Insert the needle into the loop on your left thumb.

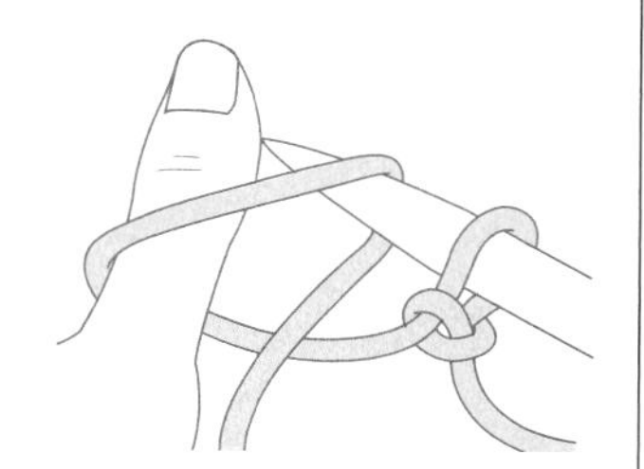

2. Bring the yarn from the ball between the thumb and needle and take it around the needle.

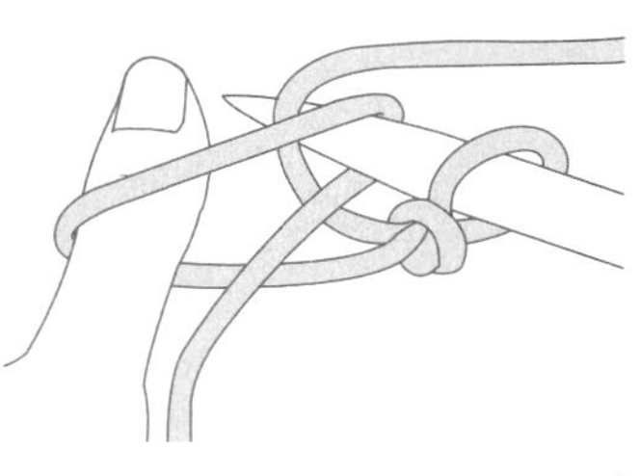

3. Gently pull the yarn through to make a stitch on the needle by sliding the left thumb away from the loop.

knitted cast on method

This is made using both needles. Make a slip knot.

1. Place the right needle into the slip knot by pushing the needle through from the front to the back, so it crosses at the back of the left needle. Support the needles in the crossed position in your left hand, take the strand of yarn with your right hand and wrap it round the back of the tip of the right needle toward the front.

2. Pull the stitch through by bringing the tip of the right needle through to the front in the crossed position again, but this time so the right needle is crossed at the front and the left needle crossed at the back. Draw a loop out by pulling gently on the right hand needle.

3. Make a stitch by catching the loop with the tip of the left hand needle under the loop, so it loops onto the left hand needle. Repeat this process until you have the required amount of stitches on the needle.

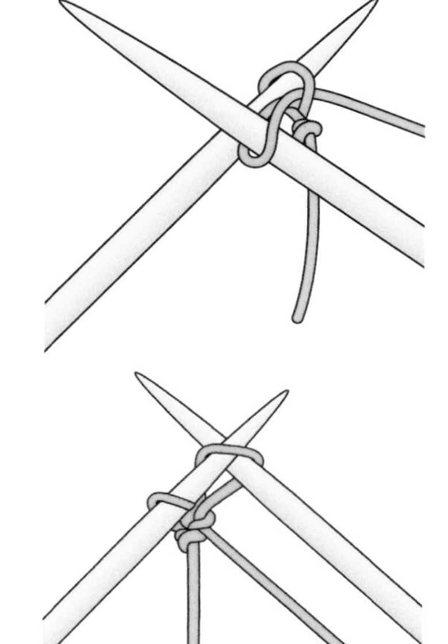

basic stitches

All knitted stitches are based on either knit or purl stitches. Once you've mastered these, the knitting world is your oyster.

knit stitch

Knit stitches are worked with the yarn at the back.

1. Place the right hand needle into the first stitch made by your cast-on row by pushing the needle through from the front to the back upward, so it crosses at the back of the left hand needle. Support the needles in the crossed position in your left hand, take the strand of yarn with your right hand and wrap it round the back of the tip of the right hand needle toward the front.

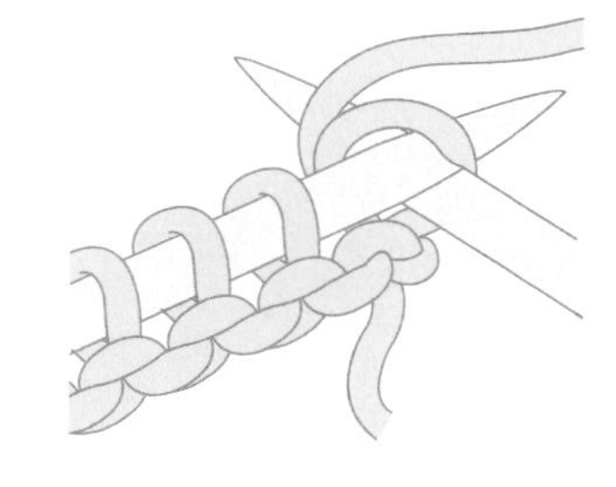

2. Pull the stitch through by bringing the tip of the right hand needle through to the front in the crossed position again, but this time so the right hand needle is crossed at the front and the left hand needle is at the back.

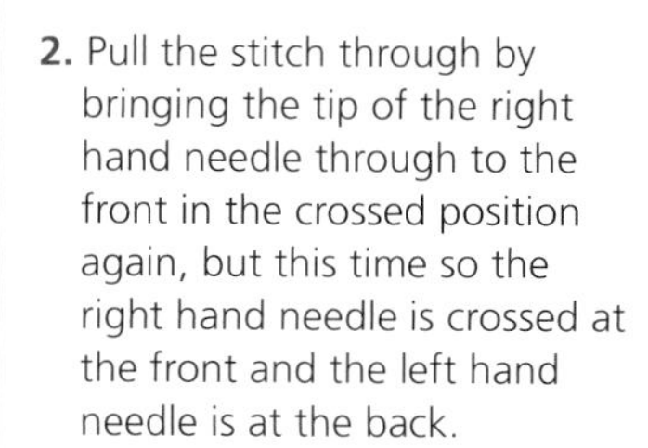

3. Gently slide the loop off the left hand needle by easing it off the tip with your left index (first) finger. Pull the stitch gently to secure in place on the right hand needle.

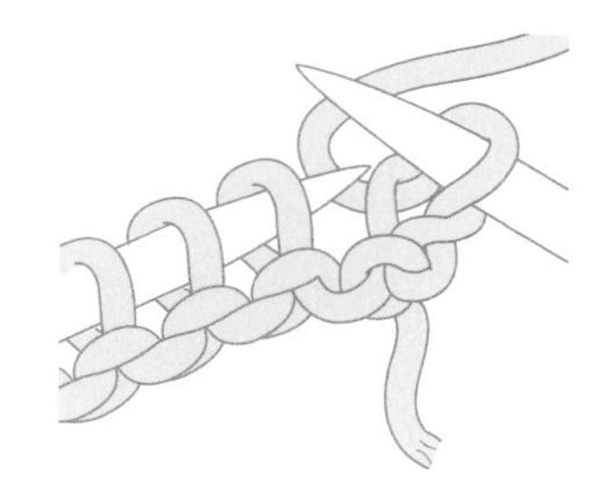

purl stitch

Purl stitches are worked with the yarn at the front.

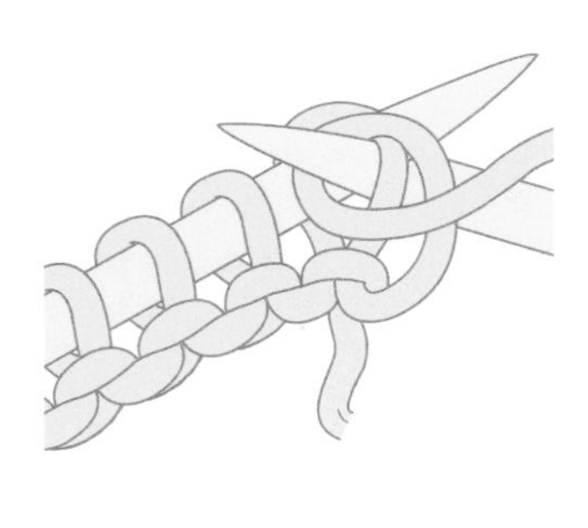

1. Place the right needle into the first stitch by pushing the needle through the loop, so the right hand needle crosses the left hand needle at the front. Support the needles in the crossed position in your left hand, take the strand of yarn with your right hand, and wrap it round through the middle of the crossed needles and around the right hand needle to the front.

2. Pull the stitch through by taking the tip of the right hand needle through to the back in the crossed position again, but this time so the right hand needle is crossed at the back and the left hand needle is at the front.

3. Gently slide the loop off the left hand needle by easing it off the tip with your left index (first) finger. Pull the stitch gently to secure in place on the right hand needle.

binding (casting) off

Working every stitch as a knit or purl will give a neat chain along the edge. For a softer edge, try casting off in the pattern that is being worked.

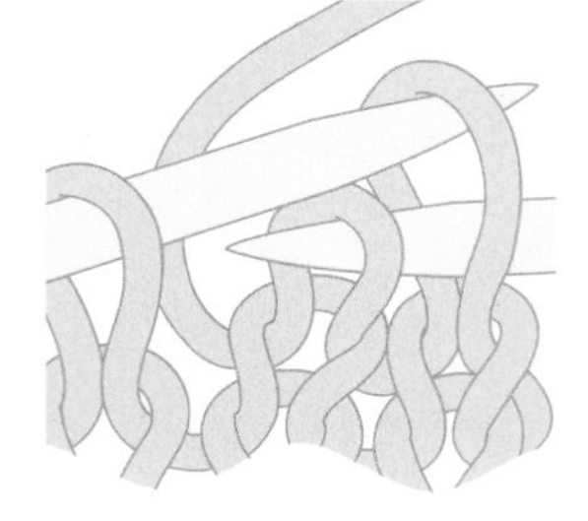

On a knit row, with the yarn at the back, knit two stitches. Using the tip of the left hand needle, lift the first stitch over the second stitch and off the needle. Knit the next stitch and continue as before until only one stitch remains.

On a purl row, with the yarn at the front, purl two stitches, put the yarn to the back of the work and using the tip of the left hand needle, lift the first stitch over the second stitch and off the needle. Bring the yarn to the front of the work, purl the next stitch and continue as before until only one stitch remains.

fasten off

Cut or break the yarn, pull the tail end through the loop, and pull gently to secure the last stitch.

measuring gauge (tension)

Gauge (tension) means how loose or how tight you knit. To achieve the exact measurements of a pattern you need to work to the same gauge (tension) as that recommended in the gauge (tension) guide or your project will come out a different size. Some patterns don't give a gauge (tension) guide, particularly if it's for a small item such as a purse or bag, but a gauge (tension) guide is particularly important if you're knitting a garment.

You can easily measure your gauge (tension) by knitting a square in the same stitch given in the pattern, and with the needle size that is recommended. Your gauge (tension) square should be at least 6 x 6in. (15 x 15cm).

When you have finished your square, lay it flat and measure the number of stitches and rows over a 4in. (10cm) square. Either use a transparent ruler and count the stitches and rows to the length, or use a tape measure and place pins to mark out the 4in. (10cm) square and then count the stitches and rows between the pin markers.

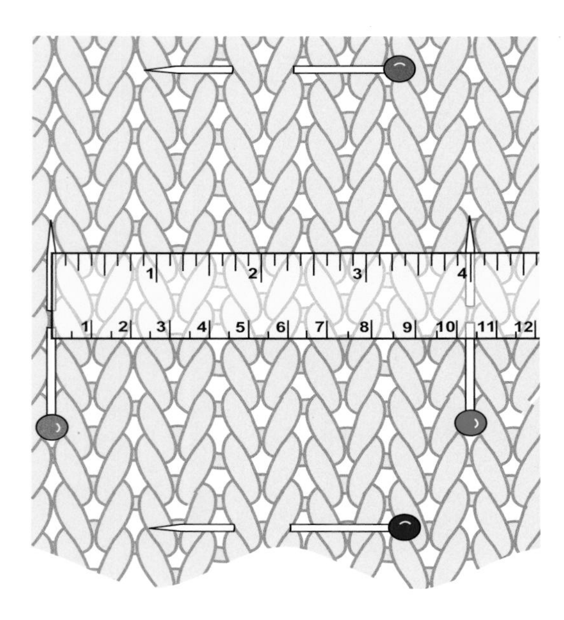

If the number of stitches and rows is less than the number specified in the pattern, your project will be too big. Change to smaller needles until you achieve the correct gauge (tension).

If the number of stitches and rows is more than the number specified in the pattern, your project will be too small. Change to larger needles until you achieve the correct gauge (tension).

increasing

Here are two methods of decreasing.

knit into the front and back

Start by knitting a stitch in the usual way, but before you drop the loop off the left hand needle, take the tip of the right hand needle behind the left hand needle and knit into the back of the same stitch, this time dropping the loop off the left hand needle.

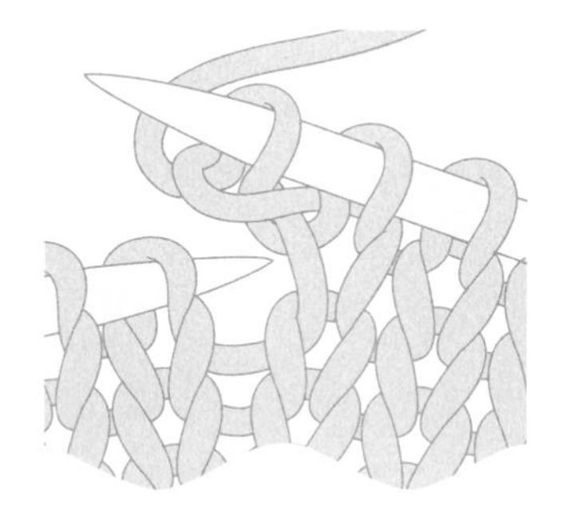

make 1 stitch (this is also called a bar increase)

Put the right hand needle through the bar (horizontal strand from the previous row, which is between two stitches) from the front to the back, slip the strand onto the left hand needle, then knit through the back of the strand. This makes one increase.

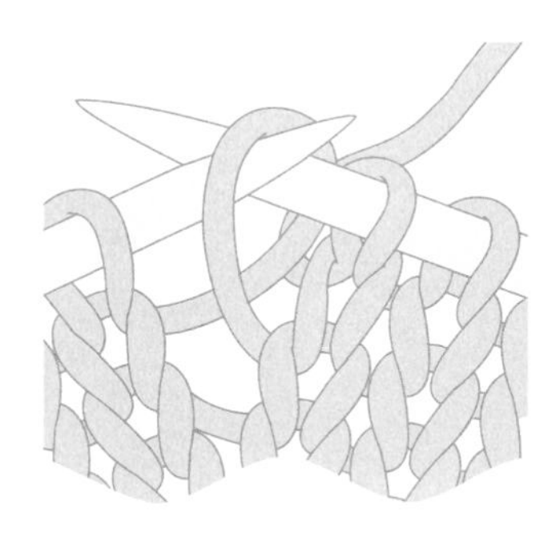

decreasing

Here are two methods of decreasing.

knit 2 together

Using the right hand needle knit two stitches together knitwise and slip them both off the left hand needle.

For purl 2 together, work in basically the same way but purl two stitches together purlwise and slip them both off the needle.

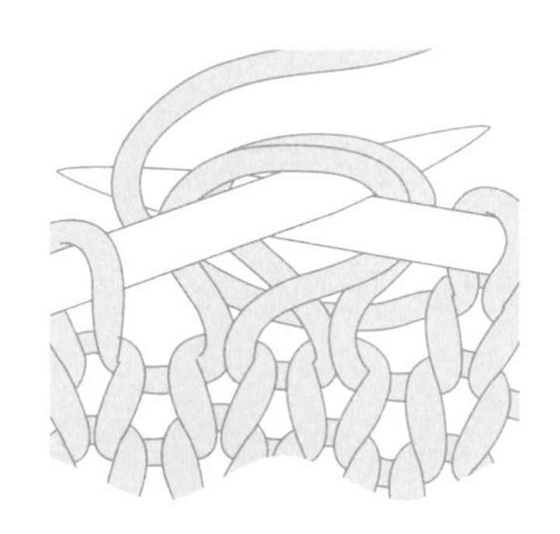

pass slipped stitch over

Slip one stitch from the left hand needle onto the right hand needle, knit the next stitch, then pass the slipped stitch over the knitted stitch, dropping the slipped stitch off the needle. Sometimes this is shown as the abbreviation skpo (slip one, knit one, pass the slipped stitch over).

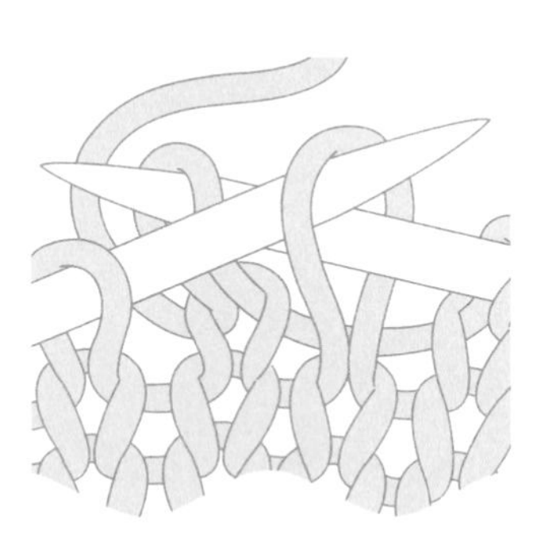

sewing seams

Generally it is best to use the same yarn to join seams that you have used for knitting, but if the knitting is particularly chunky try using a finer yarn in the same color. Use a tapestry needle when sewing seams—a blunt-ended tip is best because it is less likely to split the yarn. Use a piece of yarn no longer than 18–24in. (45–60cm), because a longer piece may start to tangle and knot. Make sure you have plenty of light before sewing up. When you have finally finished knitting your pieces at midnight, it's not a good idea to sew up with tired eyes in low light. Wait until the morning! There are many different types of sewn seams and certain methods are better than others, depending on what effect you are trying to achieve.

sewing in ends

This is such a vital part of caring for your finished item—if you don't sew in ends correctly your knitting will unravel in no time. Always leave a tail of approximately 6in. (15cm) when cutting the yarn. Thread a yarn sewing or tapestry needle with the tail and weave the end in and out on the wrong side of the garment, into the back of the stitches so that it's invisible from the right side. Weave for at least 2–3in. (5–7.5cm) on thicker yarn and 1½–2in. (4–5cm) on finer yarn. Cut the yarn off close to the work.

mattress stitch

This gives an invisible seam. Always sew with the right side facing—it's useful to do this on a tabletop or a flat surface.

To start, join the yarn to one corner of your seam and make a figure of eight to attach both edges in the bottom stitch. Put the pieces edge-to-edge and, starting on the right, take the needle up two stitches vertically; two "bars" should lie on the needle. Pull the thread through loosely (not all the way through). Take the needle back to the left and insert it into same stitch you started from, then take needle up two bars. Repeat this, working side to side but do not pull tight, leaving the loops loose. After a few inches (cm), gently pull the thread until the stitches of the separate pieces lie side by side.

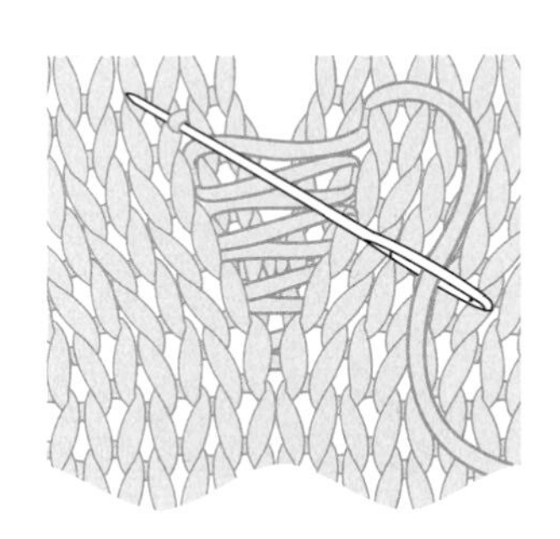

kitchener stitch/grafting

This technique copies the shape of the knitted stitch, making a seamless join and works best when joining stockinette (stocking) stitch.

Put each line of stitches on a needle (without binding/casting off) or on stitch holders.
Work as for mattress stitch, weaving the thread from one piece to the other and working stitch to stitch.

over-sewing

A very basic sewing technique that is made with wrong sides facing and right sides together. Although you will be able to see the seam, it makes a flat join without the bumpy seam that you can get from mattress stitch.

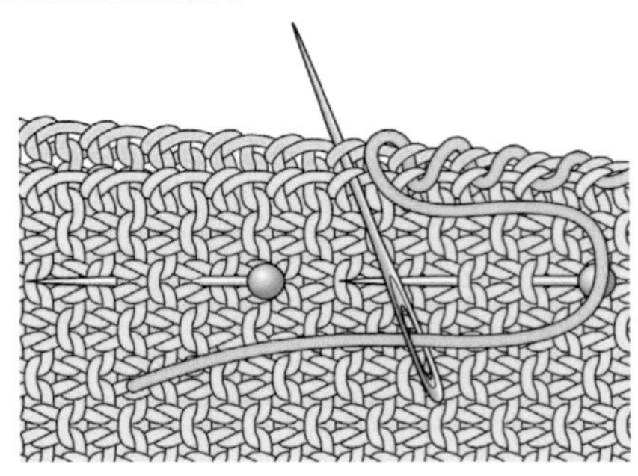

Join the wool to the edge of the seam and take the needle from front to back, taking the wool over the top and going in from front to back again, joining both knitted pieces together. Alternatively, you can sew from back to front. Continue to the end of the seam.

backstitch seam

This seam is made with right sides facing.

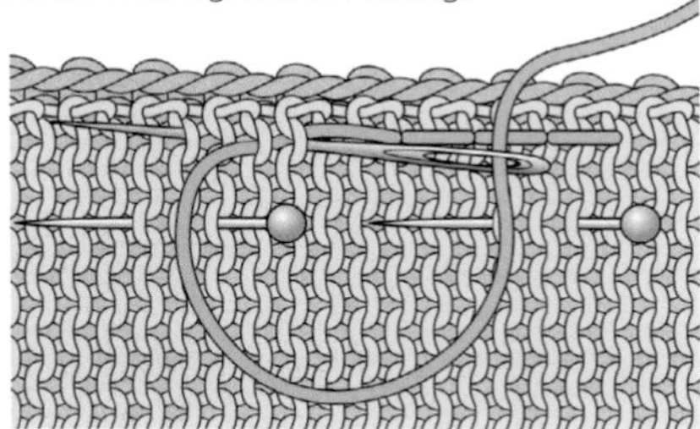

Carefully match pattern to pattern, row to row and stitch to stitch. Sew along the seam using backstitch, sewing into the center of each stitch to correspond with the stitch on the opposite piece. Sew as close in from the edge of the knitting as possible to avoid a bulky seam.

working the pattern

Before you begin, it is always a good idea to read through the pattern carefully first. Check out any special abbreviations against the key to be sure you understand them, and study any special instructions or charts.

reading a chart

When working with color, knitting patterns are generally worked from a chart. This isn't as daunting as it looks; it's a good visual alternative to reading a knitting pattern.

Start at the bottom right hand corner of the chart. Each square represents one stitch—if the chart is too small for your eyesight, enlarge it on a photocopier. If the chart hasn't already got the row numbers noted then write them on before you start knitting, starting from the bottom to the top. Using a row counter on the end of your needle is very useful because then you will be able to keep a good check on which row you're working. Work from right to left on a knit row and left to right on a purl row. I always write a big "k" on the right of the chart and a "p" on the left, just to remind me.

intarsia knitting

This is a technique used for knitting colored motifs and shapes. The color is not carried along the row—use separate lengths of yarn for each area of color and twist the two yarns together on the wrong side of the work when they meet. This will make sure that the colors are taken up as you knit and no holes are created. Using this method uses less yarn and creates only a single layer fabric.

KNIT ROW

Knit the last stitch in the old color, drop the yarn at the back, and pick up the new color, making sure that it loops around the old color. Knit the first stitch in the new color securely so the joins are neat.

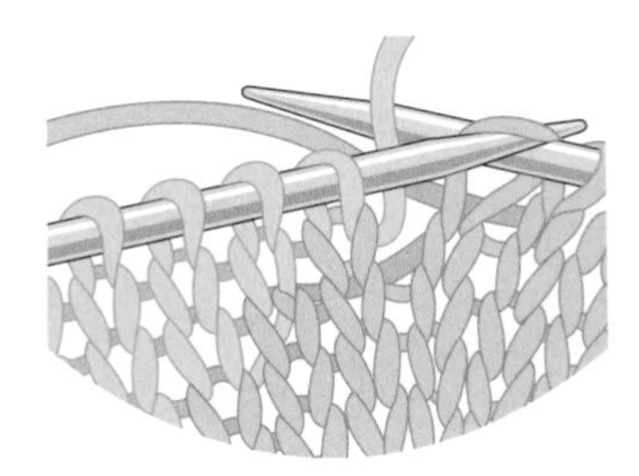

PURL ROW

Purl the last stitch in the old color. Drop the old color and pick up the new color, looping it around the old color, purl the next stitch in the new color securely so the joins are neat.

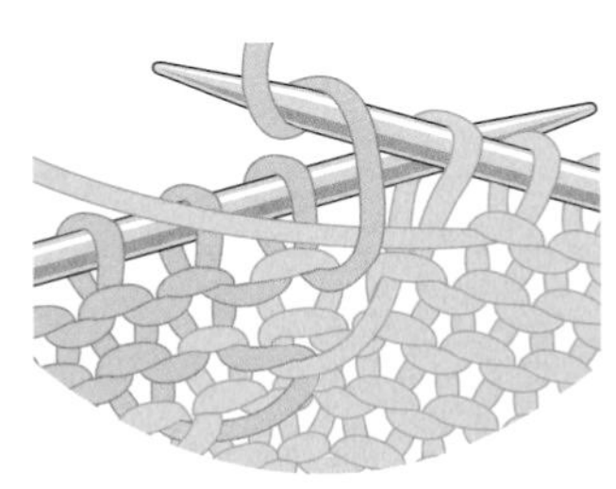

USING A YARN BOBBIN

When there are several color changes along a row, it's useful to use a yarn bobbin to avoid the colors getting tangled up. These can be store bought and are made of plastic or card. Wind small amounts of each color you need onto separate bobbins.

CHANGING COLORS

You can loop the yarns around one another if the colors change in a straight line up the work. If you are working stripes, change color at the end of row by dropping the old color at the end of the row and knitting the new color at the beginning of the row. You can either cut the old color, leaving a 6in. (15cm) tail for sewing in later, or—if the color changes fall on an even number—you can weave the yarns up the side of the work by winding them round each other, looping them up the side as you knit.

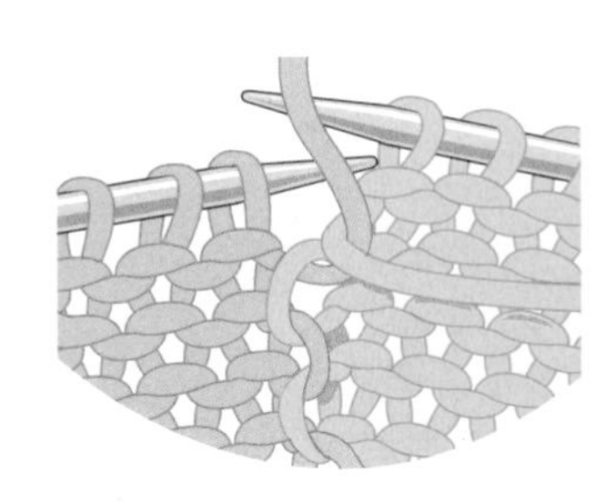

fair isle

There are two different ways of approaching this technique, depending on how many stitches there are between the color changes in a row. If there are 3–4 stitches or fewer between colors, then stranding can be used. If there are more than 3–4 stitches between colors then the spare yarn needs to be woven along the back. Both techniques create a double thickness that gives a tighter fabric and also more warmth.

STRANDING

With this technique you leave the color that you're not using at the back of the work without weaving it in to your current color. The strands stay resting at the back of the work until they are needed, then you simply drop the working yarn and pick up the resting yarn and continue to knit or purl in the usual way. This leaves a series of loops of yarn across the back of the work. When stranding, don't pull the loops tight or they will bunch up your work, and only use this technique with a maximum of 4 stitches between colors.

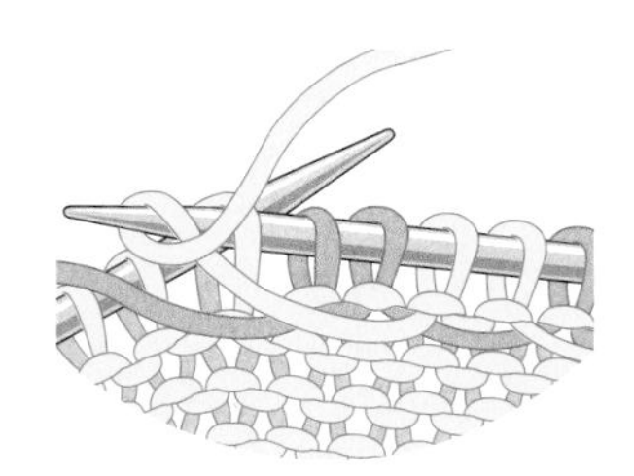

WEAVING

When the distance between the color changes is more than 3 or 4 stitches, twist the yarn. On the knit side, twist the working yarn and the resting yarn around each other once at the back of the yarn. Continue knitting with the same color until the resting color is needed.

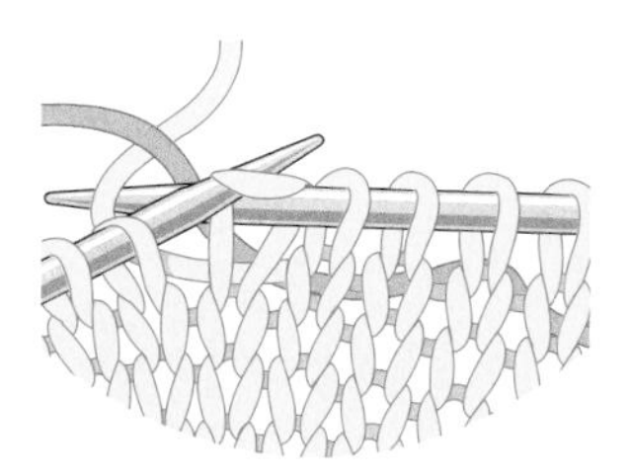

On the purl side, twist the yarns around each other as on the knit side, but at the front of the yarn.

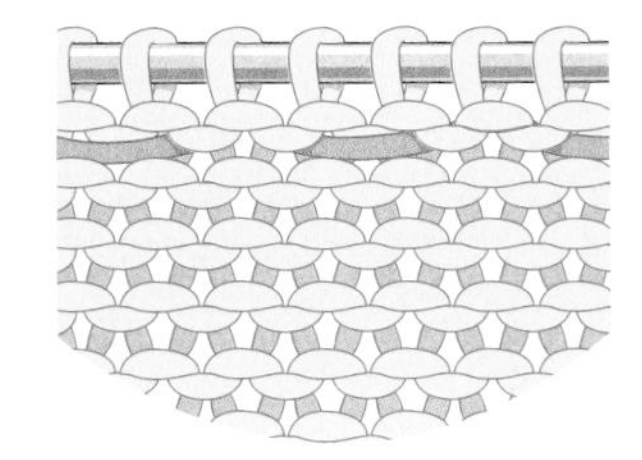

knitting with beads

When choosing beads, check that the hole is big enough for the yarn that you will be using. Thread all the beads that you need for the project onto the ball of yarn before you start knitting.

THREADING BEADS

Using sewing thread and a sewing needle, make a loop with the thread and thread the loop through the eye of the sewing needle without pulling the tail through. Put the yarn tail through the loop of the thread. Thread the bead onto the sewing needle and push the bead down until it sits on the yarn. Push it down securely and continue in this way until all the beads are threaded onto the yarn.

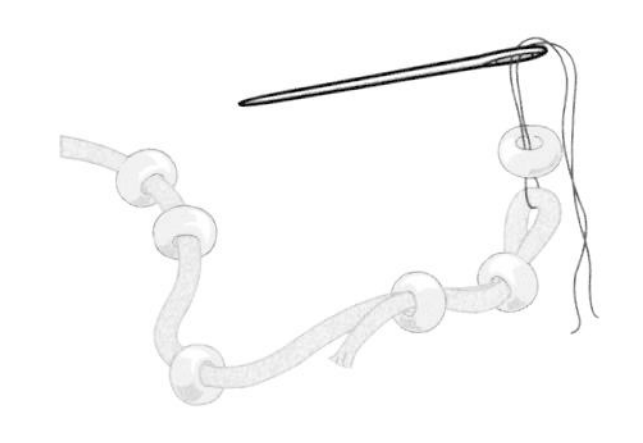

KNITTING IN BEADS

To knit in a bead, knit up to the stitch before you want the bead, bring the yarn and bead to the front of the work, slip the next stitch purlwise, bring the yarn to the back of the work, leaving the bead at the front, then continue to work in knit.

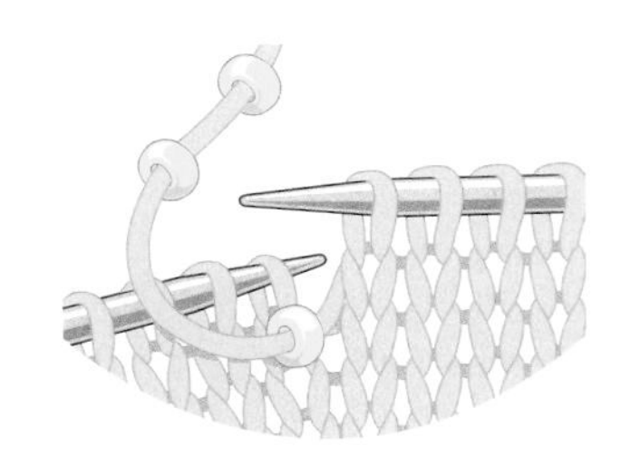

To knit a bead in a purl row work in a similar way; purl up to the stitch before you want the bead, take the yarn and bead to the back of the work, slip the next stitch knitwise, bring the yarn to the front of the work, leaving the bead at the back then continue to work in purl.

cables

There are various cables and the pattern you're working will specify which method to use. You will need a cable needle, which is straight and double pointed; some of them have a little crook in the middle to prevent the stitches from sliding off.

WORKING A FRONT CABLE

1. Slip the first three stitches of the cable purlwise onto a cable needle and keep the cable needle to the front of the work. Leave the three stitches on the cable needle in front of the work, in the middle so they don't slip off.

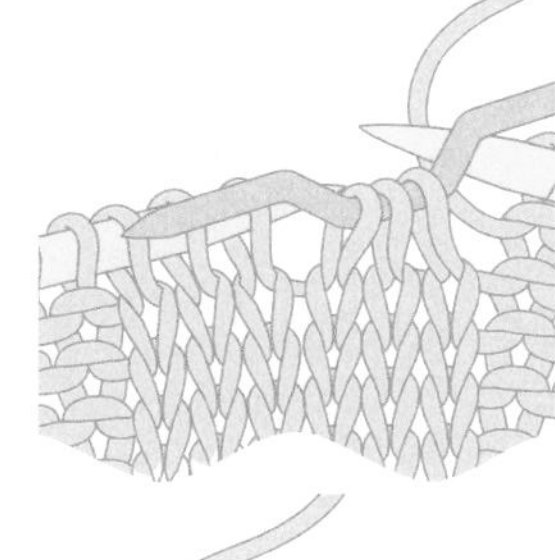

2. Pull the yarn firmly and knit the next three stitches.

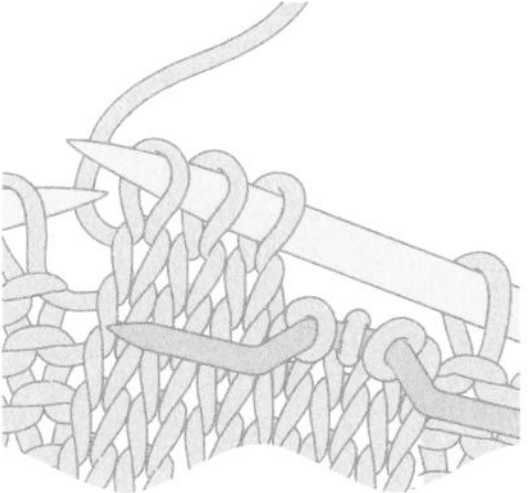

3. Knit the three stitches from the cable needle and continue working from your pattern.

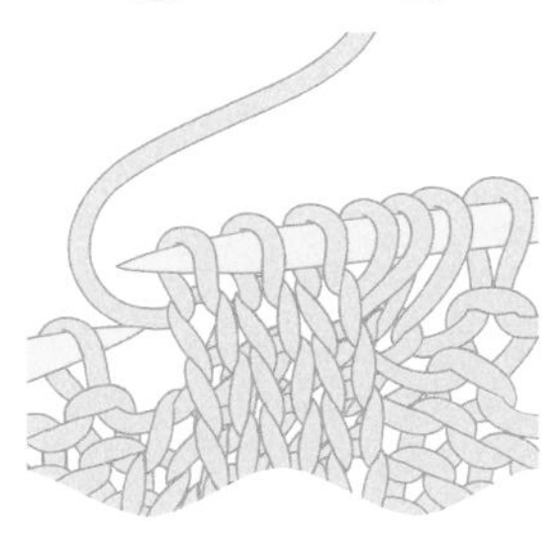

WORKING A BACK CABLE

1. Slip the first three stitches of the cable purlwise onto a cable needle and keep the cable needle at the back of the work. Leave the three stitches on the cable needle in the middle so they don't slip off.

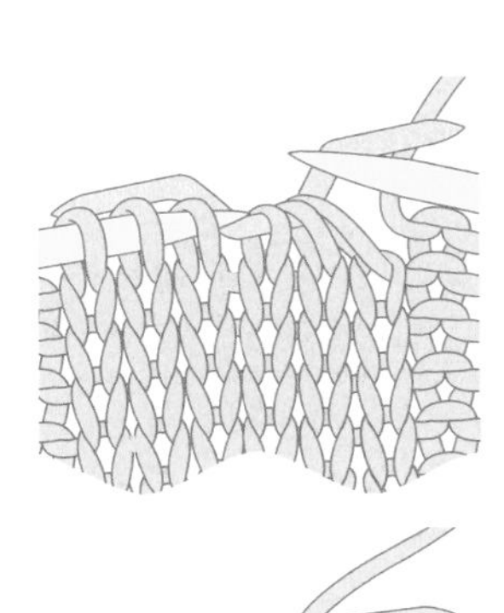

2. Knit the next three stitches on the left needle.

3. Knit the three stitches from the cable needle and continue working from your pattern.

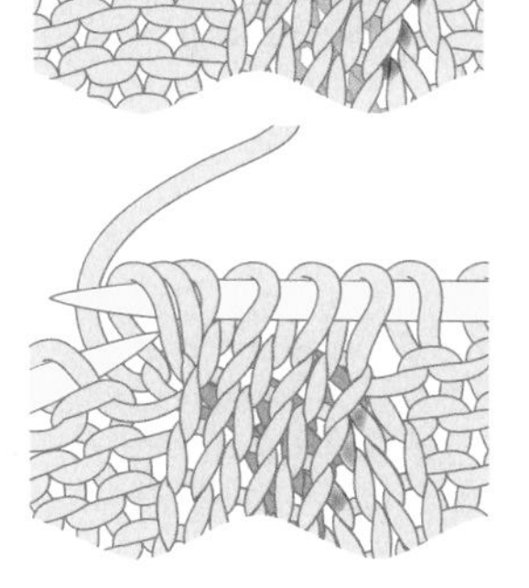

additional techniques

These are not knitting techniques, but are used in some of the projects in the book.

embroidery

When embroidering knitting it's often best to use yarn rather than embroidery floss, although embroidery floss can work well depending on the thickness of the knitting. The embroidery projects in this book use yarn that has been split. To split the yarn, rub a length of yarn to loosen the twist and then take one or two strands and pull them apart. Using these split strands of yarn, embroider the designs using a tapestry needle.

Embroidery on knitting isn't as difficult as you might think. However, you can't use a hoop because it will stretch the knitted fabric, and it is also impossible to draw your design beforehand so choose simple designs that you can follow free hand. The designs in this book are very easy and use very simple stitches.

CHAIN STITCH

Bring the needle from the back to front of the work at the center of a knitted stitch. Insert the tip of the needle next to where it came out and bring it out again in the center of the next knitted stitch to the right, but don't pull the yarn through. Loop the yarn under the tip of the needle, then pull the yarn through to complete the stitch. If you work chain stitch in a circle, as shown here, it is called lazy daisy stitch—after completing each loop, take the needle over it and back into the knitted fabric again to secure the loop in place.

RUNNING STITCH

Use small straight stitches. Bring the needle from the back to the front of the work between two knitted stitches. Pass the threaded needle over one knitted stitch and under the next one to form stitches in the length required.

FRENCH KNOT

Bring the yarn to the front from the back and hold it firmly between your left index finger and thumb and away from the knitting. With the needle pointing away from the knitting, wrap the yarn over and around the tip with your left hand. Wrapping twice will give you a smaller knot, three times a larger knot. Hold the yarn taut with your left hand, turn the needle downward and slide it back into the knitting close to where it originally came out, but not in exactly the same place or the knot will unravel. With the tip of the needle inserted in the knitting, slide the knot down the needle onto the surface of the knitting, pulling the yarn taut with your left hand at the same time. Slowly push the needle to the back of the work while holding the knot firmly in place under your thumb.

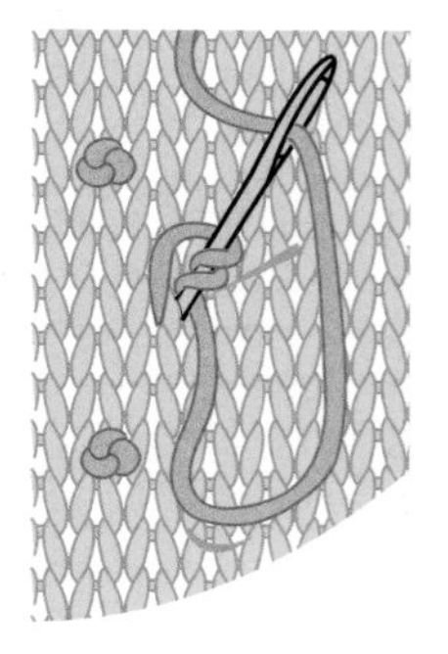

making a pompom

You can buy commercial pompom makers, but using card or your fingers is just as good, if not better. Method 1 is best for bigger pompoms, as used on the Pompom Draft Excluder on page 113, while Method 2 is better for smaller ones such as those on the Child's Pompom Hat on page 152.

METHOD 1
POMPOMS

Using card (cereal packets are ideal), cut out two circles 4in. (10cm) across with a 2in. (5cm) diameter hole at the center. The diameter of the outer circle should be the approximate size you want the finished pompom. Put the two circles together and start winding the yarn around the card through the hole. Continue to wind the yarn evenly around until the center hole is full. If you want a less dense pompom, stop winding when the center hole is not so full. Cut the yarn and then slide the tip of the scissors between the two pieces of card and cut around the yarn at the edges of the circle. When you've cut all the way round, pass a length of yarn between the pieces of card and tie it very firmly around the middle. Remove the card, fluff up the pompom and trim.

METHOD 2

To make a smaller and quicker pompom without using card, wrap the yarn around two or three fingers approx. 80 times. Gently slide the yarn off your fingers and tie a knot in the center very securely. The pompom will now have loops on either side of the knot. Cut all the loops; trim and fluff the pompom into shape.

fringing

Fringing is a popular way of decorating the edges of knitting, such as on the Fringed Shawl on page 110. For a quick way of making lots of fringing, use a CD case or a book about the same length that you want the fringe to be. Starting with the yarn tail at the bottom, wrap the yarn several times around, depending on how thick you want the fringe. Cut the yarn at the bottom only. Gently slide the wrapped yarn off the book or CD case and thread the top loops into one of the stitches of the edge of the garment. Thread the cut ends through the loops and pull gently to secure in place. When you have completed the length of fringing, trim the bottom ends level.

tassels

Cut 6 lengths of yarn approx. 10in. (26cm) long. Hold together and fold in half to create a loop. Cut another length approx. 14in. (35.5cm). Align one end so it is same length as other tails. Wrap other end around the top of looped yarn several times approx. ¾in. (2cm) down from top to secure in place. Thread this end onto the yarn needle and thread back through the tassel to secure in place.

machine felting

This is a great way of achieving a felted look without having to use traditional wet-and-rub felting techniques. Place the knitting piece into the washing machine, on a hot wash with a cold rinse. Wash once, or twice to achieve a tighter look. In this book, the Felted Hearts (page 162) were washed once and the Felted Bag (page 159) was washed twice. Allow the felted piece to dry naturally. You can then use the knitting as though it were a piece of fabric, cutting it to size without having to hem because it won't fray.

choosing or substituting yarn

One of the great pleasures of knitting—or making anything handmade—is in choosing the materials. When choosing yarn, be sure that it is the right thickness for the project you're making. If you want to substitute the yarn recommended, check to see what thickness it is. For example, many of the projects in this book are made in Rooster Almerino DK; the DK means light worsted (double knit), and so any light worsted (double knit) from another brand will generally substitute well. Check the gauge (tension) that is recommended for each brand because this will give you a guide as to whether it will knit up the same.

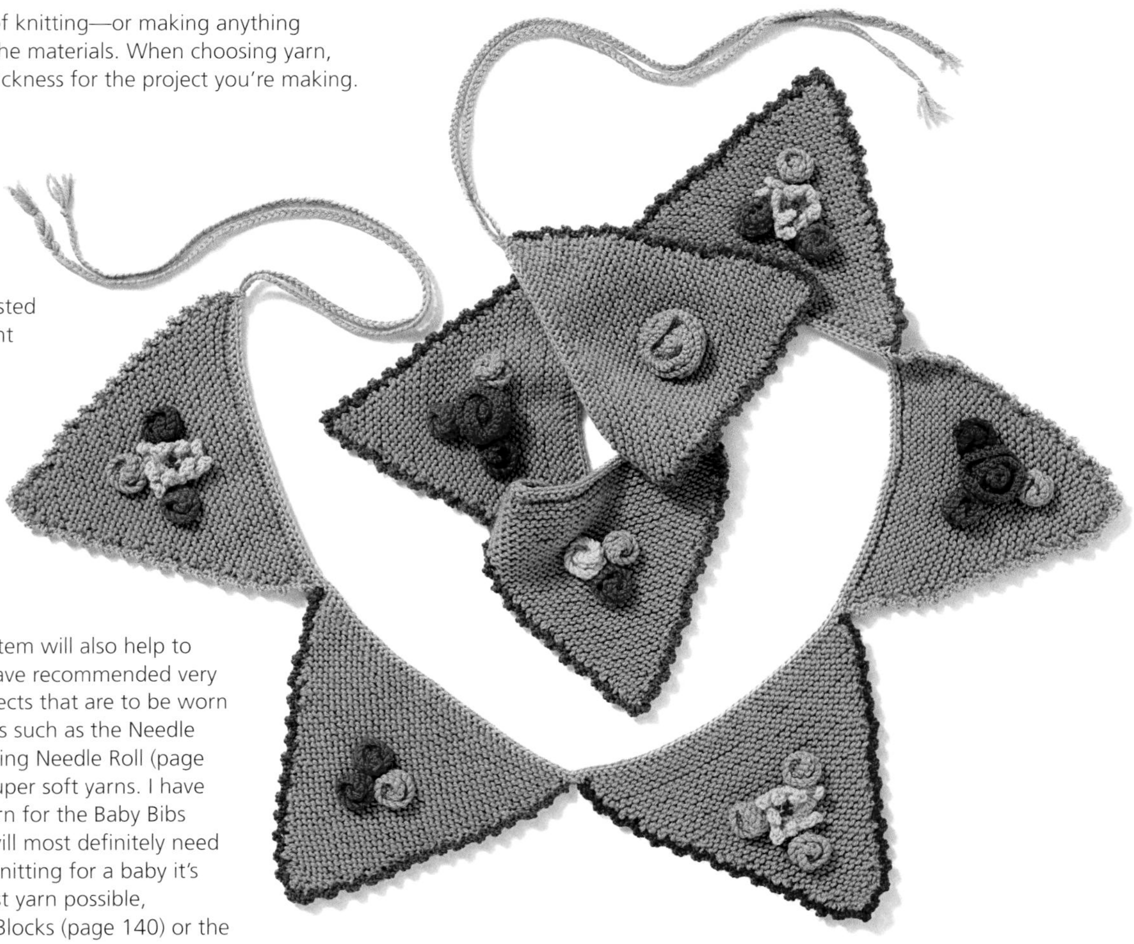

The function of the knitted item will also help to decide what yarn to use. I have recommended very soft, luxurious yarns for projects that are to be worn close to the skin, but projects such as the Needle Case (page 154) or the Knitting Needle Roll (page 136) need not be made in super soft yarns. I have also used a 100% cotton yarn for the Baby Bibs (page 122), because these will most definitely need to be washed easily. When knitting for a baby it's always best to use the softest yarn possible, whether it's for the Nursery Blocks (page 140) or the luxury Baby Cot Blanket (page 96).

I tend to be very led by color and the yarns I have used for this book are in the color palette that I'm most drawn to, but experiment by using your own color combinations and feel free to experiment and change the colors to suit your own taste.

finishing and aftercare

It would be really heartbreaking to spend a lot of time making a project, only to spoil it when sewing up or at the first wash. It really is worth taking some time at these stages so your item will give you pleasure for years to come.

blocking, pressing, and steaming

Though you can buy a ready-made blocking board, I use an old woolen blanket or the ironing board to block. I washed the woolen blanket in a hot wash, so the fibers felted together and it makes the perfect surface for blocking.

Lay your knitted fabric out flat and use pins to secure it in place, shaping it as you pin. You can then either press or steam the piece, depending on the yarn—the recommended instructions will be on the yarn label. Don't press directly onto the knitted fabric; lay a damp cloth over the top and press through it gently. To steam, turn on the steam iron and push the steam button while hovering over the top of the knitted fabric without actually touching it. Leave to dry, overnight if possible.

basic care instructions

When you've spent hours hand knitting, it's vital that you care for the item properly afterward. Check the washing instructions on the ball band of your yarn—this will determine whether you hand wash or can machine wash your item. Most of the yarns in this book are natural fibers and will require hand washing.

Buy a specific hand wash soap/detergent and use just a little—approximately the same amount as you would shampoo on your hair. Wash the item in hand-hot to cool water, then rinse well and wring out gently. Shape the item while it is still damp and leave to dry naturally. If you can, dry flat by placing on a towel—if you hang knitted items while they are still wet, you will risk them stretching or becoming misshapen. Natural fiber yarns shouldn't be pressed; instead try steaming, by holding the steam iron over the surface without touching the knitting.

abbreviations

alt alternate
cont continue
foll follows, following
inc increase
K knit
K2tog knit two stitches together
lh left hand
M1 make one stitch by picking up and working the loop between two stitches
P purl
psso pass slipped stitch over
p2sso pass two slipped stitches over
P2tog purl two stitches together
P3tog purl three stitches together
rem remaining
rep repeat
rh right hand
skpo slip one, knit one, pass slipped stitch over
Sl slip a stitch
Sl 1 slip one stitch
Sl 3 slip three stitches
St(s) stitch(es)
St st stockinette (stocking) stitch
tbl through back of loop
tog together
wyib with yarn in back (UK take yarn back) bring the yarn to the back under the needle
wyif with yarn in front (UK take yarn forward) bring the yarn to the front under the needle
yfrn yarn forward round needle – take the yarn forward and over around the needle to inc by one st between a knit and a following purl st
yo yarn over (UK yarn forward) take the yarn over the needle to inc by one st between two knit sts
yon yarn over needle—inc by one st by taking the yarn over the needle between a purl and a following knit st
yrn yarn round needle—take the yarn around the needle to inc by one between two purl sts
[ ] work the instructions within the square brackets the number of times stated

special abbreviations used in this book

Cluster 5 pass next 5 sts onto rh needle dropping extra loops, pass these 5 sts back onto lh needle, [k1, p1, k1, p1, k1] into all 5 sts tog, wrapping yarn twice around needle for each st

C4B cable 4 back—slip next 2 sts onto a cable needle and hold at back of work, knit next 2 sts from left hand needle, then knit sts from cable needle

C4F cable 4 front—as C4B, but hold sts on cable needle at front of work

C8B cable 8 back—sl next 4 sts onto cable needle and hold at back of work, k next 4 sts from lh needle, then k sts from cable needle

K1B knit into back of st on right side rows

Kfb knit into front and back of next st

Make Kiss slip right needle under 3 strands knitwise, knit next st pulling the loop through downward and under strands

MB make bobble—knit into the front, back and front of next stitch, turn and K3, turn and P3, turn and K3, turn and sl 1, K2tog, psso (bobble completed)

Pb place bead

P1B purl into back of st on wrong side rows

Pfb purl into front and back of next st

Ssk slip, slip, knit—slip next 2 sts one at a time, insert left needle into fronts of slipped sts and knit tog

T4F twist 4 front—slip next 2 sts onto a cable needle and hold at front of work, purl next 2 sts from left hand needle, then knit sts from cable needle

Tw2L twist 2 to the left—pass needle behind first st, knit second st, knit first st and slip both sts off needle

Tw2R twist 2 to the right—pass needle in front of first st, knit second st, knit first st and slip both sts off needle

index

yarn suppliers and websites

UK Suppliers

Rooster yarns, Debbie Bliss, Rowan, Blue Faced Leicester, Cascade:
Laughing Hens
The Croft Stables
Station Lane
Great Barrow
Cheshire
CH3 7JN
Tel: +44 (0)1829 740903
www.laughinghens.com

Rowan yarns:
MEZ Crafts UK
17F Brooke's Mil
Armitage Bridge,
Huddersfield
West Yorkshire
HD4 7NR
Tel: +44 (0)1484 950630
www.knitrowan.com

Various yarns:
(+44) 0845 544 2196
www.loveknitting.com

Debbie Bliss yarns:
Designer Yarns
8–10 Newbridge Industrial Estate
Pitt Street
Keighley
West Yorkshire
BD21 4PQ
Tel: +44 (0)1535 664222
www.designeryarns.uk.com

Sublime yarns:
Tel: +44 (0)1924 369666
www.sublimeyarns.com

US Suppliers

Various yarns:
Knitting Fever Inc.
315 Bayview Avenue
Amityville
New York
NY 11701
Tel: +1 516 546 3600
www.knittingfever.com

Sublime yarns:
Tel: +1-(828)-404-3705 or (828)-404-3706
www.sublimeyarns.com

Various yarns:
+1-(866)-677-0057
www.loveknitting.com

UK Classes

Nicki Trench Knitting and Home Crafts Classes:
www.nickitrench.com

author's acknowledgments

I am totally delighted with the projects and blocks in this book and it's all down to my team of talented knitters and helpers who all flocked forward to help to reach deadlines and wade through the mound of wool to turn it into something marvellous.

The knitters are: Tara Blackwell, Roberta Couchman, Tracey Elks, Christine Glasspool, Emma Lightfoot, Catherine Lohan, Gaye Mansfield, Lesley Morris, Janet Morton, Beryl Oakes, Yasmin Paul, Maddy Perkins, Zara Poole, Louise Pyke, Susan Shaw, Susan Smith, Julie Swinhoe, Judith Taylor, Geraldine Trower, and Ellen Watson. Thanks, too, to Besh Grimes for the pretty embroidery.

Huge and special thanks to Sian Brown who contributed some really lovely designs and who worked alongside me to design the blocks and projects and helped get everything finished on time.

I'm also extremely grateful to the UK yarn companies who donated the yarn for the book, particularly Laughing Hens for providing Rooster and Cascade yarns, Designer Yarns for Debbie Bliss yarns, and Rowan Yarns.

A huge thank you to Cindy Richards, Gillian Haslam, and Sally Powell from CICO Books. I was given a great deal of creative freedom and am bowled over by their trust in my ability to get the job done. Also, many thanks to Marie Clayton for her careful editing.

A credit to Vikki Haffenden for helping me work out the Designaknit program and contributing to some of the motifs on the Toddler Blanket.

There is always something new to learn about knitting, no matter how experienced you are, and this book has been a fascinating journey into not only knitting but learning how to work with my very talented mother, Beryl Oakes, whose hawk eye and meticulous attention to detail have turned her into the best pattern checker ever and probably a venture into a new career in her old age. Thanks, Mum.